THE AMERICAN CITY NOVEL

The American City Novel

THEODORE DREISER • THOMAS WOLFE

SHERWOOD ANDERSON • EDITH WHARTON

JOHN DOS PASSOS • JAMES T. FARRELL

NELSON ALGREN • BETTY SMITH • LEONARD

BISHOP • WILLARD MOTLEY • AND OTHERS

BY BLANCHE HOUSMAN GELFANT

NORMAN

UNIVERSITY OF OKLAHOMA PRESS

Library of Congress Catalog Card Number: 54-5936

Copyright 1954 by the University of Oklahoma Press,
Publishing Division of the University. Composed
and printed at Norman, Oklahoma, U.S.A., by the
University of Oklahoma Press. First edition.

TO MOLLIE HOUSMAN

PREFACE

PERHAPS I can best suggest what I have tried to do in this book by indicating some of the things I have avoided. I have avoided a geographical or topographical approach to urban life and fiction. I have not attempted a chronological survey. I have not traced foreign influences. My purpose has been to introduce a concept of a literary genre, the twentieth century American city novel. I have sought to define this genre by its intention, materials, and motifs; to suggest the social backgrounds out of which it has emerged and upon which it draws for its material; to discover the basic forms it has developed; and to consider the relationship between a social vision of the city and the aesthetics of the novel. Underlying the concept of the city novel is a concept of the American city as a distinctive and peculiarly modern way of life that has shaped the writer's vision and influenced the forms of his art.

I am happy to express here my deep appreciation to Professors Frederick Hoffman and Paul Wiley of the University of Wisconsin for their personal encouragement and for the helpful suggestions they gave me in the early stages of my work.

To my husband, Seymour Gelfant, I owe various happy memories associated with the writing of this book.

BLANCHE HOUSMAN GELFANT

Madison, Wisconsin
March 11, 1954

CONTENTS

ix

THE AMERICAN CITY NOVEL

CHAPTER 1

THE CITY NOVEL

AS A LITERARY GENRE

Intention

IN BEN HECHT's *A Thousand and One Afternoons in Chicago,* a newspaperman dreams of writing a great novel about the American city. He wants to discover the inmost and essential meaning of city life so that his novel can say definitively: "The city is so and so. Everyone feels this and this. No matter who they are or where they live, or what their jobs are they can't escape the mark of the city that is on them."[1] While the newspaperman is a thin, sentimentalized character, the literary impulse he is expressing is a real and urgent one: for out of the desire to define the city and reveal its essential "mark" upon its people the twentieth-century American novel has developed as a generic literary form. Behind the rise of the modern city novel has been the awareness—always growing stronger and more clearly articulated—that city life is distinctive and that it offers the writer peculiarly modern material and demands of him literary expression in a modern idiom. As a shaping influence upon the modern American literary mind, the city has made its impression not only as a physical place but more important as a characteristic and unique way of life. In order to give literary expression to this

[1] Ben Hecht, *A Thousand and One Afternoons in Chicago* (New York, Covici-Friede, 1922), 286.

3

way of life—to re-create its tensions and tempos, its institutional patterns, its economic structure, its system of tenuous and yet complex social relationships, its manners and moral temper, its breathless, sometimes stultifying, atmosphere, its immediate daily routines and mechanized monotony, and its total impact upon the mind, imagination, and spirit—the American novelist has drawn upon the methods of European and English writers. But his social vision and emotional complex, which are the intrinsic material of his art, derive from an experience of American life. This experience has developed an awareness of the distinctive qualities of the American city as a modern creation of industrialism, a melting pot, still inchoate and lacking in the rich historical and emotional associations that the centuries have built up about a London or Paris. Central to the city writer's interest in the distinctiveness, the American-ness, and urgent modernity of a Chicago or New York is his concern over the personal impact of urban life. His fundamental intention, phrased by Hecht's character, is to show what the American city is by revealing how it creates and definitively marks the people living in it.

This intention is realized within the novel as the city becomes a key actor in a human drama. It participates in the action as a *physical place,* which makes a distinctive impression upon the mind and senses; as an *atmosphere,* which affects the emotions; and as a total *way of life*—a set of values and manners and a frame of mind—which molds character and destiny. In Robert Herrick's *A Life for a Life,* there is an explicit, if rather dramatic, statement of the shaping influence of the city: "The City was man! And already it was sowing its seed in the heart of the youth, this night. It was moulding him as it moulds the millions, after its fashion, warming his blood with desire,—the vast, resounding, gleaming City. . . ."[2]

[2] Robert Herrick, *A Life for a Life* (New York, The Macmillan Company, 1910), 44.

Usually the city plays the role of antagonist. It exists as the obstacle to the fulfillment of the hero's desires, while, ironically, it may promote and encourage them. Sometimes it may itself be protagonist, emerging in such novels as John Dos Passos' *Manhattan Transfer* and Elmer Rice's *Imperial City* as a vital personality with an identity and life of its own, distinct from that of its people.

This active participation of the city in shaping character and plot distinguishes the city novel from what might be called urban local color fiction. In a local color city novel, the characters act against a static urban setting that is not the vital and necessary condition for their acts. The substitution of another backdrop might alter details within the novel but not the essential patterns of plot, characterization, theme, and language. An O. Henry short story, "The Defeat of the City," amusingly dramatizes the difference between the intrinsic and the spurious urban product.[3] (O. Henry, incidentally, for all the unwarranted praise that the social historian Henry Steele Commager[4] has given him as the authentic American city writer, is an excellent example of the writer exploiting urban material primarily for local color.) The hero of this story has come to New York from an upstate farm and has been transformed by the city: New York has "remodelled, cut, trimmed and stamped him to the pattern it approves."[5] When he visits the farm, however, he is overcome by a "rural atavism": he tears off his stylish clothes, wrestles buffoonishly, strums an old banjo, dances the buck-and-wing, and becomes so completely the "yokel" that no trace is left of "the immaculate Robert Walmsley, courted clubman and ornament of select

[3] O. Henry, "The Defeat of the City," *The Voice of the City* (Garden City, New York, Doubleday, Page and Company, 1919), 85–94.

[4] Henry Steele Commager, *The American Mind: An Interpretation of American Thought and Character Since the 1880's* (New Haven, Yale University Press, 1950), 62.

[5] O. Henry, "The Defeat of the City," *The Voice of the City*, 85.

circles." He stands unmasked as a "peasant gambolling inde-
corously in the valley"—this is his real self. Now, just as Walmsley seemed to be a real urbanite because he displayed the
clothes and manners of the city man, so local color city fiction
seems to be authentic urban literature because it uses urban
settings and dialects; but this urban paraphernalia does not
create city fiction, just as Walmsley's clothes did not create a
New Yorker. The ruling theme of O. Henry's work, for example, is the irony of coincidences, which do not depend
for their occurrence upon a particular locale; in *The Four
Million* and *The Voice of the City,* the coincidences only happen to occur in New York.

——Unlike a local color writer, the city novelist sees urban life
as an organic whole, and he expresses a coherent, organized,
and total vision of the city. As he is not concerned simply with
details of local color, he is also not concerned only with the
anecdotal value of city incidents (as O. Henry is in his stories).
In creating a unified impression, he uses particularized incidents as a means of arriving at underlying truths about city
life. He offers an interpretation and a judgment of the city—a
way of seeing and evaluating it as an ordered pattern of experiences consistent with the inner principles of its being.
While the interpretation inheres in the total formal structure
of the novel, the experiences that develop and comment upon
the meaning of city life are contained in the episode.

The death of little Arty in Farrell's *No Star is Lost* is a case
in point. When little Arty becomes ill, the O'Neills call Dr.
Geraghty, but even though the doctor realizes that the child
has diphtheria, he refuses to care for him. Arty dies; but the
children at the O'Flahertys', given careful medical attention,
quickly recover. The episodes dealing with Arty's illness and
death have suspense and human interest. But while each episode is a link in the narrative structure, it serves also as an
instrument of social commentary. Because of the circum-

stances surrounding this death, one begins to understand the structure and meaning of a social system. As Jim O'Neill realizes, his son is victimized by poverty. Dr. Geraghty will not come to a poor man's home,[6] but he arrives quickly enough at the O'Flahertys', not because Al O'Flaherty is his special friend, but because he knows he will collect his fee. Money is the arbiter of life and death in the South Side—this is what the unnecessary waste of Arty's life clearly reveals.

Almost invariably the city novel contains social implications. Yet its intention is not exhortatory. As a form of creative expression rather than propaganda, it is distinguishable from what may be called city *problem* fiction, fiction which presents a particular social evil in order to show the need for immediate reform. The purpose of a problem novel is rhetorical; its end is a call for social action. The standard for judging the problem novel is its exactness in reproducing the social facts and its influence upon public opinion. It is a good problem novel if, like good journalism, it presents facts clearly and correctly and if it leads to social reform. Perhaps the best example of problem literature is Upton Sinclair's *The Jungle*. It presents an accurate, if heightened, picture of social conditions that demand to be reformed. The exposé of the scandalously unsanitary conditions in the Chicago stockyards led to a government investigation and a federal pure foods act. The novel proposes a specific remedy for social evils, that is, a socialistic system. The affinity between problem literature and journalism is strong: in spirit, purpose, and material, *The Jungle* is a fictional counterpart of the muckraking journalism of Ida Tarbell, Ray Stannard Baker, and Lincoln Steffens.

Sometimes a fictional account of actual situations has been so close to journalism that it has almost defied classification. For example, *The Long Day* by Dorothy Richardson, a social

[6] James T. Farrell, *No Star Is Lost* (Cleveland, World Publishing Company, 1947 reprint), 602, 627.

7

worker, is a fictional statement of the author's experiences as a working-girl in New York.[7] As its conclusion it summarizes the young girl's problems and temptations in the city and outlines a program of social reforms. The difference between such problem fiction (and journalism) and the city novel can be seen by a comparison between *The Long Day* and Dreiser's *Sister Carrie*. Both depict the working-girl's struggles to find work, to maintain economic independence, and to protect herself against temptation. But *Sister Carrie* does not present a solution to the isolated problems of the young girl in the city because the novel is not limited to these specific problems. Rather it is concerned with a total way of life. It explores the values and manners of the modern city and reveals its total impact upon human character and destiny. It has also an intrinsic interest in the city as a unique place and atmosphere. In other words, the intention of the novel is to explore the city, to show what it is, what values it lives by, and what effect it has upon the individual's character and destiny. Consequently, it is broader in scope than the problem novel; it interprets city life as a social structure, while the problem novel records, in a more photographic manner, only the symptoms of a particular urban disorder.

City novelists have themselves pointed out that their intention is to give a personal impression of the city and not a solution to its problems. Dreiser, for example, recalls how his brother Paul had once shown him about New York and suggested that he write a novel to expose corruption and inequality in the city.[8] Because he was then "youthful, inexperienced, unlettered," Dreiser had thought that he could "show up some of these things" and perhaps help to prevent them;

[7] Dorothy Richardson, *The Long Day: The Story of a New York Working Girl as Told By Herself* (New York, The Century Company, 1905).

[8] Theodore Dreiser, *A Book About Myself* (New York, Boni and Liveright, 1922), 449.

8

but his mature reflection was that "picturing or indicating life" was no guarantee of changing it. He understood the purpose of the novel to be the *expression* of a personal vision of life, and not *exhortation*. In a preface to a bibliography of his work, Dreiser pointed out that his purpose was that of the creative artist—to re-create his "vision of life": "This is what living in my time has seemed like. . . . You may not like my vision . . . but it is the only one I have seen and felt . . . therefore it is the only one I can give."[9]

Later writers have become more aware of a complexity of motives behind the city novelist's act of creation. Farrell, for example, believed like Dreiser that the writer's purpose is to communicate a personal discovery about his world and that the primary function of the novel, as "a branch of the fine arts," is to provide "aesthetic pleasure."[10] Although the city novel deals with social disorder and personal failure, it produces aesthetic pleasure by virtue of the form it imposes upon the disorganized experiences of life. But Farrell also pointed out that as the writer reveals the confusions and disorder of modern life, his art becomes "an instrument of social influence."[11] The subject matter of the novel makes its claim upon the social conscience of the reader; he may be aroused to action as he is troubled by the vision of life contained within the novel. If the city novel exerts social influence, then, it is because of its social implications rather than because of a direct attack upon an urban problem.

A study of the literary methods of city novelists brings into sharp focus the integral relationship between their social vision and aesthetic technique. In the past some critics (Gran-

[9] Theodore Dreiser, Preface to Edward McDonald, *A Bibliography of the Writings of Theodore Dreiser* (Philadelphia, Centaur Book Shop, 1928), 12.

[10] James T. Farrell, *A Note on Literary Criticism* (New York, Vanguard Press, 1936), 11.

[11] *Ibid.*, 177.

9

ville Hicks, for example)[12] have taken the novelists' social ideas out of their novelistic context and judged them as social philosophy, while others (Mark Schorer in his comments on Farrell)[13] have taken a single formal element out of context and judged it as technique. But the city novel is an organic whole in which material and form have become one aesthetic integer. The material is the writers' particular social vision of city life; their techniques are the instruments through which they have crystallized and expressed this vision. The formal elements in their work—style, plot, tone, theme, and structure—give literary expression to their specific attitudes towards the city as a place, an atmosphere, and a way of life. To judge Dreiser's structure, for example, without relating it to his view of the city's economic structure, or Dos Passos' complex aesthetic design without relating that to his comprehensive view of a complex urban society, or Farrell's style without evaluating it as an instrument that reveals his characters' sensibility is to ignore the fundamental unity of the city novel as a work of art. It is only as we examine the relationship between material and form, between the vision of city life and technique, that we can evaluate city fiction as literary art; and then we also can see that its artistic achievement has been a considerable one. For not only has the city novel shown a keen insight into the social meaning of the city's complex and turbulent life: it has also developed a form for re-creating that life in imaginative terms that reveal its essential meanings.

[12] See Granville Hicks, *The Great Tradition* (New York, The Macmillan Company, 1935).

[13] See Mark Schorer, "Technique as Discovery," *Forms of Modern Fiction* (ed. by William Van O'Connor, Minneapolis, University of Minnesota Press, 1948), 283–300.

Form, Setting, and Language

THROUGH literary practice, if not through theory, three forms of the city novel have emerged: the "portrait" study, which reveals the city through a single character, usually a country youth first discovering the city as a place and manner of life; the "synoptic" study, a novel without a hero, which reveals the total city immediately as a personality in itself; and the "ecological" study, which focuses upon one small spatial unit such as a neighborhood or city block and explores in detail the manner of life identified with this place.

The portrait novel belongs in the literary tradition of the novel of initiation—that is, a novel tracing a young hero's discovery of life and growth to maturity. In the portrait novel, the hero is typically a naïve and sensitive newcomer to the city, usually a country youth, as in the fiction of Dreiser, Herrick, and Wolfe, although in Howell's *A Hazard of New Fortunes,* he is an older man. Structurally, the novel is built upon a series of educating incidents in which the city impresses upon the hero its meanings, values, and manners. As the hero responds to the insistent pressures of city life, his character undergoes a change: he learns what the city is, and this is his achievement of sophistication and maturity. He may adjust himself to an urban way of life and conform to its standards and seek its goals, or once he becomes aware of its social implications, he may repudiate it. The change in character, as a younger person either suffers inner defeat, achieves material success, or arrives at social wisdom, reflects the personal impact of urbanism. Dreiser's protagonists submit to the city: they learn to want that which it obviously values—money, fashion, and ease. The heroes of portrait novels of the thirties and forties usually repudiate city life for its injustices and materialism and dedicate themselves to the cause of social change.

11

Since the portrait study traces a process of social conditioning—the hero is gradually illuminated and conditioned to the city's way of life—the narrative pace may be slow and the effect documentary. Whatever the form and results of the conditioning, the forces acting upon the hero must be commensurate with the changes in his character. In Dreiser's novels, the city impresses itself upon the hero's mind and sensibility in a few climactic experiences, which are moments of recognition when the protagonist realizes what the city has to offer. But the preparation for these moments has been carefully laid, for example, in the studied account of Carrie's job-hunting or in the descriptions of Clyde's home environment. The potential weakness of the portrait novel is that the portrayal of environmental forces may be made at the expense of the interior drama, so that the hero seems an automaton, too much acted upon and not enough an actor. But at its best, the form allows for a revelation of a way of life in its greatest personal significance, that is, in its effect upon human character and destiny. It permits the reader to see and feel the environmental pressures that help mold, if they do not entirely determine, the moral identity of modern city man.

The ecological novel differs from the portrait study by having as its protagonist not a single person but a spatial unit —a city neighborhood, block, or even an apartment house. Interest thus focuses upon the social relationships and manners within a close group, although one figure may come to prominence, as Danny O'Neill does in Farrell's novels of the South Side. The title of the ecological novel often specifies the spatial unit: for example, there is Waldo Frank's *City Block,* Albert Halper's *Union Square,* Ann Petry's *The Street,* Sholem Asch's *East River,* and John Kafka's *Sicilian Street.* Sometimes the locale is implied in the title; Willard Motley's *Knock on Any Door* refers (as the epigraph states) to any door in the city's back alley and slum; and Nelson Algren's

The Neon Wilderness (a collection of stories) refers to Chicago's Skid Row. Sometimes the title designates the social group, as in Meyer Levin's *The Old Bunch.*

While the ecological form limits the range of the novel, it permits an intensive study of urban manners and of idiosyncratic urban types. The breakdown of the city into small, self-contained, and distinctive social worlds gives a sociological justification to the ecological approach. The fact that most recent writers have been born into a particular neighborhood and know its way of life intimately explains the increasing popularity of the form. This inmost kind of knowledge of a society within the city is the writer's equipment: it can make him, as it has made Farrell, a city novelist of manners. The ecological novel can reveal city life as it exists for the native city-dweller—perhaps devoid of its surface glamour, perhaps merely monotonous as in Farrell's South Side Chicago, or bitter and cruel as in the slums of Michael Gold's, Joseph Gollomb's and Isidor Schneider's East Side New York, or superficial and conventionalized as in Edith Wharton's "fashionable New York." Perhaps no city fiction gives the reader so immediate a sense of the familiar world of everyday experiences as the novels of Farrell. His ecological approach permits a detailed exploration of the manners and morals of a cohesive group of city people. Time moves slowly in his works— four novels are required to show Danny O'Neill's emergence from childhood and adolescence—and this slowing down of time in combination with the strict circumscription of space allows for a minute and comprehensive portrayal of how urban people think, act, and feel. The reader comes to understand the inner life of a community in terms of the perceptions of its people. In Farrell's works the reader can see the forces of environment slowly and inexorably shaping the youth, giving them the content of their experiences and determining their attitudes, actions, and destinies.

13

The synoptic novel makes the city itself protagonist. It is an inclusive form that presents the complex pattern of city life—its contrasting and contiguous social worlds (the ironic union of gold coast and slum, of gangland and bohemia, of Harlem and Chinatown), its multifarious scenes, its rapid tempos and changing seasons, its tenuous system of social relationships, meetings, and separations, and its total impact as a place and atmosphere upon the modern sensibility. Because it intends to be all-inclusive, the synoptic novel requires special techniques of condensation, integration, and characterization. The massive material of city life must be ordered and condensed to fit within a formal framework. Urban symbolism, used so prominently in *Manhattan Transfer,* is one method of condensing statement, atmosphere, and judgment. The awkwardness of Elmer Rice's *Imperial City* can be explained in part by his failure to develop successful methods of condensation. Unless the separate scenes and incidents of the synoptic novel are also integrated within a clearly defined formal frame, the novel will collapse into a loose series of incidents. Mood unifies *Manhattan Transfer,* but more important, an underlying interpretation of modern city life relates the varied incidents and characters to a unifying theme. Since the protagonist in the synoptic novel is the city itself, the technique of individual characterization raises a crucial artistic problem, for if the people do not emerge with sufficient importance and vitality, the novel loses the appeal of human drama. In *Imperial City,* Elmer Rice inserts biographical sketches within the narrative structure when the focus is upon the action of a particular character. But this is a crude device that results in awkward pauses within the novel and an undramatic exposition of character. *Manhattan Transfer* also does not successfully solve the problem of characterization, although it is the outstanding example of the synoptic city novel and of experimental technique. In its elaborate symbolism, its dissociated urban images, its dramatization of color in the cityscape, its experimentation with syncopated rhythms, and its impressionistic method, it reveals an artist's conscious effort to re-create the modern city through innovations in language and form.

The form of the city novel has important implications for the language as well as the setting. Since the ecological form limits the setting to a circumscribed and usually peculiar area, it may use this area's characteristic speech as a means of creating character and scene. The synoptic form, on the other hand, may rely heavily upon metaphor and symbol as a language that condenses description and social judgment. If in the portrait novel the hero makes a sweeping exploration of the city, a panoramic approach to setting may lead to symbolism as a technique of implicit social commentary and to the use of vulgar speech patterns as a technique for realizing atmosphere and character.

The urban setting may be created through three distinguishable elements: the physical facts of the scene (actual streets, structures, topography), the aesthetic impression that the scene makes upon a sensitive mind, and the urban atmosphere. Early writers felt called upon to give a detailed account of the physical facts—partly because they could not assume the reader's familiarity with them, partly because they themselves had only recently discovered these facts and found them exciting, partly because they felt that a literary theory of realism demanded close description, and partly because they believed it important to preserve the facts as a matter of historical record. Their difficulty lay in incorporating information about the setting into the narrative structure. Usually, they relied upon exposition, which was awkwardly set apart from the narrative. Dreiser, for example, sometimes halts his story and addresses the reader directly in order to inform him about the facts of the scene. But while this intrusion of exposition is

15

awkward, the facts are significant, for the physical scene affects the characters and produces in them attitudes and emotions that help explain their actions. Later writers have been able to incorporate facts into the structure more successfully not only because they have felt themselves less under the necessity of describing physical details but also because innovations in novelistic technique make it possible for them to project external facts through the minds of the character.

The facts themselves have changed with the historical development of the city. And the writer's response to them has also changed as he sees them from the perspective of his own time and his own personal relationship to them. The physical city of Dreiser's novels, described in expository passages, is a growing and vigorous world in which is heard constantly the noise of construction. There are grand mansions that thrill the newly arrived country youth, streaming crowds of well-dressed people who arouse their admiration and envy, tall and impressive office buildings that inspire wonder and awe. And in its very immensity the city also brings youth to a recognition of their smallness and essential helplessness in the modern world. In the beginning of *Manhattan Transfer,* New York is like Dreiser's Chicago a young and vigorous city with promises of a great destiny, but at the end of the novel its promise is left unfulfilled. The vision of the architects in the novel of a magnificent city of steel, concrete, and glass, beautiful in a modern way, never comes to life. New York has become a place of incessant movement, clamorous noise, stench, oppressive heat or biting wind, of dirt and garbage and grit. The physical city of Farrell's novels is a narrow and confining neighborhood far different from Dreiser's immense city of glittering contrasts. The boys play in small alleys or narrow streets, and the women live out their days in cluttered apartments. The only spot of beauty in this dismal world is a small artificial park.

When the objective scene is presented as subjective experience, it usually becomes not a statement of fact but an aesthetic impression. The setting is no longer described: it is dramatized as an inner experience. The emphasis is therefore not upon the facts of perception: it is upon the fact *of* perception —upon the way one sees the scene, the way it seems to be. The aesthetic impression reflects the quality of mind of the observer, whether it be the novelist or one of his characters. Because it gives a personal reaction, in which the selective element is significant, it also contains an implicit judgment. Whether one finds the city a place of beauty or ugliness, of harmony or discord, may be expressed through the selective process that determines the details of the aesthetic impression.

Like the aesthetic impression, the atmosphere realizes the setting as a physical place and comments on it. The difference in atmosphere between an early and later city novel is partly a historical one; but also it reflects a change in attitude towards the city and a change in the writer's knowledge. Dreiser saw the city as it was going through an exhilarating period of growth, and he saw it as a newcomer. In his novels the atmosphere plays an important part in a pattern of defeat: it arouses in youth hopes that are to be unrealized. His characters move in an atmosphere of vigor, strength, and excitement, and only gradually are they made aware of undercurrents of struggle and tensions in the atmosphere. When they begin to appreciate these currents, their hopes have already been doomed to defeat. Dos Passos' characters also move in an atmosphere of excitement and tension, but it is one that has lost its power to inspire dreams. The contrast between the atmosphere of Dreiser's city and that of Farrell's is a sharp and significant one. Farrell's young men do not step out into a city whose vigorous mood stimulates and excites them; they live in an atmosphere of stagnation in which are hidden currents of brutality. The city that inspired in characters like

17

Carrie, Eugene Witla, or Cowperwood enthusiasm and a vast eagerness to live has now become a place that makes the young people weary with the emptiness of time.

In giving expression to the city as a place and a way of life, city novelists have been concerned with the development of an idiom appropriate to their material. Because the world they deal with is a mechanized world of man-made structures, a language that draws heavily upon metaphors and symbols taken from nature seems incongruous and outmoded. Rather, the city itself has provided a vocabulary for the urban novel. While early novels like *Sister Carrie, A Life for a Life,* and *The Voice of the Street* employed urban symbols, the need for an appropriate idiom was not explicitly discussed. But a more recent novelist like Farrell, who has become fully aware of his role as city novelist, has pointed out in critical writings the need for a metaphorical and symbolic language derived from the facts of modern urban life. In a review of Edward Dahlberg's novel *Those Who Perish,* he wrote:

. . . an author does not pick his images out of a grab bag, but rather they grow out of his own background and changing experiences. . . . it is apparent that romantic literary conventions have already passed their efflorescence and that they reflect an ideology of dualism completely dead and antiquated for many of us.

Contemporary American writers, in many cases, I believe, have . . . perceived this fact about the use of romantic symbolisms. Many of them are the products of urban life. In their immediate sensory experiences they have been most affected by the sights, sounds, odors, and objects of an industrial city. In their first stages of reading particularly, they have absorbed much of the romantic poets, and in their early writing there has been some imitation of the romantics. Generally speaking, the charms and attractions of nature have been peripheral if not non-existent in their lives. Hence they often have sensed a dichotomy between the objects and sensations they have sought to describe and the language and symbolism they have inherited.[14]

Perhaps one of the most conscious experimenters with urban imagery is Dos Passos in *Manhattan Transfer*. His use of the dissociated or fragmentalized image is particularly effective in creating the sense of rapid movement within the city, while it suggests also a peculiarly modern kind of perception. In very recent fiction, the most evocative and stirring use of urban imagery has been made by Nelson Algren.

Urban symbolism equates physical elements in the setting with social or psychological characteristics of city life. The symbol not only suggests an interpretation of urban society but it usually contains an implicit moral judgment. Thus, symbolism is one of the city novelist's means of introducing his evaluation of modern life without, however, intruding himself as direct commentator. Early novels which use urban characters as symbols are H. B. Fuller's *The Cliff-Dwellers* and Ernest Poole's *The Voice of the Street*. In the former, the elusive figure of a beautiful pampered wife of a Chicago titan symbolizes the materialistic impulse within competitive Chicago, as well as the injustices and social inanities that result from this materialism. In *The Voice of the Street,* the hero, who might be taken for a kind of urban "Everyman," vacillates between two characters, who together personify the dual forces of good and evil in the city. Herrick's *A Life for a Life* makes a simple linear equation between a huge glittering sign that says "Success" and the materialistic and competitive drives within urban society. Beneath the sign there takes place an accident which indicates the high human cost of success. As in *Manhattan Transfer,* fire is symbolic of the destructive element in modern life. Dreiser made most effec-

[14] James T. Farrell, "In Search of an Image," *The League of Frightened Philistines* (New York, Vanguard Press, 1945), 156f.

19

tive symbolic use of fashion: in a society where people were anonymities, the outward signs of dress became a kind of symbolic language that communicated one's social and economic position. Perhaps no writer translated the facts of city life into symbolic gestures as much as Thomas Wolfe, although his symbolism was not always conscious and controlled; and perhaps no writer has so consciously controlled his urban symbols as John Dos Passos in *Manhattan Transfer*. In Meyer Levin's *The Old Bunch,* the Chicago World's Fair becomes an interesting symbolic counterpart to the city itself: its flimsy façades and glittering spectacles are destroyed in a final collapse, just as, Levin implies, the false values and deceptive foundations of urban society are also doomed to destruction. These are only a few examples of how the city novelist has assimilated the physical facts of the urban setting into his language.

Another development has been the use of vulgar city speech as a medium for creating character and scene. This development can be explained in part as the result of a shift in narrative point of view. When the early novelist like Dreiser or Herrick put himself in the position of omniscient author, he spoke in his own language. Dreiser characteristically shifted from a most extravagant romantic idiom to journalese and to scientific jargon. This was his own vocabulary. But once the writer projected the scene from within the consciousness of his characters, he began to employ their speech patterns, intonations, and rhythms. Particularly in the ecological novel, an idiosyncratic language—whether that of the Chicago Irish or the New York East Side Jews—has been an aesthetic medium. The effectiveness of this language depends upon the novelist's ability to make it a revelation of a state of mind and a way of life; and contrary to common critical opinion, this is the achievement of Farrell's language—it creates and comments upon the South Side and its people.

20

Themes

TWENTIETH-CENTURY life has thrust upon the modern artist certain obsessive concerns—to name some, a concern over man's aloneness and alienation, over the collapse of his community and the breakdown of tradition, the ineffectuality of love and religion, the impact of mechanization, the materialism of modern life, and the conflict between artist and society. These are the themes of modern art; they are also the themes of city fiction. Because the modern American city abstracts and concentrates the social forces that have given the artist his themes, the city novel can develop and project these themes against the background that most clearly illuminates their social origins and implications. The modern experience of alienation and aloneness is thus related to a breakdown of tradition and community nowhere so striking and definitive as in the city. The materialistic temper of the age, as well as the mechanistic basis of our modern way of life, is also most intensely expressed in the city. And the tempo and tensions of the twentieth-century world of speed and hectic amusement are revealed in the rhythms and pace of big city life. In the same way that the city epitomizes the twentieth century, city fiction focalizes the main themes of twentieth-century literature.

The comprehensive theme of city fiction is personal dissociation: the prototype for the hero is the self-divided man. Dissociation is a pathological symptom which results from, and reflects, a larger social disorder. The dissociated person has not found a way to integrate motive and act and so to organize his life's activities towards a continuous and progressive fulfillment of his desires. In contrast to inhibition, which implies coercive pressures from an organized society, dissociation arises mainly because of a lack of social unanimity: the community has failed to provide a cohesive tradition that

21

can guide the individual in his choice of goals and moral alternatives. Dissociation is also distinguishable from frustration. One experiences frustration when he is prevented from attaining his goal; but one is dissociated when he cannot even clearly define what his goal is.

In *Manhattan Transfer,* Jimmy Herf articulates most clearly the confused and indecisive feelings of personal dissociation. He is discussing his failure to achieve fulfillment with his friend Stan Emery (who expresses his own inner dissociation by seeking escape from reality in alcohol):

"The trouble with me [Jimmy says] is I cant decide what I want most, so my motion is circular, helpless and confoundedly discouraging."

"Oh but God decided that for you. You know all the time but you wont admit it to yourself."

"I imagine what I want most is to get out of this town [New York] preferably first setting off a bomb under the Times Building."

"Well why don't you do it? It's just one foot after another."

"But you have to know which direction to step."[15]

In Dreiser's characters, desire is urgent and intense, but dissociation manifests itself because the character does not really understand the nature of his desire—and consequently, he seldom makes the right decision for his own happiness. With Carrie, for example, desire and action remain essentially unintegrated: while she really wants beauty, she acts to attain only its false appearances in fashion and fame. And her dream of personal happiness and fulfillment remains as elusive at the end of the novel as it was at the beginning.

The irony, pathos, and tragedy of city fiction lie in the fact of dissociation. Ironically, the city novel shows that the

[15] John Dos Passos, *Manhattan Transfer* (New York and London, Harper and Brothers, 1925), 176. Italics mine.

chaotic conditions of urban society create man's intense need for conscious self-integration while they also constitute the obstacles to personal fulfillment. Thus, from *Sister Carrie,* the first city novel of the century, to such recent works as Nelson Algren's *The Man with the Golden Arm,* city fiction has portrayed man searching for a complete self in an urban world where personal integration or completeness seems to have become impossible. The pathos and tragedy of urban fiction lie in the inner defeat that man suffers as he becomes self-divided and perhaps even self-destructive. The "stranger motif" is another expression of the pathetic and tragic implications of dissociation. The characters in urban fiction typically feel that they are strangers moving in an alien world. Their subjective experience is one of loss and confusion: they feel as though they have lost hold of their identity, that they have failed to define and objectify themselves, and that any course of action may involve them in serious self-contradictions, if not indeed in self-destruction. The failure of personal love is both cause and consequence of an inner dissociation. As Sherwood Anderson tried to show, an incomplete man cannot love; and a man who cannot objectify himself through relationships of love cannot be sure of the reality of his identity. If the failure to conciliate motive, perceptions, and acts is final, defeat is inevitable. But if a character recognizes the cause of his floundering, he may decide upon some course of action. Like Jimmy Herf in *Manhattan Transfer,* he may leave the city for an unknown destination, or, like Farrell's Danny O'Neill, he may dedicate himself to the task of changing society.

In Tess Slesinger's *The Unpossessed,* another aspect of dissociation is very specifically revealed, and that is its relationship to a new kind of personal freedom, the freedom that results from the collapse of binding social conventions. It is partly because the individual is free—free, it seems, from coercive moral restraints, from clearly defined social responsibilities, from the forces of convention and the ties to family and community—that he suffers inner confusions and feels himself somehow lost in a social void. The heroine of *The Unpossessed,* the modern liberated woman, articulates her feelings of isolation, impotence, and sterility in an interior monologue, and significantly, she ties these together with her sense of personal freedom. She recalls that when she separated from her lover, "We wept because we could not weep, we wept because we could not love, we wept because . . . we care about nothing, believe in nothing, live for nothing, because we are free, free, free, like empty sailboats lost at sea."[16]

Although dissociation takes form as a personal failure, it has been related in both literary and sociological pictures of the city to the social context of urbanism as a way of life. This relationship between personal and social systems of disorder is expressed in the formal terms of the novel as an interaction between character and setting or milieu. It is expressed in other terms in a sociological theory of urbanism that defines the collective characteristics of the city as a way of life and describes their personal consequences for the individual. While the sociology of city life cannot validate the art of the city novel, it can illuminate the social backgrounds with which the novel is concerned and out of which it has emerged. Because the actualities of city life have shaped the city novelist's vision of life and given him the material, themes, symbols, setting, and language of his art, an understanding of the modern city's essential characteristics can further our understanding of the city novel. The following chapter gives a selective summary of these characteristics as they have been formulated and systematized in the sociological theory of urbanism.

[16] Tess Slesinger, *The Unpossessed* (New York, Simon and Schuster, 1934), 136.

CHAPTER 2

THE SOCIOLOGY
OF CITY LIFE

The Subway

IF WE WONDER why city people typically develop certain attitudes and patterns of social relationships—if indeed we question that the urban way of life is peculiar, different from the way of life in the small cohesive community—we might consider for a moment the human reactions in a crowded, hot metropolitan subway. Subway life in a way epitomizes city life: in the daily life situation within the subway are the collective physical conditions and psychological tensions that give rise to a manner of life defined as urbanism. As crowds of total strangers are herded together in a limited space, forced into a physical proximity that belies their social isolation, they are called upon to make some adequate inner adjustment to the outer conditions. Thus in the subway, as in the city, mere physical conditions regulate peculiar social and psychological responses. In a small-town bus, one may greet each of his neighbors by name; in the urban subway, one is surrounded by anonymities, and if one should speak to everyone, he would soon develop laryngitis. One cannot respond to the subway hordes with the same sociability, the same act of individual recognition, courtesy, and interest that one might show lifelong neighbors in a small community. A sheer need to conserve energy requires a pattern of reaction that expresses itself as indifference, reserve, perhaps even as outright hostility. But more than this, the competitive situation in the subway—the disproportionate number of people to seats and trains—develops aggressive behavior. The man who must punch a time clock at a certain minute has no time for courtesies; should he permit the ladies to enter the train before him, he would never get to work. The outsider who looks upon the pushing subway rider as an aggressive, rude boor would soon admire and try to achieve his elbow skill if he too had daily to fight his way into the subway.

Within the subway, strangers are forced into close physical contact: like proverbial herded cattle, they press shoulder to shoulder, buttock to buttock. The paradox of "social distance" in "physical proximity" gives rise to a peculiar sense of aloneness. One is cloaked in anonymity—"alone and lonely in the crowd." One shares a few feet of space with people with whom he may have no shared tradition or common background. Social and economic disparities are glaringly set off: one rider may get off at Wall Street and spend the day in an air-cooled office; another may get off at the garment center and spend eight hours in a close, noisy factory room. The role of fashion in the subway, as in the city, is symbolic: fashion is used to reveal or else conceal one's social status. It may be impossible, for example, to determine from a woman's dress whether she is an underpaid salesgirl or a rich young wife; for the salesgirl may try to conceal her position by lavishing all her money on clothes and grooming. While strangers communicate mediately through the symbolic language of fashion and possession, lifelong neighbors in a small town acknowledge each other on an immediate and personal basis.

If the vast subway system should suddenly go out of commission, the entire economic life of the city would be endangered. The thousands of people who ride the subways and supply the life to the city are dependent upon the machine.

26

Indeed, city life is fundamentally premised upon the fact of the machine. The mechanized quality of the urban milieu is reflected in the subway rider's experience. He breathes a fetid air and gazes at drawing tunnels and gloomy stations; he allows gaudy advertisements to impress themselves upon his mind until his response to products is mechanically conditioned. An experience of awe and wonder at God's magnificent creation can hardly overwhelm him. His experience is of tension and fatigue as the sudden starts and stops, the rumbling, grating noises, the dirty air, and close smells insult the sensibilities.

The analogy between subway and city cannot, of course, be pressed too closely; but it does illuminate certain basic aspects of urbanism as a way of life. It suggests how peculiar physical conditions—the crowding of large numbers of people in a confined and mechanized environment—give rise to certain patterns of behavior (to indifference, impersonality, competition, aggressiveness, and reserve); to a typical inner experience of aloneness and anonymity, of tension and a sense of helplessness; to a sense of the outer world as a mechanical creation of man rather than as a beauteous and divine creation of God; and to a materialistic set of values, as fashion and conspicuous consumption become symbols of success. These are generalizations: they do not at all preclude the possibility of individual variations and differences. Some singular incident or person—an inquisitive child, a drunk, or a stranger asking directions—may momentarily draw the subway riders together, so that they will smile at each other and speak. But characteristically, *in general,* there is a collective set of attitudes and a pattern of behavior to which the subway rider conforms. In the same way, there is a typical manner of life, a typical frame of mind, characteristic of the city as a whole.

27

The City

THE TYPICAL characteristics of city life are systematically stated in the modern sociological theory of urbanism. As an extraliterary tool, this theory can be useful in an interpretation of city fiction in the same way that Frederick Jackson Turner's theory of the frontier proved useful to a study of the frontier influence on American literature.[1] Turner's definition of the frontier as a physical place with psychological implications[2] allowed Lucy Hazard, for example, to trace the literary significance of the frontier as both a setting and a frame of mind—a pioneering spirit[3] which left its mark upon writers far removed from actual conditions of frontier life. The urban sociologist's concept of the city as a physical entity that produces a particular manner of life and state of mind corresponds to Turner's concept of the frontier. In the following statement of the urban sociologist's assumptions, the substitution of "frontier" for "city" would give us Turner's basic postulates: (1) the city as a physical environment produces a characteristic state of mind and pattern of manners; (2) "the total impact of urban life upon the individual is pro-

[1] Frederick Jackson Turner, "The Significance of the Frontier in American History," originally printed in 1893 and reprinted in *The Frontier in American History* (New York, Henry Holt and Company, 1920).

[2] "That coarseness and strength combined with acuteness and inquisitiveness; that practical, inventive turn of mind, quick to find expedients; that masterful grasp of material things, lacking in the artistic but powerful to effect great ends; that restless, nervous energy; that dominant individualism . . . and buoyancy and exuberance . . . these are traits of the frontier, or traits called out elsewhere because of the frontier." *Ibid.*, 37.

[3] Lucy Hazard, *The Frontier in American Literature* (New York, Thomas Crowell Company, 1927). Miss Hazard states that the successive frontiers "display a common factor," which is the "pioneering spirit: a spirit of determination, of endurance, of independence, of ingenuity, of flexibility, of individualism, of optimism," p. xviii.

28

foundly different from that of non-urban life";[4] (3) urbanism as a *way of life* is not confined to the physical city, but may be transmitted to other geographical areas; and (4) on the basis of empirical evidence and deduction, the sociologist can specifically describe the characteristics that collectively identify the city as a way of life.

Systematic investigations leading to a coherent theory of urbanism were not carried on intensively until after World War I,[5] although at the end of the nineteenth century it was already apparent that the growing American city was producing a distinctive way of life. In 1915, the prominent sociologist Robert Park wrote an influential article outlining specific problems to be investigated if the city was to be understood not merely as a physical entity but also as a "psychophysical mechanism."[6] Pioneer studies on Chicago appeared after the war, among them such classic works as Harvey Zorbaugh's *The Gold Coast and the Slum* (1929); Frederick Thrasher's *The Gang* (1927); Louis Wirth's *The Ghetto* (1929); Ruth Cavan's *Suicide* (1928); and *The City* (1925), a collection of articles by Robert Park, Ernest Burgess, and Roderick McKenzie.[7] One of the monumental works on the impact of urbanism also belongs to this period: *The Polish Peasant in Europe and America* by W. I. Thomas and Florian Znaniecki. Since this beginning in the 1920's, sociological research has been extensive. In 1945, for example, Ernest Burgess and

[4] Niles Carpenter, *The Sociology of City Life* (New York, Longmans, Green and Company, 1931), 217.

[5] Note two articles on urbanism in the *American Journal of Sociology* of March, 1912: H. B. Woolston, "The Urban Habit of Mind," Vol. XVII, 602–14; Frederick Howe, "The City as a Socializing Agency," Vol. XVII, 590–601.

[6] Robert Park, "The City: Suggestions for the Investigation of Human Behavior in the City Environment," *American Journal of Sociology,* Vol. XX (March, 1915), 577–612.

[7] For full reference see bibliography of Selected Background Readings.

Harvey Locke brought out a comprehensive study of the urban family, *The Family: From Institution to Companionship*. A highly significant article summarizing the sociological view of the city is Louis Wirth's "Urbanism as a Way of Life."[8] Published in 1938, it contains the germinal concepts of the theory of urbanism. Wirth singles out three characteristics of the urban population—its great numerical size, its density, and its heterogeneity—as having sociological implications of fundamental importance.

The significance of the numerical size of the urban population is that it weakens social ties. Instead of the close personal contacts typical of the small community, relationships in the city tend to be "impersonal, superficial, transitory and segmental."[9] In segmental relationships, a person reacts to only a part of another's personality. (For example, a purchaser in an urban department store finds himself reacting not to a sales*woman* but to a *sales*woman: the total identity is lost.) Such incomplete responses are a physical necessity. Sociologists have explained that "if the unceasing external contact of numbers of persons in the city should be met by the same number of inner reactions as in the small town, in which one knows almost every person he meets and to each of whom he has a positive relationship, one would be completely atomized internally and would fall into an unthinkable mental condition."[10] Even the conspicuous "reserve" and indifference of city people towards each other can be interpreted as mechisms for "immunizing" one's self against potential expectations from a tremendous number of people to whom it is physically impossible to respond. Because so many relation-

[8] *American Journal of Sociology,* Vol. XLIV (July, 1938), 1–24.
[9] *Ibid.,* 12.
[10] Georg Simmel, "Die Grossstädte und das Geistesleben," *Die Grossstadt* (ed. by Theodor Petermann, Dresden, 1903), 187–206, quoted by Wirth, "Urbanism as a Way of Life," *American Journal of Sociology,* Vol. XLIV (July, 1938), 11f.

ships are segmental, however, people become accustomed to reacting to each other as though they were utilities rather than human beings. The breakdown in personal relationships leaves man without objective assurance of his value—even of his identity—as a complete person. Out of the sense that one is unrecognized and unresponded to comes a characteristic feeling of aloneness, a feeling that one is wandering in a "social void."

The density of population, that is, the concentration of numbers as differentiated from the great size, reinforces the sense of social void. People are thrown physically together while they remain socially apart, and the characteristic loneliness in city life derives partly from the pointed contrast between apparent closeness and actual isolation. A further effect of density is nervous tension: "the necessary frequent movement [Wirth writes] of great numbers of individuals in a congested habitat gives occasion to friction and irritation. Nervous tensions which derive from . . . personal frustrations are accentuated by the rapid tempo and the complicated technology under which life in dense areas must be lived."[11]

Both the density and the heterogeneity of the urban population explain the segregation of social groups into small differentiated settlements. "The city . . . tends to resemble a mosaic of social worlds in which the transition from one to the other is abrupt."[12] Contrasts are startling and extreme: within a few blocks lie the city's "gold coast" and slum, the staid brownstone houses and bohemia. The ecological pattern undergoes change, sometimes slowly, sometimes rapidly, as neighborhoods deteriorate or are "invaded" by new social groups. The closeness of areas that have different cultural patterns may develop one's sense of toleration and a "relativistic

[11] Wirth, "Urbanism as a Way of Life," *American Journal of Sociology*, Vol. XLIV (July, 1938), 16.
[12] *Ibid.*, 15.

31

perspective." But one may also become confused. Faced by conflicting traditions and alternative moral codes, the individual may find himself in a moral dilemma. Without a single guiding tradition he may feel himself caught in irreconcilable contradictions. Because his own relationship to any single group can change easily—and because the entire social pattern of neighborhoods is constantly shifting—instability becomes a norm. The unchangeable element in city life seems to be change itself.

As a community, the city gives rise to the same type of relationships and attitudes that it fosters as a physical place. Just as physical circumstances have created a mosaic of segregated cultural areas, the breakdown of social institutions has resulted in (and is also the result of) a decline of community life within separate areas. From his study of Chicago's Near North Side, Harvey Zorbaugh concluded that community life was disappearing with the city's natural areas.[13] Not only had the city as an entity ceased to be a community, in the sociological sense, but also within definable separate social worlds (in the Gold Coast, the rooming-house district, the artist's bohemia, and the various neighborhoods within the slums) there was no cohesive community. The social and personal implications of this fact are best revealed through a comparison between the city and the village, for the village provides the clearest example of community life. Zorbaugh describes the village as "a homogeneous, relatively undifferentiated social group":

Its population is relatively one in social and economic status. There are few contrasts between the accepted and the outlandish. Every social situation has been defined for generations, and the person is made to conform to the traditional behavior patterns. Persons re-

[13] Harvey Zorbaugh, *The Gold Coast and the Slum* (Chicago, University of Chicago Press, 1929).

spond to situations with common attitudes. Where the person cannot meet the situation for himself, the community meets it for him. In a crisis the group acts as one.[14]

As concepts and as social realities, the community and the city are antithetical. Social unanimity, characteristic of a community, cannot survive in a milieu in which various and conflicting cultural patterns exist side by side. Because no one tradition is socially agreed upon, the individual cannot turn to tradition for a definition of his social role. The failure of the family and the church to perpetuate a guiding tradition is a consequence of the breakdown of the community; it also contributes to the process of social disintegration. While social institutions sometimes act to thwart the individual, they have the positive function of giving him moral and social guidance.[15] When they fail in this function, they throw the individual upon his own inner resources. Without a moral direction, he may make decisions that are harmful to himself as well as to society.

In a recent study of the urban family, Burgess and Locke have pointed out that "most of the factors making for family integration are absent or at a minimum in the modern urban American family."[16] Whereas members of the rural family "work as a unit with resulting family solidarity,"[17] those of the urban family work separately. The industrial system of division of labor deprives the family of economic unity and self-sufficiency, just as commercialized entertainment deprives it of an essential social function. The movies, poolroom, dance

[14] *Ibid.*, 223.
[15] See John Lewis Gillin and John Philip Gillin, *An Introduction to Sociology* (New York, The Macmillan Company, 1942), 325–31.
[16] Ernest Burgess and Harvey Locke, *The Family: From Institution to Companionship* (New York, American Book Company, 1945), 356.
[17] *Ibid.*, 71.

33

hall, or bowling alley take the individual out of the home and further the process of family disintegration initiated by working conditions. And the unsatisfactory aspects of living in small and crowded apartment-house flats either cause the family to disperse or else produce tensions within the home.[18]

Since the realities of everyday life seem to conflict with the ideals of the church, the influence of organized religion is also weakened. Caught in serious contradictions between a business ethic and the Christian ethic, an individual may find himself in a moral dilemma. Material success and spiritual salvation seem to require irreconcilable modes of behavior. Moreover, the constant pressures of a mechanized environment challenge religious convictions. Because the city man lives in a world created by man under the impulse of economic motives, he may become skeptical of supernatural explanations of life. The immediate intuition of God as a creative and fertile Principle or as a benevolent Being—often called forth by a direct perception of the abundance, variety, and beauty of nature—is hardly provoked by a mechanized urban setting. Sociologists point this out:

the city man tends to be somewhat more rational, or at least more inclined toward a naturalistic as opposed to a supernaturalistic interpretation of his universe . . . possibly because he lives in a social world which he can interpret largely in terms of cause and effect. He sees with his own eyes the material growth and functions of the city—the erection of buildings, the construction of streets and viaducts, the movement of vehicles, and innumerable other things that affect his existence; and while he may know little of the actual processes and techniques involved in the cultural changes, there is nothing particularly mysterious or awe-inspiring about them.[19]

[18] Note the recognition of this fact in William Dean Howells, *A Hazard of New Fortunes* (New York, Harper and Brothers, 1911 ed.). Mr. March says, "The flat abolishes the family consciousness." p. 73.

[19] Noel Gist and L. Halbert, *Urban Sociology,* Revised ed. (New

The effects of the scientific revolution are thus immediately experienced. Modern technology has produced the city, and the response to the products of technology is a rational and materialistic point of view which often may involve, in its negation of the supernatural, a repudiation of religious doctrines.

Besides affecting man's religious attitudes, technological advances have deprived man of the self-sufficiency usually associated with the American frontiersman and with the American character in general. Specialization, the effect of an industrial division of labor, has been called "the essence of city life."[20] While specialization has given man leisure time to cultivate the arts, it has denied him independence. Indeed, the central economic activity of his life, earning a living, typically narrows his range of achievement and makes him increasingly dependent. Since a city man develops few skills other than those required for his special work, any dislocation in the economic world challenges his security. As Louis Wirth has said, "The city discourages an economic life in which the individual in time of crisis has a basis of subsistence to fall back upon."[21] Out of a dependence upon others, a relative insignificance in a huge machine economy, an inability to perform more than a limited function, and an economic insecurity, grows a strong, if secret, sense of inadequacy. In Robert Lynd's *Knowledge for What?* we have a clear-cut statement of the relationship between economic specialization and the inner experience of helplessness:

Ours is a world of division of labor and specialization. Each of

York, Thomas Crowell Company, 1946), 346. See also Robert Park *et al.,* "Magic, Mentality and City Life," *The City* (Chicago, University of Chicago Press, 1925).

[20] Carpenter, *The Sociology of City Life,* 443.

[21] Wirth, "Urbanism as a Way of Life," *American Journal of Sociology,* Vol. XLIV (July, 1938), 21.

us works, whether scientist or business man, on a narrow sector. This enhances our feeling of helplessness, because, whatever we do, we feel ultimately coerced by larger forces not controllable within our immediate area of personal concentration. Herein lies one source of the sense of ultimate futility that haunts our private worlds, no matter how wide our knowledge, how acute our techniques, or how great our effort.[22]

Division of labor also deprives workers of a creative satisfaction in work. A craftsman can express himself creatively, but the man on an assembly line is merely an extension of the machine. As the machine standardizes his movements, it robs them of creative meaning. Engaged in only a part of a total process, man responds with only part of his personality; segmentalization of experience, typical of his social relationships, thus also characterizes his work. Moreover, since mass production calls for mass consumption, man is urged and frightened into buying standard products. As he wears the same clothes as other men, reads the same newspapers, smokes the same cigarettes, enjoys the same entertainment, he becomes a standardized product, much like an interchangeable unit on an assembly line. The machine deprives him of individuality. It acts also as a coercive force that determines the forms of human behavior:

Beginning by standardizing production processes, the machine finally standardizes ways of living. The worker must submit to stereotyped movements dictated by machines and consumers must submit to the consumption of standardized goods. In short, the machine negates all forms of behavior which do not conform to its movements. . . . This modern standardization . . . is standardiza-

[22] Robert Lynd, *Knowledge for What?: The Place of Social Science in American Culture* (Princeton, Princeton University Press, 1946), 12.

tion by reason of external compulsion and therefore becomes central to any rational explanation of modern life.[23]

The flagrant materialism of city life is integrally related not only to the economics of industrialism but also to a modern state of mind. Money can, of course, bring economic security in an insecure world. But more than this, it can give emotional security. If one feels himself an anonymity, wandering alone in a social void, dependent upon others and upon a vast impersonal mechanistic system, he can achieve some sense of identity and value through conspicuous consumption. External fineries and extrinsic possessions become a compensation for a deeply rooted inner sense of helplessness. For people who live among each other as strangers, fashion comes to symbolize status and achievement. In the small community such symbolic representation is unnecessary; people meet each other with full recognition, no matter what clothes they wear or what model car they drive. But in a world where men are virtually anonymous, they "are rated according to fixed standards, such as wealth, party, occupation."[24]

The struggle for success in the city is essentially a struggle for the possession of things (although there are always exceptions, people who measure success by nonmaterial goals). Nowhere else are luxuries so glittering and seductive; and nowhere do they exert a greater power over the imagination. The life of the rich seems glamorous and completely enviable, while the appalling contrasts between poverty and wealth accentuate the desire for material things. The qualities necessary to attain success are those characteristic of urban social relationships: competitiveness, predatoriness, impersonality, and

[23] Nels Anderson and E. C. Lindeman, *Urban Sociology: An Introduction to the Study of Urban Communities* (New York, A. A. Knopf, 1928), 181.

[24] Howard Woolston, "The Urban Habit of Mind," *American Journal of Sociology,* Vol. XVII (March, 1912), 605.

indifference. Thus, social, economic, and psychological factors reinforce each other, producing a high degree of selfishness and self-interest. Since the struggle for money further alienates man from his fellow men, it sets added obstacles in the way of the personal recognition he desires but can achieve only through the co-operation of others. Thus the acquisition of material things may not bring self-realization, while the process of acquisition may in itself intensify man's spiritual disunity.

The pursuit of success at least focalizes a person's activities and gives them organized direction. The inherent contradictions in the value systems that exist in city life may, however, lead to an inner dissociation, so that one's activities will be random and circular instead of progressive. Social psychologists have pointed out that the conflicts within the urban environment are responsible for a high incidence of certain types of personal disorder, such as neurosis, alcoholism, and suicide. Karen Horney states that "where highly contradictory values and divergent ways of living exist side by side, the choices the individual has to make are manifold and difficult,"[25] and the pattern of inner contradictions typical of the neurotic is encouraged to develop. Her discussion of the social origins of neuroses is particularly pertinent to an analysis of the urban frame of mind, for she has shown that the social milieu can either foster or prevent the types of inner tension which reveal themselves as neurotic behavior. In the modern world, she says, "man has become to so great a degree merely a cog in an intricate social system that alienation from the self is almost universal, and human values themselves have declined. As a result of innumerable outstanding contradictions in our civilization a general numbness of moral perception has developed. . . . There are too few whole-hearted and inte-

[25] Karen Horney, *Our Inner Conflicts, A Constructive Theory of Neurosis* (New York, Norton and Company, 1945), 24.

grated persons around us to offer contrast to our own scatteredness."[26]

To the dissociated person, adultery, perversions, or drink may seem to offer escape from inner tensions. The fact that one can be anonymous in the great city helps explain the easy indulgence in vice. An illicit meeting or an orgiastic party can be arranged in a hotel room, in an apartment in some distant part of the city, or in a nightclub for only special patrons. The great urban population offers partners to one's perversions. Needless to say, drink or perversion cannot solve inner problems. Temporary self-forgetfulness only intensifies the basic confusions of one who escapes from life into the unreal dreams of alcohol or drugs.

The final escape of the disorganized person—the ultimate expression of one's inability to integrate desire and act towards a progressive achievement of self-fulfillment—is suicide. Ruth Cavan, who has studied the sociological implications of the act of suicide,[27] considers it (as Karen Horney considered neurotic behavior) a form of personal adjustment to a problem situation. Suicide is a method of resolving conflicts by running away from them forever. Like Karen Horney, Ruth Cavan relates this type of adjustment mechanism to a social context, giving sociologists evidence upon which to conclude that "the city . . . furnishes the setting for the type of disorganization that leads to suicide."[28] Miss Cavan has pointed out that "rural rates of suicide are everywhere lower than urban rates, and it is probable that it is not because men till the soil that they do not commit suicide, but rather because of the integrity of the social organization in rural communities which provides for the individual in such a way that dis-

[26] *Ibid.*, 134.

[27] Ruth Shonle Cavan, *Suicide* (Chicago, University of Chicago Press, 1928).

[28] Gist and Halbert, *Urban Sociology,* 384.

organization is less apt to occur than in the confusion of social groups in cities."[29] The relationship of personal disorganization in its several forms to social disorganization, as summarized by Ruth Cavan, can conclude this discussion on the pathological consequences of city life:

Whenever community organization breaks down there is an especially good opportunity for personal disorganization to occur. Vagrant and normally inhibited impulses are permitted free reign in a way not possible in a well-integrated community where departures from the standards of conduct would bring severe criticism and social ostracism. Moreover, the community without such standards attracts those from other communities both within the city and in small towns who find themselves at odds with the restrictions of the social order and who wish to live without reference to established and conventional norms of conduct. Without the repressions of community control and with the presence of people who wish forbidden stimulations and pleasures there is a tendency for institutions to be established in these disorganized areas to cater to the peculiar demands found there. The dope peddler, the vender of alcoholic drinks, the house of prostitution, the rooming-house, and the pawnshop are such institutions the reason for whose being is both the inability of the community to oust them and the willingness of a certain portion of the community actively to support them.[30]

The sociological facts presented here give us a general picture of the social milieu in which the city novelist has found his material. Although this chapter gives a highly selective summary of the theory of urbanism, it presents some of the basic conclusions of that theory, namely, that community life is disappearing in the city and that individuals who live in the city in physical proximity remain in social and spiritual isolation. The problem of reconstructing the community is one

[29] Cavan, *Suicide,* 321.
[30] *Ibid.,* 103f.

to which sociologists are now giving serious thought, for they realize that unless the individual can feel himself a part of a cohesive social group, he cannot fulfill himself as a human being.[31] The problem of the novelist is to give artistic form to the manner of life of his times. The sociological emphasis and the literary emphasis have been upon the destructive elements in city life—upon the social disorganization that has left its effects in personal confusion and disorder. Whether both points of view have given a distorted picture of the city— the legendary place of culture, the social expression of modern man's progress—cannot here be argued. One can only point out that sociological and literary interpretations of city life corroborate each other, and an understanding of urban sociology helps to explain the basic orientation of twentieth-century city fiction—its emphasis upon the materialism and inequality in city life, upon the collapse of tradition and the community, upon the failure of social institutions, and upon the inner experience of alienation and aloneness. It helps explain also a mood of foreboding in the city novel and an attitude of social condemnation.

[31] See Henry Churchill, *The City is the People* (New York, Reynal and Hitchcock, 1945).

CHAPTER 3

Theodore Dreiser:

THE PORTRAIT NOVEL

The Personal Discovery of the City

In *A Hoosier Holiday, A Book About Myself,* and *Dawn,* Theodore Dreiser has left a record of a personal discovery of the modern American city. He has described how he came to the great cities of America—Chicago, St. Louis, Cleveland, Pittsburgh, Buffalo, New York—what he found there, and how he responded. Perhaps without his realizing it, his individual perceptions and reactions gradually fell together into a pattern that defines the meaning city life held for him. Each city writer makes this definition of the city for himself, and for each it is individual and personal. But Dreiser's interpretation of the city, growing as it did out of a typical social experience of the times, has a broad historical relevancy, as well as significant implications for the development of American fiction. His personal discovery summarizes and comprehends a social experience of the times: in coming to the city, observing it, responding to it, and evaluating and finally rejecting it, Dreiser went through a typical pattern of hope and disillusionment. In this disillusioning process of discovery, he developed an understanding of city life and an emotional complex towards it that equipped him to become the generic novelist of twentieth-century city fiction. While other novelists of his time shared some of his isolated insights into the

42

meaning of city life, none had gone through the total experience of discovery that gave Dreiser an inclusive and immediate knowledge of the modern city.

Like many hopeful young people of the time, Dreiser participated in the sweeping migration from small town and country to the city. He experienced the characteristic emotions of the ordinary youth; he subscribed to his legends and ideals, and he struggled like him for success. If he could later re-create so movingly the common disillusionments, fortuities, and defeats in city life, it was because he had lived through them as personal experience. But while he experienced typical reactions to the city, the range and intensity of his emotional responses were more extreme than that of the ordinary person. He moved from the heights of exhilaration and hope through bafflement, anger, and despair to a neurasthenic sense of helplessness. His disillusionment was extreme because he felt so strongly the startling antithesis in the city between what men hope for there and what they realize.

This participation in the common struggles of city life set Dreiser apart from novelists who were dealing with themes similar to his own. For example, while Robert Herrick dealt in novels like *Memoirs of an American Citizen* and *A Life for a Life* with the destructiveness and materialism of city life, he could not bring to his work the heightened emotional awareness which made Dreiser's novels, despite their defects, gripping and alive. Herrick's highly developed New England conscience set him apart from the success-seeking, money-fevered crowd of which Dreiser had been a part. As a university instructor, Herrick lived in Chicago behind a curtain of security and stability which kept him removed from an immediate experience of the city's sordidness, confusion, and evil. Deeply as he was affected by the fearful spectacle of city life, he was nevertheless only an observer, not, like Dreiser, a participant. While Dreiser did not create characters reflective enough, or even intelligent enough, to think in a significant way about city life,(he gave us characters who experience it intensely as they seize upon and respond to its essential and yet commonplace aspects.)

Dreiser's newspaper experience also contributed to his equipment as city novelist. Not only did his reporting duties bring him into immediate contact with the sordid elements of city life; they forced him to describe these elements fully and accurately. He was trained to tell all that he knew. If he had any natural reluctance to face and describe actual social facts, it was destroyed by the discipline of his work. Even when he witnessed the most tragic events—like an explosion of oil-tank cars that ignited men's bodies as though they were matches—he could not run away from the horror; he had to "report this, run to it, not away."[1] While others might have found it possible to withdraw from the ugliness of city life or to refuse to acknowledge it, he had daily to face corruption, vice, and injustice and to describe minutely the situations in which they were revealed. While his newspaper experience extended his knowledge of the city and intensified his sympathy for its people, it also developed a willingness to describe the dark and unhappy side of modern life. As a novelist, Dreiser was never to shrink from a minute portrayal of situations which would have been disqualified as literary material by the good taste of a mild realist like William Dean Howells. Unlike H. B. Fuller, who preferred to end his writing career rather than probe into social horrors he knew existed, Dreiser was thus steeled to deal with the tragic aspects of American life.

Another factor that gave Dreiser singularity among the novelists of his time was a quality of mind. He had a brooding and flexible mind that could absorb new material and change old ideas in order to assimilate new facts—indeed, that

[1] Dreiser, *A Book About Myself,* 158.

would throw over completely, if need be, all that it had once held. This meant that he held no theory as a certainty. He mulled over traditional views, questioned them freely, and freely rejected those that seemed unsupported by fact. His readiness to abnegate, if necessary, the traditional ideas within whose framework the literary artist had worked made him a pioneering figure. He gave up intellectual certainty for uncertainty—this was his modernity.

Dreiser's philosophy of life (the term can be applied only loosely to the totality of his beliefs) developed empirically. Formal scientific theory confirmed—it did not give him—his views on life. That Dreiser knew and was deeply impressed by Darwinian theory is clearly indicated by the mixed scientific jargon in his novels and the images based on Darwinian concepts. It is also indicated by Dreiser's explicit remark that his discovery of Huxley, Spencer, and Tyndall "quite blew me, intellectually to bits."[2] But Dreiser spoke of these scientific thinkers as having *"verified"* his "gravest fears as to the unsolvable disorder and brutality of life."[3] Moreover, he was reading them at a time of great personal disappointment and failure, when his own struggle for existence was most severe. He discovered Huxley and Spencer while he was preparing himself in Pittsburgh for a second try at New York, the city that had shown him callous indifference. He was struggling bitterly, stinting himself to save money—living, he said, "upon so little that I think I must have done myself some physical harm."[4]

Dreiser began to seek confusedly, but persistently, for a philosophy of life as soon as he found himself in the strange and bewildering world of Chicago. Here he experienced a way of life that could not be rationalized by the conventional ideas he held as a small-town boy. He had accepted his father's religious assumption of a moral order, but this assumption

[2] *Ibid.*, 457.   [3] *Ibid.*, 458.   [4] *Ibid.*, 457.

45

seemed entirely negated by the chaotic and changing scene before him. As he studied this scene, he felt forced to question and reject a set of beliefs that belonged to a world from which he was now removed. His mature views took shape under the impact of urban life: they constituted his discovery of the city. His attitude towards the city specifically changed as his knowledge of it grew. His social, political, and religious attitudes also changed and developed, so confusedly and frequently that he came finally to hold incongruous, even contradictory, views. His observations of the great inequalities permitted by urban society led him in a straight line of development to social awareness and a belief in the need for reform through political action. His joining of the Communist party shortly before his death was the final step in this development. At the same time, however, he followed a circuitous path away from, and then back towards, a rather vague religious ideal of moral order, which in his childhood had been associated with Catholicism and which came to be associated in his age with cloudy concepts of an Inner Light.

The fundamental change in Dreiser's knowledge of, and attitude towards, the city was one of which he later became fully aware. As a man of sixty, reflecting upon his youthful reactions to the city, he recalled his romantic idealization of Chicago:

The City of which I am now about to write [he says in *Dawn*] never was on land or sea; or if it appears to have the outlines of reality, they are but shadow to the glory that was in my own mind. Compassed by a shell or skull, there was a mirror inside me which colored all it reflected. There was some mulch of chemistry that transmuted walls of yellow brick and streets of cedar block and horses and men into amethyst and gold and silver and pegasi and archangels of flaming light. There was lute or harp which sang as the wind sings. The city of which I sing was not of land or sea or any time or place. Look for it in vain! I can scarcely find it in my own soul now.[5]

Dreiser was twelve when Chicago made its first impression upon him as a glorious "land of promise, a fabled realm of milk and honey."[6] His family had moved to the city from the small Indiana town of Evansville; but financial difficulties brought their stay to an abrupt end, and they were soon back in Indiana. Four years later Dreiser returned to Chicago: a youth of sixteen, he was on the timeless quest for fortune, fame, and adventure. His early feelings of infatuation were strongly reinforced. Once more Chicago seemed a miraculous city, pulsating, alive, and full of promise. Dreiser saw himself the blazing hero in the American dream-story of success. Though he was callow, poor, inexperienced, and untrained, he dared dream of a sudden and spectacular rise from rags to riches.

His attitude was typical of this period of rapid urban growth. Just as the Far West had excited youth's hopes in the early part of the century, so now the city held out promise of fabulous success. As Arthur Schlesinger, historian of the rise of the cities, has written: "It was the city rather than the unpeopled wilderness that was beginning to dazzle the imagination of the nation."[7] Since Warsaw, Dreiser's home town, was close to Chicago, he was in a position to be deeply stirred by the general atmosphere of hopefulness and excitement. He saw his friends leaving for the big city, while he himself was "fascinated by descriptions . . . in the Chicago daily papers of . . . city life."[8] Finally, a "trivial" incident—his reading of a "Sunday newspaper account of Halstead Street's

[5] Theodore Dreiser, *Dawn* (New York, Horace Liveright, 1931), 156.

[6] *Ibid.*, 229.

[7] Arthur Schlesinger, *The Rise of the City: 1878–1898* (New York, The Macmillan Company, 1933), 61.

[8] *Dawn*, 293.

47

life and activities"[9]—determined him to join the pilgrimage to the city.

Once in Chicago, Dreiser experienced the typical reactions of the small-town boy to the big city's glamour. He wandered in a dream world of surging crowds, theatres, glowing restaurants, strange and contrasting neighborhoods, and long stretches of streets lined with awesome stone buildings. The atmosphere of the expanding city was, he said, "different from anything I had ever known; it was a compound of hope and joy in existence, intense hope and intense joy."[10] Because the scene was new and strange, it seemed to him entirely praiseworthy:

In Evansville was no such congestion, no such moving tide of people, no such enthusiasm for living. I was lost in a vapor of something so rich that it was like food to the hungry, odorous and meaningful like flowers to those who love. Life was glorious and sensate, avid and gay, shimmering and tingling.[11]

Thus, Dreiser gave unqualified praise to Chicago. His first reaction was one of simple uncritical wonder and gratification. His dream lay before him, and for a while nothing could interfere with the pleasure he took in it. He was like an art-lover before a beautiful work of art: he noticed and responded to the aesthetic elements of the urban scenes (being as yet too naïve to grasp their social implications). While he was deeply moved by the spectacle of city life, he maintained the detachment of an observer. For example, when he saw a group of streetcar strikers, he did not react (as the mature Dreiser would have) with sympathy or concern. He enjoyed the sight of the sober, idle men because it was "an odd spectacle."[12] Even when he was looking for work, any commonplace urban scene could distract him. Men digging, a train

[9] *Ibid.*, 294.   [10] *Ibid.*, 159.
[11] *Ibid.*   [12] *Ibid.*, 327.

48

pulling into its station, a crowd gathering in the street, a flock of pigeons suddenly wheeling into the air—these pleased him for their aesthetic qualities, their "material facial textures."[13] Years later, he attributed his uncritical attitude as much to ignorance of social facts as to an aesthetic sensibility. In his early acceptance of city life he saw evidence of an unawakened social conscience: "Placed before a given series of facts which, had I been in the least economically or society or individually-minded, must have given rise to at least some modest social speculation, I saw only the surface scene, and other than artistically my mind was a blank."[14]

But as his relationship to the surging spectacle of city life changed, the scene lost its surface glamour. From an onlooker he became a participant in the city's struggles, and close contact with the ugly realities of city life shattered his romantic image. Disillusionment grew out of a contrast between reality and a country boy's dream, and it proved as bitter as the illusion had been bright. His failures to achieve economic security, let alone success, gave him a new perspective on the city: he saw Chicago from the position of the underprivileged, and it was a frightening sight. While his adolescent dreams had been of the fabulous pleasures of the rich, real life was forcing him to observe the plight of the poor—and to sympathize with them. Now that he himself had become one of the city's poor, a slum neighborhood that had previously excited aesthetic pleasure evoked instead horror, fear, and a sense of helplessness.

In the long days of job-hunting, as he walked the streets with his brother Al, his social conscience was awakened. "That keen appreciation of the storms and stress of life that later may have manifested itself in my writings was then being forced on me [he wrote]. For so often I was touched by the figures of other seekers like myself and Al—their eyes,

[13] *Ibid.*, 528. [14] *Ibid.*, 327.

worn faces, bodies, clothes, the weariness of them in line at so many doors! As a matter of fact, this was but the beginning of a long observation of the struggles and fortunes of man."[15] The work he finally did find drew him even more closely into contact with the tragic side of city life. As dishwasher, laundry-driver, rent-collector, he was forced to observe the sordidness of the city, to see its "pimps and prostitutes, dope fiends and drunkards," and to sympathize with the "unsatisfied dreams of its people."[16]

His experiences as a newspaperman gave the final touch to his disenchantment. To his cynical newspaper friends, the facts of urban vice and corruption were commonplace. They "looked upon life as a fierce, grim struggle in which no quarter was given or taken, and in which all men laid traps, lied, squandered, erred through illusions."[17] This was the point of view with which Dreiser himself soon "heartily agreed." What he did not absorb from them, he learned from his own reporting experiences. Assigned to write an article on "Chicago's vilest slum," he observed "slovens, slatterns, prostitutes, drunkards and drug fiends" caught up in a "horrible life" of vice and degradation.[18] In St. Louis, Cleveland, Pittsburgh, and New York, his newspaper duties forced him into contact with the lowest and most sordid elements of society; and in each of these cities the disillusionment born in Chicago grew more profound. As he changed from a spellbound youth to an experienced reporter, a man who had known intimately the evil of the city, he came to realize that poverty and degradation were not isolated social phenomena: they seemed inevitable consequences of a social structure in which "indescribable poverty" existed, and was expected to exist, alongside "indescribable wealth."[19] Individual perceptions of city life were thus beginning to fit together into a total picture of

[15] *Ibid.* [16] *A Book About Myself,* 107.
[17] *Ibid.,* 70. [18] *Ibid.,* 66. [19] *Ibid.,* 459.

urban society, a sordid and offensive picture, but one of whose truth he was convinced.

Dreiser's mature concept of the "real" city grew out of these early disillusioning experiences and observations. His own disappointments, following high expectations and hopes, may have distorted his view of city life by leading him to exaggerate its "darker phases." But there was a fundamental validity to his picture of the city; the unerring way he discovered the essential characteristics of modern urbanism reflects an acuity of observation and a readiness to absorb new and disturbing facts. Fundamental to his concept of the real city was a recognition of an appalling, almost unimaginable, inequality in the distribution of wealth. Dreiser had seen and experienced poverty in Indiana, but the poor there had never sunk to the abysmal depths of slum life as it existed in Chicago, Pittsburgh, and New York. Nor had the rich risen to such extraordinary luxury. In each city to which he came, in his gradual pilgrimage to New York, he was shocked anew by the contrast between poverty and wealth. In Chicago he was first bewildered by the unforgettable sight of "harlots . . . smirking and signaling creatures . . . ready to give themselves for a dollar, or even fifty cents . . . this in the land of this budding and prosperous West, a land flowing with milk and honey."[20] In St. Louis, he encountered, "daily if not hourly," contrasts so sharp as "to cause one to meditate on the wonder, the beauty, the uncertainty, the indifference, the cruelty and the rank favoritism of life."[21] In Pittsburgh, as he compared mansions on the east side with "hovels" at Homestead and Monongahela, he felt that "never in my life . . . was the vast gap which divides the rich from the poor in America so vividly and forcefully brought home to me."[22] And finally in New York came the climactic awareness of the economic extremes in the city:

[20] *Ibid.,* 66.   [21] *Ibid.,* 147.   [22] *Ibid.,* 392.

51

Never before had I seen such a lavish show of wealth, or, such
bitter poverty. In my reporting rounds I soon came upon the East
Side; the Bowery, with its endless line of degraded and impossible
lodging-houses, a perfect whorl of bums and failures; the Brooklyn waterfront, parts of it terrible in its degradation; and then by
way of contrast again the great hotels, the mansions along Fifth
Avenue, the smart shops and clubs and churches.[23]

This recognition of economic inequality had far-reaching
consequences for Dreiser's social and political views as well
as for his art. His novels dramatize his own startled awareness
of the fact of inequality. Structurally they are built upon contrasting episodes that thrust forth the contrasts between poverty and wealth. His personal commitment to an ideal of
social justice led him in his last years to join the Communist
party because it was the one party that professed economic
equality as its goal. But he thought, curiously, that he could
be a Party member and yet not necessarily conform to the
Party line. To signify that he meant to maintain his individuality, he took the name of "equitist."[24] His equitism indicated
not only a desire to see economic equality established in American society but also a fundamental loss of faith in the American system of free enterprise and capitalism. He had seen the
consequences of this system in the way of life in the big cities,
and this convinced him that only a radical change of system
could reinstitute the basic principles of democracy.

While Dreiser sympathized with the poor (and participated in their causes), he envied the rich. He realized that he
lacked the "temperament" and the "skill" necessary for one
to "join the narrow, heartless, indifferent scramble" for great
wealth.[25] Nevertheless, he fully appreciated the reasons for

[23] *Ibid.*, 480.
[24] See the article on Dreiser's equitism by Alva Johnston in the
New York *Herald Tribune,* November 22, 1931, 2.
[25] *A Book About Myself,* 459.

the materialistic impulse in modern man. He saw with devastating clarity the total difference between the life of poverty and the luxurious life of weath; and he realized that this difference gave man his terribly urgent desire for money. But the consequences of this desire, as he saw it, lay in brutal economic war between the money-lords (which he described in the Cowperwood novels) and in daily struggle among the common people (which he also described in *Sister Carrie, Jennie Gerhardt,* and *An American Tragedy*). So long as the worlds of the rich and poor remained so widely separated, men would engage in "wolfish" competition for wealth, and the brutalities committed in the name of free enterprise would make the city a jungle of preying and preyed-upon animals. To Dreiser, as to his character Frank Cowperwood, the battle between lobster and squid, in which the stronger animal devoured the weaker, provided a perfect analogy to human relationships in modern society.

The people caught and defeated in an internecine economic struggle seemed to Dreiser driven and helpless, as though overpowered by forces beyond human, or certainly individual, control. Dreiser's sense of man's helplessness in the great city grew out of his own experience of defeat (which had reduced him to a state of neurasthenia), as well as out of observation. He understood man's smallness and insecurity in the city. Even after he had been conditioned to the size and impersonality of Chicago, St. Louis, Cleveland, and Pittsburgh, he had found himself unprepared for the heartlessness of the greatest city of them all—and the most terrifying— New York. New York "strangely over-awed [him] and made [him] more than ordinarily incompetent by its hugeness and force and heartlessness."[26] "A sense of incompetence and general inefficiency seemed to settle"[27] upon him there, so that he was distressed by "a strong sense of my own unimpor-

[26] *Ibid.,* 479. [27] *Ibid.,* 480.

tance."[28] In *A Book About Myself* (as in *Sister Carrie*), Dreiser asked, "Whatever one might have been elsewhere, what could one be here" in New York?[29] Hurstwood is his answer. He personifies Dreiser's fear of the power of the city to reduce man to his essential nothingness. Hurstwood was conceived under the influence of one of the most sobering sights in New York—the sight of the city's ruined and homeless men spending their days on the benches in Hall Park, while behind them loomed the overpowering forms of the city's great buildings. In *A Book About Myself* Dreiser describes this inception of the character of Hurstwood:

About me on the benches of the park was, even in this gray, chill December weather, that large company of bums, loafers, tramps, idlers, the flotsam and jetsam of the great city's whirl and strife to be seen here today. I presume I looked at them and then considered myself and these great offices, and it was then that the idea of *Hurstwood* was born. The city seemed so huge and cruel.[30]

The fact that Dreiser could give birth to the idea of a Hurstwood shows how far he had come from the first vision of the city, when she had lain before him veiled in mists of wonder and beauty. Now she appeared a modern jungle where men carried on savage competition. If one failed in that competition, he was reduced to a life of poverty and struggle. If he succeeded, he corrupted himself and defeated his fellow men. The whole struggle for success then became ironic, for even if one achieved his dream of material possession, he was victimized by the loss of inner spiritual unity. In some way—physically, spiritually, economically—he was reduced to insignificance by a world too big and terrible for him.

Dreiser's personal sense of bafflement, as he tried to adjust to social facts he could not deny, resulted in an articulated

[28] *Ibid.*, 481.   [29] *Ibid.*, 437.   [30] *Ibid.*, 463 f.

belief that the universe, as well as society, was dominated by huge irrational forces. Such a belief contradicted the religious assumption of a cosmic moral order, but in the presence of evils that shocked his sensibilities, Dreiser felt he could not continue to accept a religious view of life. While writing his first newspaper articles on Chicago's blighted areas, he began to question the existence of a divine force which could permit such human degradation as he saw before him:

I had been reared on dogmatic religious and moral theory [he wrote in *A Book About Myself*], or at least had been compelled to listen to it all my life. Here then was a part of the work of an omnipotent God, who nevertheless tolerated, apparently, a most industrious devil. Why did He do it? Why did nature, when left to itself, devise such astounding slums and human muck heaps? . . . What had brought that about so soon in a new, rich, healthy, forceful land—God? devil? or both working together toward a common end?[31]

Moreover, as the city removed him from the influences of nature, he lost the immediate intuition of beauty and order which the natural scene had always inspired in him. As a boy in Indiana, his religious sensibilities had been acted upon not only by his father's Catholicism and the inculcation of the doctrines set forth in the catechism and by his mother's dreamy "mysticism" but also by his own intimate relationship with nature. In *A Hoosier Holiday* and *Dawn,* he described himself as an inquisitive and responsive youngster who would awaken at three or four in the morning to explore the mysteries and beauties of the woodlands. The natural scene stirred him to "a rich, emotional mood, tremulous, thrilling"[32] (just as later the cityscape lifted him to an emotional fervor). He describes his responses to nature in his most extravagant manner: he was "a harp on which nature idly strummed her melodies; a flower form into which she blew her endless sugges-

[31] *Ibid.,* 66. [32] *Ibid.,* 60.

tions of color; an ear attuned to infinite delicacies of sound; an eye responsive to the faintest shadows of meaning."[33] Out of his pleasure in the forms of nature came a vague apprehension of some more deeply interfused principle, a glimpse of "something immense and inscrutable . . . wherefrom these various forms emanated and to which they returned."[34] Such intuitions marked his growing faith in a divine creative principle which had designed the world for a good and purposeful end.

But once he was removed from the natural scene to the mechanized environment of Chicago, this self-identification with a divine creative force came abruptly to an end; and he was not long in redefining what he meant by nature. The term that once had stood for a rich variety of beautiful and changing forms now came to signify the savage and competitive instincts in man or the blind and impersonal force that actuated those instincts. In the Indiana woods he had sensed the harmony and oneness of all life forms, but here as he observed only a brutal struggle for survival, he was predisposed to accept a materialistic explanation of nature's beauty. He yielded to the physicist's view that "our glorious sunsets are accidents of dust, . . . that all scenery, as we know it, is chance, never to appear perhaps anywhere again."[35] If this explanation was correct, then nature was deprived of purpose and beauty. It did not occur to Dreiser that the fact that man could respond aesthetically even to purely physical elements was as significant as the fact that nature was a physical phenomenon. When he considered the scientific explanation of natural beauty, and when he observed, moreover, the predatory habits of man—"life living on life"—he felt revulsion. His early idealism gave way to a kind of cynical despair, which is suggested in this quotation from *Hey-Rub-A-Dub-Dub:*

[33] *Ibid.*, 63. [34] *Ibid.*, 62. [35] *Ibid.*, 588.

Common dust swept into our atmosphere makes our beautiful sunsets and blue sky. Sidereal space, as we know it, is said to be one welter of strangely flowing streams of rock and dust, a wretched mass made attractive only by some vast compulsory coalition into a star. Stars clash and blaze, and the whole great complicated system seems one erosive, chaffering, bickering effort, with here and there a tendency to stillness and petrifaction. This world as we know it, the human race and the accompanying welter of animals and insects, do they not, aside from momentary phases of delight and beauty, often strike you as dull, aimless, cruel, useless? Are not the processes by which they are produced or those by which they live (the Chicago slaughter-houses, for instance), stark, relentless, brutal, shameful even?—life living on life, the preying of one on another, the compulsory aging of all, the hungers, thirsts, destroying losses and pains. . . .[36]

In forsaking the organized Christian philosophy, Dreiser gave up a coherent pattern of beliefs for which he never found an adequate substitute. He fell into a twentieth-century mood of incertitude to which he tried to reconcile himself by retreating to an agnostic position. When his bafflement over the incompatibility between a knowledge of evil and a faith in God became too great for him to cope with, he staved off his own inner questioning by saying that "all we know is that we cannot know."[37] The short negativistic credo at the beginning of *A Traveler at Forty* has often been quoted as Dreiser's definitive philosophical position. Dreiser writes there: "For myself, I accept now no creeds. I do not know what truth is, what beauty is, what love is, what hope is. I do not believe anyone absolutely and I do not doubt anyone absolutely."[38]

As a matter of fact, this statement is too clear-cut to suggest

[36] Theodore Dreiser, *Hey-Rub-A-Dub-Dub* (New York, Boni and Liveright, 1920), 11.

[37] *Ibid.,* 21.

[38] Theodore Dreiser, *A Traveler at Forty* (New York, The Century Company, 1913), 4.

Dreiser's philosophical position. Throughout his lifetime, he vacillated in his views, and unavoidably he contradicted himself. Sometimes he tried to reconcile agnosticism with a profession of faith in some evolutionary force. Sometimes he wrote, in the vaguest terms, of some higher being which was ineffable: "There is something controlling, of which we are a part and not a part; there is the mystery to which we belong yet which will not show to us its face."[39] Dreiser's philosophical difficulties were as much peculiar to his age as they were personal. He was a transitional figure, trying by a deliberate effort of mind to bridge the gap between the different points of view of the nineteenth and the twentieth centuries. The most curious aspect of his intellectual position is that he could hold conflicting points of view simultaneously, as well as alternately. In his last years, he found a personal consolation in the return of his faith in a divine order that gave human suffering meaning and purpose. But if, as Lionel Trilling points out, Dreiser's final mood of "acceptance" derived from emotions with which one cannot argue as one argues with an intellectual conviction,[40] this mood did not lead him to produce his greatest work. His novels take their strength from his anger at irrational forces and social injustices and from his sense of uncertainty and disturbance. Ford Madox Ford has said that Dreiser's significance to the modern reader lies in his portrayal of the uncertainty that follows a loss of faith: "It is because he renders for us this world of fantastic incertitude that Dreiser's work is of such importance."[41]

Dreiser's indecisive rejection of orthodox religion is only one reflection of his break with traditional ways of thinking. This break is reflected also in his examination and repudiation

[39] *Hey-Rub-A-Dub-Dub,* 22.

[40] Lionel Trilling, "Reality in America," *The Liberal Imagination* (New York, The Viking Press, 1950), 3–21.

[41] Ford Madox Ford, "Theodore Dreiser: Excerpt from *Portraits from Life,"* *American Mercury,* Vol. XL (April, 1937), 495.

of both social and literary conventions. Rather than blindly accept conventional attitudes, he tested them by the realities he saw about him; and when the facts of modern life did not support the conventional theories, he rejected convention and insisted upon the need for new standards to be arrived at empirically. The "small-town mind" seemed to cling most tenaciously to outmoded codes and attitudes, while the urban mind adjusted itself more readily to the circumstances of twentieth-century life. "The small mind of the townsmen," he wrote, "is antipolar to that of the larger, more sophisticated wisdom of the city."[42] When he visited his fiancée in a "small town in the backwoods of Missouri," he saw townspeople apparently oblivious to reality, people "suspended in dreams, lotus eaters."[43] He compared their vision of life with his own, which had grown empirically out of experience and observation in Pittsburgh, Chicago, and New York. While he had learned that in modern society "self-interest and only self-interest ruled," they still believed that "the Christian ideal was right and true, and that it really prevailed in life, and that those who did not agree with it were thieves and scoundrels."[44]

In particular, he felt that sexual taboos imposed unwarranted restrictions upon the individual. In order to show the insipidity of the conventional view that "each of us was to take one wife or one husband to our heart and hearth,"[45] he "called attention to Pittsburgh, Chicago and New York . . . to the endless divorces and remarriages and all the licence of the stage and the hungry streets of harlots and kept women."[46] Here in the city were actual facts and practices that seemed to him to demand a readjustment in the attitude towards sex. His typical protest against conventional opinion was that "we were being dominated mentally by a theory that had no re-

[42] Theodore Dreiser, *A Hoosier Holiday* (New York, John Lane Company, 1916), 113.
[43] *A Book About Myself*, 426.   [44] *A Hoosier Holiday*, 279.
[45] *Ibid.*, 119.   [46] *Ibid.*, 120.

lationship to life whatsoever."[47] While he advocated a new freedom for the individual, public opinion condemned his personal behavior as well as his literary practice. It is understandable that one of his chief themes is the individual's struggle against convention and social restraints; and it is also understandable that this theme owes its prominence to his early perceptions of the disparity between the social ideals of "rural America" and the social practices within the modern city.

Paralleling his revolt against social conventions was his repudiation of the literary conventions of his time. Again, it was the contrast between an outmoded theory and a current practice—between the conventional view of life presented in literature and his own knowledge of social realities—that led him to examine and then reject the convention. His creative desire traced back, so he remembered, to his first weeks in Chicago when the spectacle of this "roaring, yelling, screaming whirlpool of life" stirred him to artistic expression. Under the influence of Eugene Field's daily column in a Chicago newspaper, he invented "word pictures" in free verse which he sent to Field, who, incidentally, never acknowledged them.[48] Three years later, as a reporter in Pittsburgh, he made a breath-taking discovery of Balzac. Balzac's novels of Paris left an overwhelming impression upon his aesthetic sensibilities: but more important, they suggested to him the use of the city as material for fiction. As he contrasted Balzac's Paris with the vital world about him, he became convinced that Pittsburgh had as much to offer the American novelist in inspiration and material as Paris had offered the French master.[49] Meanwhile, he started writing a series of mood studies that gave him his first taste of what it meant to be a creative artist.[50]

[47] *Ibid.*, 280.
[48] *A Book About Myself*, 3.   [49] *Ibid.*, 411.   [50] *Ibid.*, 413.

While Dreiser recognized in Balzac's novels characters and situations that were real to him, he found contemporary American fiction depicting an alien and fanciful world. He was appalled to realize that his deepest convictions that life was grim and sad, haphazard, casual and cruel[51] found no confirmation in current magazines and novels. Rather, fiction gave grand assurances that "beauty and peace and charm were to be found in everything."[52] Dreiser's statement in *A Book About Myself* defines clearly the difference between the vision of life that he thought should be expressed in literature and that which he found in contemporary fiction:

I was never more confounded than by the discrepancy existing between my own observations and those displayed here, the beauty and peace and charm to be found in everything, the almost complete absence of any reference to the coarse and the vulgar and the cruel and the terrible. How did it happen that these remarkable persons . . . saw life in this happy roseate way? Was it so, and was I all wrong? Love was almost invariably rewarded in these tales. Almost invariably one's dreams came true, in the magazines. Most of these bits of fiction, delicately phrased, flowed so easily. . . . They seemed to deal with phases of sweetness and beauty and success and goodness such as I rarely encountered. . . . In *Harper's* I found such assured writers as William Dean Howells, Charles Dudley Warner, Frank R. Stockton, Mrs. Humphry Ward, and a score of others, all of whom wrote of nobility of character and sacrifice and the greatness of ideals and joy in simple things.

But as I viewed the strenuous world about me, all that I read seemed not to have so very much to do with it.[53]

Even when Dreiser wished to write stories like those he was reading, he "could not think of any."[54] He could not bring himself to falsify experience in the way it seemed to him falsified by contemporary American fiction. The years

[51] *Ibid.*, 140.   [52] *Ibid.*, 490.
[53] *Ibid.*   [54] *Ibid.*, 491.

of poverty, struggle, and disillusionment and the strong irri-
tating awareness of evil and injustice had predisposed him
to look upon the "darker phases" of life. These appealed to
him as literary material. If he had anything to express, it was
his vision of man's struggle in a cruel and chaotic world.
Others should be free to express whatever vision seemed vital
and real to them. The "scope of fiction," he asserted, should
be determined by the author in accordance with his individual
point of view;[55] the writer of fiction must "interpret life as it
appeals to him or not at all."[56] His own preference was for
realistic literature: "I am for the type of fiction that confines
its attempted interpretations to not only the possibilities, but
the probabilities and I have no reading patience with anything
that does not compel me by the charm of its verisimilitude."[57]

As he tried to create a realistic literature, he broke with
current traditions, and, as Sinclair Lewis put it, he "cleared
the trail from Victorian and Howellsian timidity and gentility
in American fiction to honesty and boldness and passion of
life."[58] Dreiser's strict fidelity to the real thing helps to explain
a certain primitivism in his art—a general simplicity, even
crudeness, of design and manner. He had found the real world
as vivid and intense as he hoped to make the fictional; and
he felt no need to impose an elaborate aesthetic form upon
his material. The conflicts he had observed between the individual and society seemed to him inherently dramatic; he believed the drama could be projected even if (and perhaps only
if) his story gave a close and simple transcript of real life.
Thus, his literary picture of the city is best illuminated not
by references to aesthetic theories but by an analysis of the

[55] Theodore Dreiser, "The Scope of Fiction," *New Republic,* Vol.
XXX (April 12, 1922), 8–9.
[56] *Ibid.,* 8.   [57] *Ibid.,* 9.
[58] Sinclair Lewis, in his speech accepting the Nobel Prize for 1930,
quoted in *After the Genteel Tradition,* (ed. by Malcolm Cowley, New
York, Norton and Company, 1936), 14.

impact of urbanism upon his mind and feeling. The material of his art was based, as was his philosophy of life, upon empirical experience. His novels re-create the city he had discovered in a journey that took him from callow youth to maturity, and from illusion to social reality.

The Tragic Pattern of Inner Defeat

WITH THE publication of *Sister Carrie,* the twentieth-century American city novel came into being. While other novels of the time showed insight into modern city life, none combined the major urban themes, attitudes, and moods to create a new kind of fiction that clearly broke with nineteenth-century literary tradition. H. B. Fuller's *The Cliff-Dwellers,* written seven years before *Sister Carrie,* reveals the corrupting materialism of urban society; but the pattern of characterization and plot (the moral nature of the hero, the penance for crime, and the victorious emergence from sordid experiences) keeps it within the convention of the nineteenth-century novel. In Will Payne's *The Story of Eva,* published a year after *Sister Carrie,* the story of a young girl's seduction in the big city closely parallels the story of Dreiser's novel; but again the moral framework of the novel is conventional—there is a happy ending complete with reformations in character and wedding bells. Stephen Crane's *Maggie* lifts the material of slum life to an aesthetic level never before attained in slum fiction (compare, for example, Jacob Riis' stories), but it is fragmentary, lacking the serious intention and the scope of the city novel. *The Voice of the Street,* an early novel of Ernest Poole which prepares for *The Harbor,* is a slight work, interesting for its symbolism, but rather superficial in its exploration of city life. Frank Norris' works vividly reproduce urban scenes from San Francisco and Chicago, but the naturalistic intention, in its original Zolaesque definition, dominates his novels more than the specific intention of the American city writer. William Dean Howells' *A Hazard of New Fortunes* perhaps comes closest to anticipating twentieth-century city fiction, but it still remains confined to the genteel tradition of Howells' realism.

Sister Carrie brought together all the isolated insights into city life presented in these earlier and contemporary novels; and in combining them into a coherent vision of city life, it created the twentieth-century city novel. It embodied an empirical approach to urban life. In examining social actualities, it questioned the basic assumptions of moral and social traditions, as well as, implicitly, the assumptions of the nineteenth-century novel. It showed an intrinsic interest in the city, in urban character types, urban atmosphere, moods, tensions, and structures. Even more important, it was concerned with the impact of urbanism as a way of life: it traced the personal implications of materialism, economic inequality, and social indifference. In developing without equivocation the modern theme of personal dissociation and urban victimization, it explored a peculiar pattern of defeat within the city. It dealt too with the thwarting of individual desire for beauty, and it revealed an essential helplessness of man in an overpowering and alien world. In a way, all the assumptions and motifs of modern urban fiction were implicit in *Sister Carrie*. It was the generic novel of twentieth-century city fiction, just as Dreiser was its generic novelist.

Formally, *Sister Carrie* contained the essential elements of Dreiser's art. As a portrait novel, it revealed Dreiser's method of creating and judging the city through its impact upon a naïve and sensitive register. Carrie, like all of Dreiser's protagonists, was a dramatic presentation of an aspect of his own personal discovery of the city. Like Eugene Witla, Frank Cowperwood, and Clyde Griffiths, she lives through Dreiser's experience of arriving at the city, responding joyously to its

64

atmosphere of hope and growth, delighting in its spectacle, and then discovering within it undercurrents of struggle, irrationality, and injustice. Carrie reflects Dreiser's insight into the seductive power of the city's vanity fair—just as Hurstwood dramatizes Dreiser's fear of its destructive force, Jennie and Clyde his sense of social injustice, Cowperwood his awareness of the drive to power, and Eugene Witla his sense of bafflement and cosmic irrationality. Significantly, no one character moves through the total pattern of personal discovery as Dreiser himself had experienced it. None arrives at his mature sense of social responsibility. The total pattern of Dreiser's discovery of the city is given literary expression in a tragic pattern of inner defeat. This is fundamental to all his novels, and this had marked *Sister Carrie* as a new and original kind of fiction. Since Dreiser has been severely criticized for artistic deficiencies, it is quite illuminating to see how successfully social vision and aesthetic form are integrated in his work. Just as individual characters are dramatizations of his social insights, so the formal elements of his art—plot, theme, setting, tone, and tragic pattern—are integral expressions of his personal discoveries and vision.

As a form of city fiction, Dreiser's novels are perhaps the best example of the portrait study, the novel that reveals city life through its impact upon a single protagonist. In his responses and in the total pattern of his destiny, each of Dreiser's protagonists becomes a register of, and a judgment upon, urbanism as a way of life. While Dreiser turned to the novel with a hero because it was the conventional literary form of the time, it had peculiar appropriateness to his talents and his theme. As a form which achieves an inherent unity by virtue of a single hero, it placed least demand upon Dreiser's architectonic skill. (Even so, *Sister Carrie* has a rather shaky structure and a tenuous unity.) In focusing upon one hero, the portrait novel also expressed Dreiser's individualistic point of view—his thematic concern with the individual and his private search for happiness. Moreover, even with its conventional framework, the portrait novel allowed Dreiser a means to express an unconventional view of life and to create a new and unconventional type of hero.

Dreiser's heroes are a radical departure from literary tradition. Emotionally intense, romantic, and sensual, they are all driven by instinct rather than reason or duty; they are highly amoral; they rarely, if ever, achieve spiritual stature; and they all live through a tragic pattern that brings them to inner defeat. How unique this hero is can be seen by a comparison with the protagonist of H. B. Fuller's *The Cliff-Dwellers*. Fuller presents a young man who succumbs, like Dreiser's characters, to the temptations of city life. But he experiences a strong sense of guilt that leads him to do penance for his mistakes. He emerges from his sordid experiences morally victorious, and his ending is from this point of view a happy one. While the specific nature of his struggle is determined by the urban milieu, his nature as a fictional hero—his growth through experience with evil to moral stature—is essentially no different from that which we find in the novels of Fielding or Thackeray.

Underlying Dreiser's characterization are dual concepts of temperament and character. Temperament is inborn and physical; character is the acquired product of social experience and conditioning. When Carrie Meeber and Eugene Witla first step off the train into Chicago, when Jennie Gerhardt first presents herself for work at the hotel, and when Clyde Griffiths first stands with his parents on the street corner, they are simply creatures of temperament, endowed with a certain kind of sensibility and driven by certain innate needs and desires. But in their final scenes—as Carrie sits in her rocker, Eugene withdraws to his studio, Jennie faces "a vista of lonely years," and Clyde faces the executioner, they are social products. In the process of responding to the world about them, they have acquired a character. Because this world has offered them only certain alternatives and pressed upon them a certain scale of values, it has been crucial in shaping their character, and in turn it is reflected in what they have become and in what has become of them. Dreiser's heroes are always conformists: even when they defy convention they conform to the basic values of their society. But in doing so they fail to satisfy their peculiar temperamental yearning for beauty. In effect, temperament and character remain unreconciled, and the tragedy of Dreiser's heroes is the tragedy of the dissociated personality.

Yet in their initial responses, Dreiser's young people are among the most wholehearted and zestful in modern literature, quite different from the jaded characters of later fiction and from all the twentieth-century fictional people who feel guilt or nausea, rather than joy, at the fact of their existence. The intensity of Dreiser's heroes is temperamental, springing from a peculiar soul-hunger, a deep, romantic yearning for beauty. Dreiser is always vague or ambiguous about the exact nature of this beauty towards which his characters yearn. It is, we gather, a spiritual quality. But if its nature remains nebulous, the fact of desire for it is the central, the fundamental, fact of Dreiser's novels. His characters burn with incandescent desire for some glimpse, some fulfillment or realization, of an ideal of beauty. (Perhaps the clearest expression of this kind of intense yet indefinitive vague yearning is in Winston Churchill's description of the heroine of *The Dwelling-Place of Light:* "She was one of the unfortunate who love beauty. . . . Desire was incandescent within her breast. Desire for what? It would have been some relief to know.")[59]

Dreiser views Carrie's career as "an illustration of the de-

[59] Winston Churchill, *The Dwelling-Place of Light* (New York, The Macmillan Company, 1917), 13.

67

vious ways by which one . . . may be led in the pursuit of beauty."[60] He describes her in characteristically extravagant terms as a youthful dreamer, "ever hearkening to the sound of beauty, straining for the flash of its distant wings."[61] Jennie, like Carrie, is a woman of emotion rather than intellect, also susceptible (to the point of tears) to the beauty of life. So strong is her unconditioned response to the aesthetic elements of nature that Dreiser has her "clenching her fingers in an agony of poetic feeling" and weeping over the sheer loveliness of the evening "in that halcyon hour when the Angelus falls like a benediction over the waning day."[62]

If Dreiser tended to become rather mawkish in describing the aesthetic sensibility of his women, he was firmer and more incisive in dealing with his male protagonists. They find the fulfillment of beauty in women, so that sex in Dreiser's novels is usually related to a quest for an ideal. For example, Cowperwood's flagrant promiscuity is explained as a "seeking" in women for "the realization of an ideal."[63] Cowperwood reaches towards a beautiful woman as an art-collector reaches towards a flawless masterpiece. Until he meets Berenice Fleming, a woman who can give him intellectual companionship as well as sex, Cowperwood is little interested in women "aside from their value as objects of art."[64] This merging of aesthetic and sexual desires is seen again in Eugene Witla. His "inborn" sense of beauty is so intense "that the only two things that matter to him are "his love of the beauty of life which was coupled with his desire to express it in color,

[60] Theodore Dreiser, *Sister Carrie* (Cleveland, World Publishing Company, 1946 reprint), 557.

[61] *Ibid.,* 555.

[62] Theodore Dreiser, *Jennie Gerhardt* (Cleveland, World Publishing Company, 1946 reprint), 18.

[63] Theodore Dreiser, *The Titan* (New York, Horace Liveright, 1925 ed.), 201.

[64] *Ibid.,* 118.

and his love of beauty in the form or face of a woman."[65] While Clyde Griffiths lacks Cowperwood's force of character and Eugene's artistic talents, he is temperamentally related to both in his aesthetic feelings. When he is most in love with Sondra Finchley, he is least motivated by the sexual need which had been the main basis for his relationship with Hortense Briggs and Roberta Alden. Sondra appeals to him as the incarnation of beauty. As he sits beside her in silent adoration, he thinks, "Oh, if only I could say to her how beautiful I really think she is"; his thoughts now are "without lust": his desire is "to constrain and fondle a perfect object."[66]

As the characters undergo experience in the social world, however, they sublimate this innate desire for beauty to a desire for wealth. The city directs their vague yearning towards a specific goal as it holds out the glittering spectacle of fashion and luxury. Like forlorn urchins standing in front of a window display of shiny toys, Dreiser's naïve newcomers to the city stand outside the world of mansions, theatres, and glowing restaurants and yearn towards its glitter. They do not see that it is the glitter of tinsel; they do not know that they must pay for vanities with their chance for happiness, their integrity, their honor, and even their lives. As they burn with "incandescent desire," they reach towards what seems to them the highest social expression of beauty—beauty in the life of luxury and ease—and the desire for an ideal thus becomes the commonplace struggle for material success. But the incompatibility between spiritual desire and materialistic goals determines their peculiarly American tragedy. Society offers an individual of aesthetic and romantic temperament satisfactions which cannot fulfill his innate needs. Indeed, the more eagerly Dreiser's hero pursues fashion and wealth, the more

[65] Theodore Dreiser, The 'Genius' (New York, Garden City Books, 1935 ed.), 295.

[66] Theodore Dreiser, An American Tragedy (Cleveland, World Publishing Company, 1947 ed.), Book II, 397.

irrevocably he dooms himself. This, then, is the tragic pattern of inner defeat: an individual of strong but nebulous aesthetic yearnings is subjected to and conditioned by a materialistic urban world; he learns to sublimate his desire for beauty to a desire for wealth; he pursues material success blindly, at the expense of all moral considerations, and whether or not he achieves this success, he loses spiritual unity and suffers inner defeat.

Thus Dreiser shows modern man caught helplessly in the grip of two forces: the forces from within, the compulsions that are experienced as temperamental drives, and the forces from without, the social influences that act upon the character as conditioning factors. His portrayal of these forces reveals his weakness and strength as a city novelist. In explaining the soul-hunger for an undefined spiritual quality, he is usually vague and ineffectual. His language tends towards a strained elegance in which generalities substitute for concrete definitions. Moreover, his discussion of the temperamental drives is expressed in now outmoded constructs, for his mechanistic theories of "chemic compulsions" and of nebulous soulful yearnings are not in the contemporary vein. But his dramatization of the process of social conditioning is incisive and fully realized. His choice of the intense and sensitive individual as hero is particularly strategic (although he was probably simply using himself as prototype) because such an individual would be most susceptible to the specious glamour of fashion and wealth. Moreover, he, rather than a completely materialistic person, would experience personal dissociation, since even if he did achieve worldly success, his innate desires would remain unsatisfied. Because his motives and acts would not be integrated he would find himself caught up in self-contradictions and confusions. Thus, there are tragic implications in the life of Frank Cowperwood, who pursues disparate ideals of beauty and power, which are not suggested by the life of

Herrick's character Van Harrington. Van Harrington brings unhappiness to others, but within himself he remains an integrated and fulfilled personality because his desire for wealth is uncomplicated by any conflicting needs.[67]

Within the pattern of defeat the role of the city is that of antagonist to the hero. As an atmosphere it stirs in him false hopes; as an economic structure it educates him to want money and success; and as a way of life it engulfs him in its own disorder and leaves him helpless and alone. The atmosphere of the young and growing American city exerts a seductive attraction upon the hero. He feels his own mood of hopeful enthusiasm objectified and intensified by an electric atmosphere of growth and excitement. Eugene Witla's response to Chicago is characteristic, and it also recalls the early reactions of young Dreiser himself:

Chicago . . . offered a world of hope and opportunity to the beginner. It was so new, so raw; everything was in the making. . . . The section was running with a tide of people which represented the youth, the illusions, the untrained aspirations, of millions of souls. When you walked into this area you could feel what Chicago meant—eagerness, hope, desire. It was a city that put vitality into almost every wavering heart: it made the beginner dream dreams.[68]

The thrilling moment of arrival in the city, when the atmosphere makes its strongest emotional impact, is usually recreated in an extravagant language of superlatives. Details of setting and mood are enumerated in short exclamatory phrases that build up a rhythm and a sense of rhapsodic excitement suggestive of Whitman and Sandburg. Here is an illustration from *The 'Genius'* which could he matched by passages from *Sister Carrie* and *The Titan*:

[67] Robert Herrick, *Memoirs of an American Citizen* (New York, The Macmillan Company, 1905).

[68] *The 'Genius,'* 39. See also *Sister Carrie*, 16; *Jennie Gerhardt*, 103; *The Titan*, 4 ff.

the beat of a hundred thousand hammers; the ring of a thousand trowels! . . . Long, converging lines of telegraph poles . . . factory plants, towering smoke stacks . . . broad highways of the tracks of railroads . . . engines clanging, trains moving, people waiting at street corners—pedestrians, wagon drivers, street car drivers, drays of beer, trucks of coal, brick, stone, sand—a spectacle of new, raw, necessary life. . . . Here was the substance of a new world, substantial, fascinating, different.[69]

But while the atmosphere stirs hope and enthusiasm, it also conceals undercurrents of tension. Eugene Witla, for example, soon realizes that in this vigorous, bustling Chicago "youth and hope and energy were setting a terrific pace. You had to work here, to move, to step lively. You had to have ideas. This city demanded of you your very best, or it would have little to do with you. Youth in its search for something—and age—were quickly to feel this. It was no fool's paradise."[70]

The inner effects of a tense atmosphere of competition and struggle are reinforced by the effects of the physical locale. The looming buildings, strange, endless streets, and surging impersonal crowds, the impregnable mansions, restaurants, and hotels "swarming with patrons," the vastness, variety, and strength of the physical city—these facts impress upon the characters a sense of smallness and ineffectuality. Carrie and Hurstwood react most strongly with a feeling of helplessness. Hurstwood's response to New York recalls Carrie's "sense of helplessness amid so much evidence of power and force."[71] Once again Dreiser's characters dramatize his experience of

[69] *The 'Genius,'* 37. See also *The Titan,* 6. For an extravagant use of this technique of enumeration, see Felix Riesenberg, *East Side, West Side* (New York, Harcourt, Brace and Company, 1927). Riesenberg tries to achieve the rhapsodic effect by long enumerations of urban details, but he succeeds only in ruining the pace of the novel and attaining a rather hysterical tone.

[70] *The 'Genius,'* 39. [71] *Sister Carrie,* 18.

city life: he knew from his own period of despair in New York how overbearing the great city could be, how it could awe and frighten the individual and reduce him to a feeling of impotence. Carrie cannot at first adjust herself to Chicago's "vast buildings . . . strange energies and huge interests": "for what purpose were they? She could have understood the meaning of a little stone-cutter's yard at Columbia City, carving little pieces of marble for individual use, but the yards of some huge stone corporation . . . transpierced by docks . . . and traversed . . . by immense trundling cranes of wood and steel . . . lost all significance in her little world. It was so with the vast railroad yards, with the crowded array of vessels . . . at the river . . . the huge factories . . . the great streets . . . the vast offices . . . ."[72]

In actual contact with the city, Carrie experiences a fear that conflicts with her hopes. Her emotional confusion at the spectacle of this strange new world is preparatory to the moral confusion that leads her to an illicit relationship with Drouet. The physical facts of the city are thus crucial to the unfolding of plot. Although Dreiser is awkward in introducing these facts, bringing them in in intrusive expository passages, they are essential to the development of the thematic antagonism between man and the city. Hurstwood's failure in New York is also foreshadowed by a general and seemingly digressive discussion of New York as our most heartless and demanding city; but though this discussion, like the earlier one on Chicago, slows the narrative pace, it proves to be more than mere realistic documentation; it is integral to the character's education to city life and his ultimate victimization by it.

While the city imposes itself as an atmosphere that stirs hope and a physical place that gives rise to fear and a sense of helplessness, it makes its greatest and most dramatic impact as an economic structure—a society which holds a most star-

[72] *Ibid.*

73

tling contrast between poverty and wealth. The moments of recognition of this contrast leave a lasting impression upon the hero's mind. They constitute his main education to the city, and they determine his motives and course of action. While Carrie and Clyde seem to drift into their situations, the directions in which they drift were already determined in the moments of awareness when they saw the total difference between poverty and wealth. What Dreiser had learned of indescribable luxury and indescribable degradation in his discovery of Chicago, Pittsburgh, and New York is crucial to the education of his characters. Structurally, the novels are built upon a simple paralleling of characters and incidents that contrasts poverty and wealth. In *Sister Carrie* (which contains a double parallelism as Hurstwood relives in New York Carrie's essential experience in Chicago), chapter is balanced against chapter. For example, Chapter II, called "What Poverty Threatened," which depicts Carrie's predicament as a poor wage-earner, is to be set against Chapter VIII, "The Lure of the Material," which shows her comparative luxury as Drouet's mistress. Incidents balance each other as Carrie moves through Chicago and then New York, always contrasting her position with that of those better (and sometimes worse) placed than she in the social scale. When she is job-hunting in Chicago, she stares enviously at the great mansions of the idle rich; when for the first time she herself wears fine clothes, she contrasts her appearance with that of the poor shopgirls; when she is out riding on the North Side, she again makes the invidious comparison between her own small comforts and the luxuries of great wealth; and when she comes to New York, the discovery of inequality takes place all over again, and once more, the knowledge that poor and rich live side by side but separated by an unscalable wall renews both her unhappiness and her ambition. The second half of the novel recapitulates the first as Hurstwood relives in New

York the experiences which Carrie had undergone in Chicago: he too enters a new and terrifying city, seeks futilely for work, and becomes aware of his helplessness. He too finds a place for himself only to lose it, and then suffers a decline that parallels and underscores Carrie's moral defeat.

In *Jennie Gerhardt,* the first contrast is between poverty in Jennie's home and luxury in Senator Brander's hotel. This contrast is sharpened and reinforced as Jennie comes in contact with the wealthy homes of her employers and later with that of her lover, Lester Kane. Jennie sees and reflects the injustice of a society which fosters great inequalities in wealth. She had yielded to the Senator in innocence, through gratitude for his generosity; but she must pay heavily for her mistake. She had given Lester Kane the most satisfying love he had known; but she loses him to a woman of wealth and social position. Jennie comes to realize that throughout her life, her true antagonist has been economic inequality: "Wealth and position . . . were typified to her mind as a great fence, a wall, which divided her eternally from her beloved. Had it not always been so? Was not her life a patchwork of conditions made and affected by these things which she saw—wealth and force—which had found her unfit?"[73] The one selfless character in Dreiser's gallery of egoists, she too suffers because of the materialistic temper of modern society.

An American Tragedy makes fullest and most effective use of parallel structure to express Dreiser's underlying social concepts. The fact of inequality is dramatized through contrasting characters, settings, and situations. Rich and poor characters are juxtaposed: Asa Griffiths is contrasted with his rich brother Samuel; Clyde with his cousin Gilbert; and Roberta Alden with Sondra Finchley. The home environments of the two Griffiths families are set in illuminating opposition as the first chapters of Book I depict Clyde's background, and

[73] *Jennie Gerhardt,* 430.

the opening of Book II gives a corresponding description of the lavish home of the Lycurgus Griffiths. Later, the Alden's small, dilapidated farm appears more pitiful because it contrasts so violently with the mansions of the Lycurgus debutantes. The most startling antithesis is between the murder scene and the country club party. Both occur simultaneously: Sondra is happily anticipating Clyde's arrival at the same moment that Roberta is meeting her death. The full implications of the gulf between poverty and wealth are dramatically realized as Clyde leaves the murder scene—where Roberta has has suffered the consequences of poverty as much as of sin— and joins the country party. Finally, the closing scene, by paralleling the opening one, raises the question of whether this American tragedy must inevitably recur.

Within the parallel structure of *An American Tragedy* are climatic moments of illumination when Clyde suddenly feels the full seductive attraction of wealth. Like Carrie and Jennie, he views the glittering spectacle as a forlorn and yearning observer, standing on the outside looking in. As a poor bellhop in a lavish Kansas City hotel, he has his first climactic glimpse of the life of the rich. One time he peeks into a hotel room to see young people his own age reveling in a gay party; looking through this door at "young fellows and girls . . . not so much older than himself, laughing and talking and drinking" was like "looking through the gates of Paradise."[74] His early impressions of a fabulous life are strengthened as he daily watches the stream of well-groomed and cared-for hotel patrons, all apparently intent upon pleasure. Brought face to face with this "grandeur," Clyde is typically overwhelmed: "This, then, most certainly was what it meant to be rich, to be a person of consequence in the world—to have money. It meant that you did what you pleased. That other people, like himself, waited upon you. That you possessed all

[74] *An American Tragedy,* Book I, 58.

76

of these luxuries. That you went how, where and when you pleased."[75]

Characteristically, Clyde's response to the spectacle of wealth is hedonistic, that is, he sees money simply as a means of self-gratification, and the idea of social responsibility attached to wealth never remotely suggests itself to him. Money is equated with pleasure, pleasure with possession, and possession with success and the fulfillment of innate yearning. The symbol of possession is fashion—and it is fitting that clothes, which play so large a symbolic role in urban society, should take on symbolic value in the city novel. The role of fashion in Dreiser's tragic pattern is strategic, for as the characters respond to the obvious appeal of silks and furs and jewels, they make their first crucial mistake in identifying beauty with material possession. Carrie, for example, has always equated outer fineries with the inner fulfillment she only vaguely defines but intensely desires. She has made "the average feminine distinction between clothes, putting worth, goodness, and distinction in a dress suit, and leaving all the unlovely qualities and those beneath notice in overalls and jumper."[76] Old clothes epitomize poverty. Dressed in the fine little jacket and new buttoned shoes that Drouet has bought her, she is repelled by the appearance of working-girls to whose class she has until this moment belonged: "Their clothes were faded and loose-hanging, their jackets old, their general make-up shabby."[77] And when she considers the moral disgrace of her relationship with Drouet, she loses the will to leave him once she thinks of having to "put on the old clothes—that torn pair of shoes."[78]

Dreiser's insight into what he called "the psychology of clothes" derived from his own observations of the parades of fashion in the city streets—and more specifically, from his ex-

[75] *Ibid.*
[76] *Sister Carrie*, 44. [77] *Ibid.*, 87. [78] *Ibid.*, 111.

perience as editor of a popular woman's magazine. He not only made clothes a key symbol of false values: he made his character's attitude towards fashion a revelation of his sensibility and values. How his people react to dress indicates on one level their actual economic position and their taste; on another more important level, it reveals their moral sense of values. The difference between Drouet and Hurstwood is immediately projected through the difference in their clothes: Drouet's are expensive but flashy, slightly vulgar; Hurstwood's costly but subdued, in finer taste. Hurstwood's moral deterioration is traced through the increasing shabbiness of his dress; in his case, outer appearance and inner moral state are truly equated. The stripping of his fine clothes represents a loss of initiative, self-respect, and dignity. From the realistic point of view, this change in appearance is natural, since he can no longer afford an extravagant wardrobe. But his increasing indifference to appearance is also symbolic: the first sign of his deterioration is a willingness to wear an old jacket and shabby slippers—and sit at home—rather than to put on his good suit and face the outer world in a struggle for success.

The attempt to satisfy innate aesthetic and spiritual desires with materialistic ends—fashion, wealth, and power—is the basic irony, as well as the tragedy, in Dreiser's novels. Dreiser saw youth conforming to the values of his society and thus being ironically driven to pursue happiness along the lines that could bring only empty rewards. The basic theme of all his novels is that the subjective experience of happiness and fulfillment is not achieved, and is not measurable, by materialistic standards. But his characters pursue disparate goals of beauty and wealth without realizing that one is not interchangeable with the other. Dreiser's vision of cosmic irrationality is related to this spectacle of a mad pursuit of opposing values. In depicting the irony of his heroes' situations, he often turned to a supernatural explanation in terms of irrational and impersonal controlling forces. He seemed to need some cosmic framework in order to rationalize a complex social situation. Like the character who most resembles him, Eugene Witla, he viewed man's furious and vain strivings towards disparate goals as one indication among many that the world is a meaningless creation, or at least an inscrutable one. But his high-flown concepts of cosmic irrationality rise out of his perceptions of the irrationality and the irony in commonplace social situations; and his importance as a city novelist lies not in his vague philosophizing but in his dramatic presentation of these concrete situations and of the social void in which they occur.

The social explanation of man's ironic and apparently irrational position lies in the breakdown of the community. When Dreiser's protagonist arrives at the city, he has left an environment in which his place was clearly defined by tradition. In Chicago, Detroit, or New York, he needs to discover a new place for himself; but as he looks about him for an order and for guiding standards and values, he sees that society lacks coherence and unity—it is simply an aggregate of isolated individuals, each of whom pursues his own self-interest and pleasure. The hero never becomes part of a social group because group life does not seem to exist. He never develops a social conscience, a sense of social responsibility, or a pressing awareness of social problems. He is among the most egocentric, individualistically minded, and hedonistic characters in twentieth-century fiction. In his egocentricity he reflects the decline of social institutions and the fact of a social void that has been left by the breakdown of a unifying tradition.

A minor theme that emerges in Dreiser's novels is the collapse of the family and the conflict between the ideals of the older generation, brought up to conform to a tradition, and their children, let loose in a chaotic modern world. The main

79

tie between parent and child is pecuniary; and where that tie is frayed, the parents lose control. The emotional nexus is weak. In *Sister Carrie,* the failure of emotional ties helps explain the course of Carrie's and of Hurstwood's actions. Had Carrie's sister been capable of giving Carrie an outgoing warm love, Carrie might never have drifted into her relationship with Drouet. In the Hurstwood family, convention and economic advantage are the only family links: The Hurstwood household, Dreiser says, "ran along by force of habit, by force of conventional opinion. With the lapse of time it must necessarily become dryer and dryer—must eventually be tinder, easily lighted and destroyed."[79] Hurstwood's desertion of his family has sometimes been considered an irrational act of impulse characteristic in the naturalistic novel; but the simple explanation is that the emotional links with his family had been so weakened that he felt no real hesitation in running off with a woman he loved.

The most extensive portrayals of the decline of the family are in *Jennie Gerhardt, An American Tragedy,* and *The Bulwark*. In all three novels, the parents have strong religious inclinations: William Gerhardt is a strict Lutheran; Asa Griffiths, an Evangelist; and Solon Barnes, a Quaker. They believe that man's primary concern is to attain salvation by following the ways of God. But their children do not conform to their religious ideas because the everyday material world seems to them more important than the distant hereafter. They realize too that the pursuit of spiritual salvation interferes with sensuous pleasures and material success—and these values of course seem to them the highest that their world has to offer. Fundamentally, they are caught in the contradictions inherent in a society that gives lip service to a Christian ethic while it fosters a business ethic. The parents' attempt to make the children adhere to a religious tradition results in their rejec-

[79] *Ibid.,* 100.

tion of it. In a changing and bustling world, the younger generation refuses to be bound by a moral code that seems incongruous with the social facts. Thus, while the elder Gerhardt, for example, accepts his poverty because he believes in a Heavenly reward—and more simply, because he has been trained to an unreasoning acceptance of God's will[80]—his son rebels against it. He wants success. Modern America demands of him aggressiveness, not meekness; a competitive spirit, not brotherly love; and consuming interest in the practical world of business, not in some distant Heavenly Kingdom. Like young Bass Gerhardt, Clyde Griffiths also rebels against his parents' strict code of self-denial. But this rejection of a Christian morality leaves him morally rudderless. Inherently weak in will and judgment, he is incapable of guiding himself through the temptations of the world and preserving moral integrity. He suffers the full consequence of the failure of the family, and of society as a whole, to give the individual adequate guidance. Thus, although his own acts bring about Roberta's death and his own terrible end, there is also social guilt for the waste of these two young lives. The family had failed him when he needed guidance and example, and society itself had taught him only the value of pleasure, fashion, and wealth.

Alienation from the family is preliminary to alienation from society as a whole. When Dreiser's hero repudiates his parents' moral codes, he is tacitly expressing his individualism, in effect, declaring himself a free moral agent who recognizes no social restrictions other than those he chooses to impose upon himself. "I satisfy myself," the declared creed of Frank Cowperwood and Lester Kane, sums up the philosophy of Carrie Meeber, Eugene Witla, Clyde Griffiths, and Etta Barnes. Some of the characters are quite unconscious of the extreme individualism that separates them from society, while

[80] *Jennie Gerhardt,* 54 f.

others justify their position by an articulated theory of life. Carrie, Jennie, and Clyde have so little awareness of the meaning of a social order that they do not seem to realize that they are violating social convention. They drift into their situations, doing what at the moment seems expedient; and because they act upon impulse rather than reason, they seem to lack volition. They are simply helpless before the inner demands of temperament and the outer influences of society. On the other hand, Lester Kane, Eugene Witla, and Frank Cowperwood consciously rationalize their alienation from society. Lester Kane has found in the apparent chaos of modern life license for an attitude of simple hedonism. Having been confounded by "the multiplicity of things, the vastness of the panorama of life, the glitter of its details, the unsubstantial nature of its forms, the uncertainty of their justification,"[81] he arrives at his individualistic point of view. Since the only certainty he experiences is in the persistence of his own impulses towards pleasure and away from pain, he decides to be guided by this one certainty. He will achieve consistency in a society full of inconsistencies by choosing always to satisfy his own desires. His world is not a social world in which he takes his place among other people: it is a small self-contained unit that rotates around the axis of his desires.

Eugene Witla has also asked himself if there is any valid reason why he should *not* satisfy his own desires. What is to be gained by self-renunciation? (He is thinking of his desire for Suzanne Dale):

A sense of personal purity? It did not appeal to him. The respect of his fellow-citizens? He believed that most of his fellow-citizens were whited sepulchres. What good did their hypocritical respect do him? Justice to others? Others were not concerned, or should not be in the natural affinity which might manifest itself between two people. That was for them to settle. Besides, there was very

[81] *Ibid.,* 133.

little justice in the world. As for his wife—well, he had given her his word, but he had not done so willingly. Might one swear eternal fealty and abide by it when the very essence of nature was lack of fealty, inconsiderateness, destruction, change?[82]

Eugene's vision of society is Dreiser's naturalistic vision of a world in which only change is real and permanent. Purity, justice, fidelity are mere abstractions of the mind, fictions rather than truths; and man is a fool if he thinks he must sacrifice to them his urgent and natural desires. Thus, out of a disenchantment with society Eugene's individualistic philosophy takes shape: to the man who dares take what he wants "all apparently was permitted."[83]

Cowperwood's individualism grows out of a vision of society as a jungle in which men mercilessly prey upon each other. Like Van Harrington in Robert Herrick's *Memoirs of an American Citizen,* he is convinced that "the strong must rule: the world was for the strong."[84] He believes in power, but not in social responsibility. Not that Cowperwood is unmoved by ideals—on the contrary, his ideals are so strong that he will oppose all the forces of organized society in order to realize them. But what is insidious about them is that they are products of his "conception of individuality," and as such they clash with the ideals of democracy. Thus, the Governor of Illinois, whom Cowperwood has tried unsuccessfully to bribe, feels that he must resist Cowperwood because "ideals were here at stake—the dreams of one man as opposed perhaps to the ultimate dreams of a city or state or nation—the grovelings . . . of a democracy slowly, blindly trying to stagger to its feet."[85] In order to remain faithful "to the trust imposed on him by the great electorate of Illinois," he must fight Cow-

[82] *The 'Genius,'* 286. [83] *Ibid.,* 726.
[84] Herrick, *Memoirs of an American Citizen,* 94.
[85] *The Titan,* 485.

perwood and veto the bill that would be advantageous to him.[86] Here the conflict between private and public interest is most clearly presented. Cowperwood represents the final stage in the estrangement of the individual from the social group. He flouts social codes and justifies himself by his concept of individuality; he preys upon weaker elements in society and believes himself right to destroy them because they are weak; and as a ruthless and self-seeking capitalistic power, he menaces the fundamental democratic principle of a growing nation.

Dreiser's attitude towards the individual's alienation from society was characteristically ambiguous. He realized he was coping with a complex situation in which principles of individual liberty and of social responsibility were involved, but he found it difficult to define a point of equilibrium at which both principles could be realized without one encroaching upon the other. He believed that the natural impulses of man, being natural, should be allowed free expression. Because he saw man as helpless before his inner compulsions, he condemned society's attempt to inhibit him from satisfying his temperamental needs. Moreover, he saw little value in many of the social conventions, for he felt that convention itself had often become a mere empty shell—existing through force of habit, unrelated to actualities in social life, and at worst, exercising an invidious power over the individual. Therefore, he sympathized with the efforts of his characters to release themselves from the bonds of convention. On the other hand, however, he saw that the social consequence of unrestrained self-interest was a continuation and extension of social inequalities. A society operating on the principle of self-interest was nothing more nor less than a wild jungle in which bestial forces prevailed. Weak characters like Clyde Griffiths would destroy themselves, while strong ones like Cowperwood

[86] *Ibid.*

would destroy others. And the ultimate irony was that even if one were strong and did find a way to achieve material success, he would not find inner contentment. For the goals that modern society set before man, these very goals that turned him into a destructive agent, must inevitably fail to satisfy his deepest yearning for a complete human fulfillment. The defeat of the two characters who attain worldly success, Carrie and Cowperwood, must not be overlooked.[87] Their failure gives the final condemnation to twentieth-century society. If they, who achieve success, must suffer an inner defeat as strong as that of the failure, then there is no chance for personal fulfillment as long as one pursues the materialistic values placed so high on the social scale.

Carrie's spiritual defeat is overshadowed by the much more spectacular decline of Hurstwood. Like a Renaissance tragic hero, he has fallen from high position. Having lost his money, dignity, and will, he suffers the final ignominy of burial in Potter's Field. Meanwhile Carrie has risen to fortune and fame. Nevertheless, there is a strong parallel between their inner lives, not only because they had the same emotional reactions to a strange city but also because they have both failed to make the city yield them happiness. Although Carrie has her "gowns and carriages, her furniture and bank account,"[88] her inner feeling is still one of longing and incom-

---

[87] Critics often point to Carrie as an example of Dreiser's amorality because they consider her to have achieved complete success despite her immoral relationships with two men. Percy Boynton, for example, says that at the end she is anything but "a stricken soul," *America in Contemporary Fiction* (Chicago, University of Chicago Press, 1940), 138. Charles Walcutt also thinks that Carrie emerges completely unscathed at the end of the novel and he believes that the fortuity of her rise and Hurstwood's decline is typical of Dreiser's naturalism. He speaks of Carrie as "an example of the amoral accidents of real as opposed to Sundayschool life," "Naturalism in 1946: Dreiser and Farrell," *Accent,* Vol. VI (Summer, 1946), 264.

[88] *Sister Carrie,* 554.

pletion. "Amid the tinsel and shine of her state," she is lonely and unhappy.[89] Moreover, the beauty that evades her even now will always remain elusive; she must "dream" of a happiness that she "may never feel."[90] While Dreiser dramatized her rise to fame but only stated her failure to find inner contentment, his intention is clearly indicated at the end: he wished to show that Carrie had pursued in money and fashion *"false* representations" of her ideal of beauty. There is, thus, a suggestion of futility in Dreiser's summing up of Carrie's life. The apparently crucial experiences in her career are called mere "incidents": "Chicago, New York; Drouet, Hurstwood; the world of fashion and the world of stage—these were but incidents. Not them, but that which they represented, she longed for. Time proved the representation false."[91]

Cowperwood is the greatest material success among Dreiser's characters, but he too experiences an inner division between his desire for beauty and his desire for wealth. Indeed, the very structure of the Cowperwood novels reflects this division by the alternation of erotic episodes with episodes from business life. While Dreiser briefly suggests at the conclusion of both *The Financier* and *The Titan* that Cowperwood will never find what he is looking for in life, the implications of his inner conflict are not fully revealed until *The Stoic.* Cowperwood's life ends on the same note of futility that brings to a close all of Dreiser's novels. Of his plans and possessions, nothing remains "but a tomb, and memories."[92] His estate is taxed and divided among creditors; his art collection is dispersed; his charitable projects are never carried out. Berenice Fleming resolves the conflict between material and aesthetic aspirations only by repudiating worldly desires. She reaffirms the spiritual value of self-denial, and through her,

[89] *Ibid.,* 556.   [90] *Ibid.,* 557.   [91] *Ibid.,* 555.
[92] Theodore Dreiser, *The Stoic* (New York, Doubleday and Company, 1947), 303.

Dreiser expresses his final, rather nebulous view that all life is spiritually united and that true beauty is a reflection of the Divine spirit. Significantly, this view of life finds expression in terms taken from another culture. Berenice has learned true values from the Yogi: "Cowperwood must know, [she thinks] if he had not known when he was here in the flesh that his worship and constant search for beauty in every form, and especially in the form of a woman, was nothing more than a search for the Divine design behind all forms—the spirit of Brahma shining through."[93]

In his posthumous novels, Dreiser introduced a view of life which denied the irrationality, irony, and futility of the tragic pattern implicit in his earlier novels. He reaffirmed the existence of a moral order and asserted man's freedom to act as an independent moral agent, rather than as a driven creature of temperament and mistaken social ideals. In the ideals of the Quaker and the Yogi he found a negation of all that he had actually experienced in American secular life. Social realities had shaped his vision of a world that was materialistic, amoral, disordered, and individualistic; but the doctrines of Quakerism and Yoga gave him another point of view. They brought him back to a mystical and ascetic vision of life; they affirmed a universal moral order and the capacity of man to unite himself with a divine power outside of and greater than himself. The posthumous novels thus move in full-swing away from the rest of his work, especially insofar as they maintain that man has the power for good and for evil within him and that the external world and its social influences would be completely ineffectual if the individual conscience were guided by the Inner Light. But while these last novels reveal a renewal of Dreiser's personal faith, their literary importance is negligible in comparison with the novels that appeared during his life. The novels from *Sister Carrie* to *An American*

[93] *Ibid.,* 305.

Tragedy, which dramatize the social attitudes that are the backbone of Dreiser's art, are the ones that brought him fame and that exerted a critical influence upon the direction of American fiction. They communicate the intensity of Dreiser's awareness of man's disunity and defeat. And out of the force of his feeling about the tragedy inherent in this defeat comes the original quality of his work and his significance to American letters. But while his overwhelming sense of the tragic in modern life gives him his power, there are serious weaknesses in his work that rise out of his failure to consider factors other than those existing in the pattern of defeat. In his failure to view man's plight in a larger perspective, he arrived at an illogical social point of view which led to serious deficiencies in his art.

In magnifying the compulsive influence of the environment, Dreiser distorted the relationship between the individual and the outer world. He deprived the individual of any power to resist the environment or to impose upon it his own will. He painted the environment as a fatally irresistible force. His people, caught up in the stream of urban life and carried along in its rushing currents, are powerless to find their own direction or even to struggle against the running tide. Dreiser assumed that because society set up material success as man's highest goal, the individual was helplessly and irresistibly conditioned to pursue it. In inspiring this pursuit, society had of course duped the individual, for it had set before him false ideals and given him a direction that could lead only to spiritual disunity and moral defeat.

In denying responsibility to the individual Dreiser makes it impossible to condemn him as a moral actor. Yet Dreiser's position is profoundly moralistic, for he is indicting a whole society. While critics have pointed out that amorality is essential in Dreiser's art, the fact is that all of Dreiser's work is based upon an act of moral judgment. His novels carry a mass condemnation for all of modern urban society—for its inequalities that evoked inordinate desires for money; for its spiritual confusion and desolation; for its cultural barrenness and its failure to show man beauty in any form other than that of material things.[94] Thus, his real villain is the city itself. It has created Hurstwoods and Carries, Cowperwoods and Witlas, and weaklings like Clyde. It has taken the human being, with his deep urge to live and feel pleasure in life, and brought out the worst that is in him, selfishness and the power to destroy. In his novels, the city has transformed the fundamental virtue of all of his characters, their enthusiasm and zeal for life, into their greatest fault, for his heroes, in their very eagerness to live fully, have become completely susceptible to the glittering attractions of urban wealth. Dreiser's judgment was that man deserved better than this. There was a moral need to change society so that it could give man ideals and goals that could bring him to self-fulfillment.

But in the desire to show the moral guilt of society as a whole, Dreiser fell into the illogicalities inherent in an extreme mechanistic position. He reduced his characters to mere mechanisms. They are like passive, resistless putty before the shaping force of the environment. Utterly helpless, they cannot resist or turn away from external stimuli. Their tropistic responses to the materialistic attractions of society are essentially no different from the response of the sunflower to the sun. In thus dramatizing a mechanistic psychology, Dreiser almost defeated his own ends. For if men are so completely conditioned creatures, unable to resist the destructive influ-

[94] In *Memoirs of an American Citizen,* Herrick states that one reason why life in Chicago, as differentiated from life in the small New England town, centers about the materialistic struggle for success is that the city is ugly and culturally barren and does not inspire man with spiritual and aesthetic ideals. As his young New England lawyer says: "Whatever was there in Chicago in 1877 to live for but Success?" p. 52.

ences that exist in society, from where will come the force that can eradicate these influences? Dreiser condemns society, but he ignores the fact that society is composed of these self-same helpless creatures whom he has pitied and absolved of guilt, that it has no autonomous life of its own, and that it cannot change or improve itself. Thus, so long as he insists that the individual was not morally responsible for his acts, his condemnation of society loses much of its force.

In making his characters succumb helplessly to the forces acting upon them, Dreiser necessarily minimized or negated the two dramatic factors of human choice and human struggle. But the drama of literature inheres in the portrayal of man's struggle against whatever forces challenge him, and the suspense grows out of an interest in seeing what choices he makes. In Dreiser's novels, however, there is no fundamental clash of forces and few conscious and responsible human choices. When the hero is brought into contact with the impersonal forces of his environment, he submits to the pressures of the outer world with little if any struggle. Structurally, Dreiser's novels are built not upon the dramatic meeting of conflicting forces, but upon a series of educating incidents. The hero sees an aspect of city life and learns from his observation the fundamental lesson that money and success are the greatest values in life. He assimilates this lesson passively; he does not question or doubt its truth; he does not reflect upon its implications; and he never consciously regrets that he has learned it so well. *An American Tragedy,* for example, shows a series of incidents in Kansas City, Chicago, and Lycurgus which impress Clyde with the desirability of wealth; through these incidents the novel reveals separate and conjunctive influences acting upon character and evoking responses only of acceptance and acquiescence. The reader feels much less suspense over the question of what Clyde will do in reaction to these influences than he does over the question of what more the outer influences will do to Clyde. At the two most critical moments in Dreiser's novels—the moment when Hurstwood steals the money and when Clyde lets Roberta die—the issue of choice is obscured because the situation is framed in such a way that sheer accident plays the decisive role. We never know whether Hurstwood was morally capable of opening the safe and stealing the money, for the safe is left open accidentally and Hurstwood is in a bemuddled and drunken state when he takes the money. We never know whether Clyde was capable of deliberate murder because Clyde does not have to decide whether or not to push Roberta into the water; she falls in accidentally. This critical moment in Clyde's life, which might have become a dramatic revelation of the inner man, becomes another example of how chance circumstance entraps the individual. As Dreiser's hero lacks the power to choose, he is deprived of a vital part of his humanity; and the novel cannot achieve one of its highest effects—the revelation of man's character through the dramatic presentation of his moral decisions. Because Dreiser's heroes are so completely creatures of society, they lack any rich and personal inner life. What life beats within them is the life of the city as it is reflected through their prismatic personalities. Consequently, almost all of them have the same moral composition, for they are all reflections of the same influences,[95] and they have all been deprived of the opportunity to exercise their will and moral judgment in a way that will identify them as distinct personalities.

Moreover, Dreiser fails to bring to life the one quality in his characters which has not been socially conditioned but is peculiarly their own—their sensitivity to beauty. While he

[95] Jennie Gerhardt is a singular Dreiserian protagonist in her selflessness and generosity. She does not reflect directly the materialism of city life, although she suffers from it indirectly. She too, however, does not reveal her character through free moral choices.

dramatizes their social reactions, he merely states that their temperaments are aesthetic. Although he shows that Cowperwood collected masterpieces, and that Carrie became an actress and Eugene Witla a painter, he does not explore the inner feelings that give these people the capacity to appreciate and express aesthetic values. His own ineptness at handling language, revealed in the flatness and banality of his style, contributes partly to this failure in characterization. Neither his journalese nor his scientific jargon—both of which give him a medium and figurative language for expressing clearly, if gracelessly, his characters' social reactions—is adaptable to the dramatization of a rich inner life. This banal language is made to function dramatically in Farrell's novels because Farrell works from within the mind of his character, and the language pattern of the novel thus becomes an expression of a character's sensibility. When Dreiser tried to rise to poetic heights in expressing aesthetic reactions, he became merely vague and extravagant. Consequently, although we may know that his heroes have an aesthetic temperament because he has told us often of their longings for beauty, we do not realize this as a dramatic fact.

Dreiser's success with his characters comes rather from his power to dramatize the typicality of their existence as city-dwellers. He re-creates vividly in his people the hopes and fears which the city inspires and which any man might experience there. His characters function, therefore, as type figures; they do not exist in order to bring the reader into contact with a private and peculiar inner world: rather they reflect the outer world and reveal its significant implications for the human being. Yet in this very treatment of the typical human reactions to city life lies the reason for Dreiser's importance. He penetrated to the central meaning of urban society in its personal consequences, and his works focalize struggles, sentiments, and defeats characteristic of this area

92

of American life. Since Dreiser, writers have developed new ways of expressing the same material he has treated, but they have added essentially little to what he has said about the city. He stands out as a germinal figure in American urban fiction, a figure to whom later writers have turned for inspiration because they have found in his novels a fictional world that is familiar to them, that is the world they themselves have experienced. He recaptured the hope and excitement of the urban atmosphere that has always drawn young men and women to the metropolis. He brought to life the people who were attracted by this atmosphere and became part of it, and he created early urban types from the factory girl to the financier. He explored the hopes and disappointments of these people and traced their struggles. He showed how once they moved behind the glamorous façade of city life they were enclosed by chaos and were lost. He was among the first to reveal in fiction the other side of the American Dream of success; he showed the intensity of that dream and also the pathos of everyday failure. Earlier writers spoke of the American opportunities for success; later writers stressed the failures of an economic system that offered fewer and fewer opportunities for the rise from rags to riches. Dreiser drew together the Horatio Alger legend and the legend of human defeat before great impersonal forces of environment. His works reveal the grand illusion that has always existed about the city and the terrible realities that seem to be an inextricable part of it.

As he explored the inner meaning of city life, leaving behind wishful dreams and literary conventions of sentimentality, he voiced questions which have become thematic in twentieth-century city fiction. What place can man make for himself in a great materialistic industrial society? What hope is there to find beauty and inner peace in such a money-crazed world? What responsibility must society take for man's ineffectuality, confusion, and moral obliquities, now that it has reduced him by its own overpowering forces to his essential nothingness? In dealing with such questions, Dreiser assumed the attitude of social concern prominent in contemporary writers. He assessed the failures of urban society and condemned the destructive elements in it that keep man from finding inner contentment and leading a rich full life. He expressed the modern tragedy of man crushed in a mechanized, impersonal, and alien world that values technology rather than art, science rather than religion.

Dreiser is not merely a key figure in American city fiction, for while he takes his material from American urban life, he has much in common with the noteworthy writers of our time who have revealed and deplored the wasteland elements in the twentieth-century world. In exploring the inner emptiness of city life, he gave an early and significant expression to the sense of loss and uncertainty that seems to be the common subjective experience treated in modern literature. He depicted the confusions of the individual adrift in a society which had rejected past traditions but had not yet replaced them with new ones; and like many contemporary writers, he protested against the human price being paid for social chaos. If his works cannot rank with the greatest of twentieth-century writings, it is mainly because the art of a new realism is still primitive in them, and because the very confusions of a mind suffering the loss of faith reveal themselves as intellectual and aesthetic deficiencies. Even his faults as a novelist help, however, to illuminate his fundamental strength, for they arise out of his original insights into the appalling implications of our machine-created society. These insights give him his place in twentieth-century literature, and they show how deeply he had penetrated to the heart of the problems that thrust themselves upon us today.

CHAPTER 4

Sherwood Anderson,
Edith Wharton,
and Thomas Wolfe

Three Literary Views of the City

THE THREE writers discussed in this chapter, Sherwood Anderson, Edith Wharton, and Thomas Wolfe, form strange company. And it may seem strange that with their varied interests in the small town, the international scene, and the South, they should be included in a study of the city novel. But they are brought together and given place in this study because they have made, each in his own way, unique and significant contributions to twentieth-century urban fiction. Whatever other experiences they may have had and whatever other interests may have controlled their art, each of them, nevertheless, had his own peculiar contact with the city, Anderson with Chicago, and Edith Wharton and Thomas Wolfe with New York. The city as they personally experienced it and as they re-created in the novel has much in common with the city of which major urban novelists had written and are still writing. But each of these writers had also his own peculiar perspective, and each spoke in his own language, so that while their works enrich and enlarge the tradition of city fiction, they stand also as unique expressions of a modern vision of city life.

95

The themes of personal dissociation and the failure of love, as they are organic to modern city fiction, are fundamental to Sherwood Anderson's novels. In *Winesburg, Ohio,* Anderson developed these themes against the setting of the small town—although he had found actual prototypes for the grotesque characters of Winesburg in a rooming house in Chicago. In *Dark Laughter,* again a study of dissociation, Anderson used Chicago as a significant point of reference: it was here that the action of the novel started as Bruce Dudley went through the disintegrating experiences from which he tries to recover. In *Poor White,* a novel most critics consider one of Anderson's best,[1] Anderson did more than dramatize the fact of dissociation: he related it to social and economic sources. He showed how the rise of industrialism, which transformed America's dreamy towns into ugly and aggressive industrial centers, destroyed the social community and deprived man of the relationships he needed for self-fulfillment. In re-creating the historical process of change by which the town became the city, *Poor White* presents the dynamics of urbanization. Past and present are laid side by side—and one of the finest achievements of the novel is the delicate evocation of the past of rural America, with its large lovely landscapes, quiet towns, and homey warmth. This past gives a perspective on the present. Anderson's way of making us know what the city is, is to show what it has destroyed. *Poor White* may stand as Anderson's technical masterpiece, for in few other works has he so successfully integrated theme and form. The city in the state of becoming—this is his difficult theme; how it is given complete dramatic reality through a

---

[1] See Irving Howe, *Sherwood Anderson* (New York, William Sloane Associates, 1951), 130; James Schevill, *Sherwood Anderson: His Life and Work* (Denver, University of Denver Press, 1951), 127; Horace Gregory, Introduction, *The Portable Sherwood Anderson* (New York, The Viking Press, 1949), 15f.

variety of brilliant strategies will be discussed here as Anderson's contribution to city fiction.

Edith Wharton also dealt with a process of social transition, and she too traced the destructive consequences of the change from an old way of life to the new industrialism. The characters, like Lily Bart, who most strongly feel the tensions between past and present also suffer an inner dissociation. But the drama of conflicting values is acted out on the level of polite, high society—and it is Edith Wharton's insight into the workings of the destructive element in New York society that makes her novels unique in city fiction. She knew from the inside a world that was closed not only to most city novelists but to most city people. Her novels of New York, *The House of Mirth, The Custom of the Country,* and *The Age of Innocence,* invade the old, impregnable homes of the Five Hundred and reveal that even here one is immersed in the destructive element of twentieth-century urbanism. The tensions and conflicts within exclusive New York society parallel those found in commonplace, middle-class life. Here too one saw the breakdown of tradition and the disintegration of the community, the pressures of a new industrialism with its materialistic drives, the conflict of values and ideals—and above all, the aloneness of man wandering in a social void. These conditions assume human importance in Edith Wharton's novels by virtue of what they destroy, and Edith Wharton's claim to a place in city fiction is in her portrayals, incisive, ironic, and indignant, of the destructive elements in urban high society.

In *The Story of a Novel,* Thomas Wolfe wrote, "I saw that I must find for myself the tongue to utter what I knew but could not say."[2] Perhaps Wolfe himself never realized

[2] Thomas Wolfe, *The Story of a Novel* (New York and London, Charles Scribner's Sons, 1949), 35. Originally published serially in *The Saturday Review of Literature* in December, 1935.

how completely the language he finally discovered for himself was dominated by urban imagery and symbolism. Whatever he had to say of man's wandering and aloneness, of youth and love, of incertitude, evil, and death, and of the artist's quest, he expressed in terms of the city as symbol. The city seemed to have become part of his imaginative and expressive processes. As he himself said in an early letter to his mother, "This great city [New York] has fed my imagination."[3] New York gave him facts which imagination converted into dramatic and symbolic realities; and it gave him the language for stating these realities.

One reason why the city exerted this extraordinary influence upon him is that he himself tried deliberately, with characteristic obsessive desire, to absorb the city into his consciousness. "When I am on the streets of this city," he wrote his mother, ". . . I try to burn myself into the 'innards' of everyone I see, I listen in on everything I hear, I get their way of talking and looking."[4] But more than this, the city had a peculiar appropriateness to his needs. Its changing and varied panoramas seemed to correlate with—just as they also provoked—his volatile and intense moods; and he could use the outer scene to objectify inner states of being. The sociological characteristics of the city seemed a translation of man's spiritual condition in the modern world: anonymity, impersonality, instability, isolation—these were another way of stating Wolfe's theme of man's aloneness, homelessness, and incertitude. Moreover, because the city was a tremendous sprawling and vital world, it seemed to have a relationship to the Faustian hunger of youth and the artist: it was commensurate with this hunger, great enough to inspire it and also to satisfy

[3] *Thomas Wolfe's Letters to His Mother Julia Elizabeth Wolfe* (ed. by John Skally Terry, New York, Charles Scribner's Sons, 1943), 79. The letter is dated June, 1924.
[4] *Ibid.*, 46. The letter is dated March, 1923.

it. In denying it, however, it symbolized the ultimate irony of youth's aspirations and the inevitable frustration of his mad hopes to conquer time. What we see, then, in *Of Time and the River, The Web and the Rock,* and *You Can't Go Home Again* is the novelist transforming facts of city life into a complex symbolic statement of his meanings—and the concern here will be with the city as one of the key symbols through which Wolfe found the articulation he was seeking.

A Novel of Becoming

IN HIS introduction to the Modern Library edition of *Poor White,* Sherwood Anderson wrote: "There was a town in the state of Ohio. The town was really the hero of the book.... What happened to the town was, I thought, more important than what happened to the people."[5] Anderson's main strategy for dramatizing what happened to the town, as industrialism hit it and it became a city, is to identify the process of urbanization with his central character, Hugh McVey. Hugh is not merely the inventor who brings social change to Bidwell; he is the human counterpart to the historical process of change. What happens to him, as he becomes something he was not, is, conversely, what happens to the town. The changes within Hugh are set against the background of shifting relationships among the people of Bidwell. Their actions represent the dynamics of urbanism as a way of life. What happens to them, as they accommodate their values, relationships, and manners to the demands of a new mechanical age, is again a dramatization of the process of social change. The subplots (like the short fables Anderson introduces into the narrative) reinforce, through particular-

[5] Sherwood Anderson, Introduction, *Poor White* (New York, Modern Library, 1925), vi. *Poor White* was originally published in 1920.

ized incidents, the theme of becoming. The story of the harness-maker and his helper summarizes the tensions and conflicting values that arose with the transition from craftsmanship to machine production; and the marriage between Hugh and Clara implies the wider failure of love, which is thematic to the novel. All of the action is heightened by the changes in setting, as the large lovely landscapes, the apple orchards, and farm fields disappear to make room for factories and crowded shoddy houses. With the change in landscape comes also the disintegration of the old way of life of rural America. The most lyrical and evocative passages in *Poor White,* passages that are implicit judgments upon the new life, re-create the quiet mood and pace of the town, the satisfying activities, both arduous and joyous, of the farm folk, and the freshness and sensuous beauty of the natural scene. Against this harmonious past are set the tensions and conflicts of the growing city; and the nostalgic mood of the novel reinforces the theme of loss.

The condition of modern man, as Anderson sees it, is summarized in the character of Hugh McVey. Hugh is necessarily one of Anderson's grotesques, for he is less a human being than the human equivalent to a state of social change. His early stupor is hardly credible; yet his lethargic state of vague dreaming is evocative of America's slow sleepy towns. His complete isolation and fumbling inarticulateness are also unbelievable; yet they too become a satisfactory projection of man's inner dissociation in the world of machines. As Hugh changes from the lazy giant who slept by the mudbanks of the Mississippi to a busy inventor always making "definite" things, he embodies the *process* of urbanization. And it is significant that he is prodded out of his dreamy lethargy by a woman from New England. The driving practicality, enterprise, and shrewdness that overtake and transform the Midwest have come from the bustling centers of the East, where industrialism first took hold. In his own slow awakening to the consequences of industrialism, Hugh embodies a *moral attitude* towards the process of social change. At first, he had lacked any moral referents by which to judge the growth of cities: "he had seen towns and factories grow and had accepted without question men's word that growth was invariably good."[6] But as he catches the "disease of thinking," he begins to question the value of what he has helped to bring to Bidwell; and his awakening to the social and personal implications of the machine age is representative of a collective growing awareness. In his own failure to establish satisfactory human relationships, Hugh also embodies the *human consequences* of industrial urbanism. The hope behind his activities as inventor was that he could make for himself a place within the community. Isolated by his grotesqueness and inarticulateness, he had always been "seeking a place where he was to achieve companionship with men and women."[7] But his isolation is not broken by his success with the machine. Rather it is consolidated, for the place he makes for himself is in the shop, in the midst of machinery parts, and not in the community among friends and family. Indeed, his mechanical achievements destroy not only his own chances for human companionship: they destroy the very community of the town. "The people who lived in the towns," says Anderson, "... [had been] like members of a great family."[8] That family is disintegrated under the impact of industrialism and the competitive codes it imposes.

The larger collapse of the community is represented through the gallery of townspeople, all of whom undergo a change as Bidwell becomes industrialized. While the secondary characters are more credible as human beings than the grotesque hero, they too are human correlatives to a process of social change. Steve Hunter, once just a "noisy

[6] *Ibid.,* 369.   [7] *Ibid.,* 32.   [8] *Ibid.,* 46.

boastful youth," embodies the new spirit of business enterprise, exploitation, and individualism. Ben Peeler, who no longer has time to chat with his neighbors now that he has become a capitalist, represents the uncertainties and insecurities of the business man. He is "nervous and irritable," always worried about the security of his property. Tom Butterworth turns away from the farm that had sustained him, leaving it in hired hands, while he attends to matters of money-making. Ed Hall, "who had been a carpenter's apprentice earning but a few dollars a week ... [and] was now a foreman,"[9] betrays the workers. Having been one of them, he knows how fast they can work and on how little they can live, and he uses this knowledge strategically by imposing a speed-up system and fighting the demand for fair wages. As these people move with accelerated pace, as they become avid for money and indifferent to human values, and as they grow apart from family and community, they incorporate the attitudes and relationships of urbanism as a way of life. They live by a new business ethic, which permits them to cheat and exploit each other. They establish new relationships of inequality, of capitalist and worker, employer and employee. They become strangers moving in a strange new world, for as they transform the country into an ugly, smoke-clouded, mechanized cityscape, they lose their relationship with nature—and they grow frightened, silent, and haggard. Their situation is summarized in Anderson's fable of the country mice who come to the city and grow weak and afraid under their unnatural conditions of life. "Modern men and women who live in industrial cities," Anderson says, "are like mice that have come out of the fields to live in houses that do not belong to them."[10]

The total change within Bidwell is pictured in miniature in the subplot of the harness-maker and his helper. Jim Wains-

[9] *Ibid.,* 213.   [10] *Ibid.,* 114.

worth represents the craftsmanship which the machine destroys. As Wainsworth is being displaced, the personal rewards of craftsmanship—integrity, independence, pride, self-respect, and honesty—are also disappearing. Significantly, Wainsworth is "the first man in Bidwell to feel the touch of the heavy finger of industrialism."[11] This fatal touch turns him into "a silent disgruntled man," for it is, in reality, the opening blow against the age of craftsmanship that he represents. When Joe Gibson, a worthless drunkard, comes into the shop to be Wainsworth's helper, the full weight of industrialism is thrown upon the harness-maker, and he is never to lift himself from it. Gibson has the one faculty worshipped above all others in the new Bidwell—"the faculty for making money." His pleasure lies in the process of money-making; the money itself means little to him. In his indifference to the end of money-making and his excitement over the means, Gibson is the personification of the irrational drive for profit that seemed to Anderson a peculiar madness of the modern age. Gibson introduces the harness-maker to the new way of doing business: for honesty and neighborliness, he substitutes shrewdness and impersonality; for integrity, promotive skill; for the pleasure in creative work, the sterile pleasure in mere money-making. Under the strain of trying to readjust to Gibson's modern ways—if only in order to survive—Wainsworth cracks. He makes a wild and futile attempt to murder the new age by attacking the people who symbolize it, Steve Hunter, the business organizer, and Hugh McVey, the practical inventor. The failure of his attempt suggests the futility of trying to turn back twentieth-century "progress."

Just as the harness-maker represents the passing age of the craftsman, the farm hand, Jim Priest, represents the dying past of rural America. This past is recaptured in beautiful genre paintings of country life that are enframed within the nar-

[11] *Ibid.*, 134.

rative. These picture the awakening of life at dawn, the men washing at the pump, the women stirring in the kitchen, the animals grunting in their sheds and contentedly eating; the family working in the fields, and the "great hay wagons loaded with children, laughing girls, and sedate women"[12] going out to the fields for picking; the quiet Sunday afternoons in town, made colorful with the young folk dressed in their courting clothes; the tired gathering of family and farm hands around the great supper table at night; and the slow growth of the small boxlike farmhouses that "became almost beautiful in their humanness."[13]

One of the most memorable folk scenes is the wedding celebration for Hugh and his wife. The union of man and woman calls for elemental joy—for dancing, eating, drinking, and love-making. Jim Priest dominates the scene as the animated (and slightly inebriated) spirit of the folk. Here, in its color, gay action, and crowdedness is a verbal equivalent to a Breughel genre painting:

He began to dance a heavy-footed jig on a little open place by the kitchen door and the guests stopped talking to watch. They shouted and clapped their hands. A thunder of applause arose. The guests who were seated in the parlor and who could not see the performance got up and crowded into the doorway that connected the two rooms. Jim became extraordinarily bold, and as one of the young women Tom had hired as waitresses at that moment went past bearing a large dish of food, he swung himself quickly about and took her into his arms. The dish flew across the floor and broke against a table leg and the young woman screamed. A farm dog that had found its way into the kitchen rushed into the room and barked loudly. Henry Heller's orchestra, concealed under a stairway that led to the upper part of the house, began to play furiously. A strange animal fervor swept over Jim. His legs flew rapidly about and his heavy feet made a great clatter on the floor.

[12] *Ibid.,* 45.   [13] *Ibid.,* 131.

The young woman in his arms screamed and laughed. Jim closed his eyes and shouted. He felt that the wedding party had until that moment been a failure and that he was transforming it into a success. Rising to their feet the men shouted, clapped their hands and beat with their fists on the table. When the orchestra came to the end of the dance, Jim stood flushed and triumphant before the guests, holding the woman in his arms. In spite of her struggles he held her tightly against his breast and kissed her eyes, cheeks, and mouth. Then releasing her he winked and made a gesture for silence. 'On a wedding night some one's got to have the nerve to do a little love-making,' he said.[14]

The irony of Jim Priest's comment is that the newlyweds are incapable of "a little love-making." The failure of love is the corollary in the novel to the rise of industrialism. The bizarre relationship between Hugh and Clara externalizes man's inner state of dissociation in the machine age. Modern man and woman do not know how to move towards the consummation of their desires. Clara's search for love is frustrated by an antecedent failure in man. She cannot find a lover and husband; only her mannish woman-friend can give her the understanding and companionship she needs. Thus, *Poor White* anticipates the theme of Anderson's later novel *Perhaps Women* by showing that man has become incapacitated and the hope for the future lies in and with the woman. –

The end of *Poor White* reveals Hugh and Clara groping towards a union, but the solution to the problem of the failure of love is not a facile one; and the novel leaves the situation still unresolved. The central purpose of the novel does not require, of course, that the problems raised should be solved. One could hardly expect Anderson to present a solution to the problems that emerged with the rise of industrial urbanism, especially since they are so manifold and complex. One of the remarkable things about *Poor White* is that it does state almost

[14] *Ibid.*, 303.

every problem involved in this transition from agrarianism to urbanism: the growing struggle between workers and capital, the increasing inequality of wealth, the rise of an amoral business code, the growing mania to produce (as symbolized by Clara's aunt who knits hundreds of pairs of socks which no one will ever wear), the mushrooming of ugly crowded cities whose shoddy houses are to become the nation's slums, the breakdown of community spirit and the growing sense of individualism and alienation, the aesthetic loss in the transformation of the large undulating orchards into harsh, smoke-ridden cityscapes, the loss of man's independence and pride as he is transformed from craftsman to machine-hand, and finally, the failure of man's inner world.

These are the problems central to the whole body of twentieth-century city fiction. But the mere exposition of social problems is not the achievement of *Poor White*. The achievement of the novel lies in its dramatization of a historical moment of transition. The past that *Poor White* re-creates provides a perspective upon the present; it is also a judgment of what America has become with the emergence of industrial urbanism. Perhaps this past of small towns and rural countrysides was never as lovely as Anderson creates it. But his image has the quality of a collective memory, for in moods of nostalgia or dissatisfaction, we evoke an image of yesterday such as that captured and made timeless in the novel—the image of an endless American landscape of fresh beauty and quiet charm, of people walking peacefully in the fields, drawing their strength from the soil, of men living in social harmony and at one with their community and with themselves. The meaning of the city lies not only in the tensions and disharmonies of the present as the novel portrays them emerging in Bidwell but also in the loss of a romantic past as the town succumbs to the forces of history and becomes the city.

The Destructive Element in "Fashionable New York"

EDITH WHARTON's remarks on her literary decisions concerning the material of *The House of Mirth* are extremely revealing, for they define her approach as novelist to the American city. She had chosen, she says, to write of "fashionable New York" because this was "the material nearest to hand, and most familiarly my own."[15] But this material was by her own judgment shallow, flat, and futile, lacking in "human significance." Her problem was to find an approach to her subject that would make it yield a deeper meaning than superficially it seemed to have. She worked out her approach by asking first, "In what aspect could a society of irresponsible pleasure-seekers be said to have . . . any deeper bearing than the people composing such a society could guess?" The answer was "that a frivolous society can acquire dramatic significance only through what its frivolity destroys. Its tragic implication lies in its power of debasing people and ideals."[16]

Deliberately, then, Edith Wharton decided that her emphasis must be upon what New York society destroys; and this emphasis places her novels of New York in the tradition of the main stream of city fiction. Her fictional city is, like that of the ecological novelist, a special, circumscribed, and unique little world. But within its confines its influence is all-pervasive and irresistible; and its action is ultimately destructive. What Percy Lubbock wrote many years ago of the role of New York in *The House of Mirth* applies also to *The Custom of the Country* and *The Age of Innocence* (and his remark points to the essential nature of these novels as city fic-

[15] Edith Wharton, *A Backward Glance* (New York, Appleton-Century, 1934), 206.
[16] *Ibid.*

tion): "In 'The House of Mirth' New York is no background; it is an urgent and voluble participator in the drama."[17]

The action of Edith Wharton's New York lies in what it is as a social structure as much as in what it effects. It is a world bound together by convention but lacking an inner coherence. Within the in-group, the group that *is* fashionable New York by virtue of family background, two sets are fundamentally in conflict with each other: the old conservative aristocracy, represented by the Dagonets and the van der Luydens, and the young rich and somewhat vulgar pleasure-seekers, represented by the Dorsets, Trenors, and Van Degans. The insularity of both sets is being challenged by outsiders, as the *nouveaux riches,* attracted by the exclusiveness of high society, try to buy or bribe their way into it. Some of them, like Rosedale in *The House of Mirth,* are finally invading the inner circle; others, like the Gormers, are still on the periphery; and others, like Undine Spragg, have not only invaded the circle but have judged and condemned it, while they have defiled it simply by their own vulgar presence. Against all three American elements, providing a larger perspective on fashionable New York, stands the ancient European aristocracy, its age-old traditions represented by the Marquis de Chelles, its cultural fulfillment beautifully suggested by the Countess Olenska.

In all three novels, a young woman is placed by anomalous circumstances in a position where she must declare her alliance with one of these groups. Her choice has moral implications; and it is the dramatic fulcrum of the novel. It reflects the social tensions in which she is caught (because of her own circumstances, as well as the lack of unity within fashionable New York) and her sensitivity to the ideals of the various groups. Lily Bart is placed in her peculiar position because she is an insider without money; Undine Spragg be-

[17] Percy Lubbock, "The Novels of Edith Wharton," *Quarterly Review,* Vol. CCXXIII (January, 1915), 187.

cause she is a beautiful outsider with money; and Ellen Olenska because she is trying to escape from an unfortunate marriage.

Each of the women is tutored by a young man of certain characteristic traits. He has affinities with the old conservative aristocracy, although he mingles with the rich young set. He has rather vague artistic leanings, but enough detachment to see the cultural sterility of his world. He is a gentleman of modest income, yet not under any urgent necessity of making a living. He loves what is best in these women, but he can never consummate this love. His relationship with the woman is essentially that of a social mentor; he illuminates the ideals of the old society, and he does this usually in pointed, though sometimes elusive, conversations which follow a curious line between overt love-making and clarification of a social ideal. The final success of Lawrence Selden or Newland Archer lies not in action but in making Lily or Ellen *see,* in the Jamesean sense of the word. Ralph Marvell's failure is that he can never lift Undine Spragg, the beautiful young barbarian, to moral and social perception.

What Selden makes Lily see is the unworthiness of the values of the rich young pleasure-seekers. Brought up with the expectation of belonging to their set, Lily wants what they have, " 'I want admiration,' " Lily cries to her friend; " 'I want excitement, I want money—yes, *money!* That's my shame. . . .' "[18] Like Dreiser's Carrie (who, of course, cannot compare to Lily in intelligence and moral sensibility), Lily identifies wealth with beauty and harmonious living. Her desire for money has certain aesthetic implications. Perhaps this is most clearly indicated by her thoughts as she gazes at the perfection of precious jewels laid in settings that enhance their individual beauty:

[18] Edith Wharton, *The House of Mirth* (New York, Charles Scribner's Sons, 1905), 268.

... the milky gleam of perfectly matched pearls, the flash of rubies relieved against contrasting velvet, the intense blue rays of sapphires kindled into light by surrounding diamonds: all these precious tints enhanced and deepened by the varied art of their setting. The glow of the stones warmed Lily's veins like wine. More completely than any other expression of wealth they symbolized the life she longed to lead, the life of fastidious aloofness and refinement in which every detail should have the finish of a jewel, and the whole form a harmonious setting to her own jewel-like rareness.[19]

A "life of fastidious aloofness and refinement"—this is what it seems to her money offers as its ultimate reward. But this is not the kind of life that her rich frivolous friends lead. It is only as she sees the rich from Selden's point of view, "scanning her little world through his retina,"[20] that she becomes aware of the trivialities and stupidities, as well as the "vacuity," of a life of wealth and fashion. Because she can see that Selden's ideal of personal freedom and integrity—of the achievement of "a kind of republic of the spirit"—is higher than her own, she cannot take the decisive step into a marriage of wealth. The thought of Selden separates her first from Percy Gryce and then from Rosedale; it leads to the renunciation that is her costly moral victory.

In *The Age of Innocence,* Archer helps Ellen to see an ideal of social conduct—which is, simply, that one must give up private happiness for the sake of preserving the social unity as it is expressed through the continuity of tradition. This is the principle Ellen flings back at Archer as the great obstacle to their love: " 'Isn't it you who made me give up divorcing— give it up because you showed me how selfish and wicked it was, how one must sacrifice one's self to preserve the dignity of marriage . . . and to spare one's family the publicity, the

[19] *Ibid.,* 144.
[20] *Ibid.,* 87.

scandal?' "[21] What Ellen sees is that "happiness bought by disloyalty and cruelty and indifference"[22] is not happiness but a kind of horror. Renunciation becomes her positive ideal, for it is not simply a giving up, a loss; it is a means towards conserving and sustaining a social structure.

Both Lily and Ellen renounce personal happiness in order to live up to an ideal of conduct. But the social context which could give the act of renunciation wider meaning—which could give, that is, a social value to personal sacrifice—is missing in Edith Wharton's New York. The characters make their moral decisions under an implicit assumption that they are part of a social order; but the underlying irony in their choices is that order is gone. Under the converging impacts of inner and outer pressures, order has given way not only to disorder but to void. And the essential destructive element in the novels is social void, an emptiness left by the collapse of a way of life. Traditions that were once rich and meaningful have been shattered or have become merely empty conventions of form. Social manners have deteriorated into mere external signs and gestures without the inner significance that gives them value. And the individual, for all that he seems so preeminently a social and a socialized creature, is as much alone and adrift here in fashionable New York as anywhere else in the city.

The most poignant dramatization of the fact of social void is in the character of Lily Bart. Set apart by her own higher intelligence and moral sensibility as much as by her poverty, she has directed all her efforts towards finding a place for herself. She wants marriage because this only can give her social position; but the pathos of her struggle is that she cannot fit herself into any of the openings offered her by Percy Gryce,

[21] Edith Wharton, *The Age of Innocence* (New York, Appleton, 1920), 169.
[22] *Ibid.*, 172.

Gus Trenor, Rosedale, or even Selden. At the end of her short life, she realizes that she has always been rootless and alone—that she has suffered from this fact more than from her poverty. This is her final insight into her situation: "It was indeed miserable to be poor. . . . But there was something more miserable still—it was the clutch of solitude at her heart, the sense of being swept like a stray uprooted growth down the heedless current of the years. That was the feeling which possessed her now—the feeling of being something rootless and ephemeral, mere spin-drift of the whirling surface of existence, without anything to which the poor little tentacles of self could cling before the awful flood submerged them."[23]

It is significant that Lily's social isolation is so integrally connected with her lack of money. Money makes possible fashionable New York. It is as much a dramatic pivot in Edith Wharton's novels as it is in Dreiser's, although here the references to money-making are vague and elusive, and open discussion of money is considered vulgar. The manners of society demanded that one should "never talk about money, and think about it as little as possible."[24] This injunction could be obeyed as long as money flowed from its obscure coffers, but for Lily and Undine Spragg (this is also true of Halo Spear in *Hudson River Bracketed* and Lizzie Hazeldean in *New Year's Day*) the concern over money is constant because there is never enough. It is the function of some people in Edith Wharton's fictional world to do little else but supply money; men like Mr. Bart or Abner Spragg daily disappear into some shadowy office in Wall Street, engage in mysterious business, and produce funds for new Paris gowns and winter trips to Newport. When they fail to do this, they die, like Mr. Bart; or they sink into oblivion in their own homes. The most acceptable way to come upon money is to inherit it. The fact of

[23] *The House of Mirth*, 515.
[24] *A Backward Glance*, 57.

inheritance or disinheritance has serious moral implications: a crucial choice may be contingent upon it. Thus, when Lily is disinherited by Mrs. Peniston, she is forced to face moral alternatives that inheritance would have eliminated. Her renunciation of the offers of both Rosedale and Trenor is a moral victory made possible only by the fact of her poverty. Others in *The House of Mirth* are not as fastidious as she about using Rosedale as a source of income. Although Edith Wharton herself believed that one of the basic standards of New York society was its "scrupulous probity in business and private affairs,"[25] her novels show that the young rich were not above the persuasions of wealth, if the rewards were great enough. Thus, Gus Trenor makes room within the exclusive golden circle for the "vulgar" Mr. Rosedale because his "tips" bring Trenor a half-million dollars.

Just as Lily's renunciation of money illuminates the materialism of others, so her mere presence—her being what she is—throws into relief the faults and deficiencies of other characters; and Ellen's presence also has this illuminating effect. Thus, the dullness of Percy Gryce becomes flagrant because he is a possible, and highly incongruous, husband for Lily. The vulgarity of Gus Trenor and Julius Beaufort becomes inexcusable because they have designs upon women nobler than they. The selfishness of Bertha Dorset becomes a deliberate evil because she attacks Lily from behind the security of her "impregnable bank account." And the narrow conventionality of May Welland becomes a destructive force because she defeats Ellen's chance for personal happiness.

But beyond the insipidity or cruelty of individuals are the collective weaknesses and hypocrisies of the group. The social void in which Lily flounders is created by, and projected through, the total pattern of manners to which the group conforms. In this pattern, behavior has become so convention-

[25] *Ibid.*, 21.

113

alized that it cannot adapt itself to individual situations of stress. No one wants to hear about Lily's or Ellen's private difficulties, for these have no place within a convention. One must pretend, under the veneer of politeness, that such difficulties do not exist. Thus, Lily's best friends know and yet hypocritically refuse to acknowledge her poverty. They give her dresses and invite her to parties, but they avoid showing any deeper recognition of her plight. In *The Age of Innocence,* Mrs. Welland, the embodiment of narrow convention, refuses to hear and acknowledge any unpleasant facts of life to which Ellen's history might introduce her; and Ellen finds herself living under the fiction that nothing terrible has happened to her, that nothing terrible, ugly, or immoral exists in the world. Even May Welland's bland innocence has something frightening about it. Archer sees his future wife as a "creation of factitious purity,"[26] an artificial being living in an unreal world in which evil and accident have been exorcised by the simple process of having been hushed. When the group must choose between recognizing or ignoring a reality which conflicts with its conventional fiction about life, it preserves the fiction rather than face up to the fact. Those who urge Ellen to return to her presumably monstrous husband may not have fully appreciated the strains of her life with him, but that is because manners have become an obstacle to full human understanding and sympathy.

Indifference and narrowness are never entirely innocuous; but this society is guilty of more positive evils—hypocrisy and the deliberate sacrifice of an innocent to the vulnerable. Lawrence Lefferts in *The Age of Innocence* represents calculated hypocrisy concealed under a sanctimonious observance of manners. He deliberately draws social red herrings before the group to deflect attention from his own affairs, just as in

[26] See Wharton, *The Age of Innocence,* 42f. for an illuminating discussion of "innocence."

The House of Mirth, Bertha Dorset points the accusing finger at Lily in order to keep away suspicion from herself. It is ironical that Ellen should feel herself safe in the purity of New York society (this is a repetition of Madame de Malrive's feeling in *Madame de Treymes*) when Lefferts is there to sacrifice her to his own security, Beaufort to use her for his own designs, and May Welland to send her away for the sake of convention.

Hypocrisy, indifference, pettiness, narrow convention, and insensibility—these are not merely the flaws within a society: they *are* fashionable New York. Whatever was once fine and dignified about the social aristocracy survives only in attenuated form—in the aging van der Luydens who live now in semiretirement and in the ineffectual young men who find reality in their secluded libraries. The failure of the aristocratic ideals to survive in the present is symbolized in the failure of Ralph Marvell. When Marvell marries Undine, he is under the gallant delusion that he is saving her from the clutches of the vulgar. But actually he is delivering himself into Undine's grasping hands, just as fashionable society as a whole is slowly delivering itself over to the new vulgar plutocracy. Marvell's suicide is his recognition of Undine's victory and of the victory of all that she represents and destroys. His suicide represents also the symbolic death of the traditions that had once dignified upper society. There is no place for a young man of moral and aesthetic sensibility in the rushing, pleasure-fevered new world, just as there is no place now for ideals of honor, social solidarity, and human dignity.

The vulgar outsiders, the Gormers, Spraggs, Rosedales, and Moffatts, add the final destructive touch to a society that is already only a shell of convention and manners, the real substance having been destroyed by attrition and inner weakness. A vital new blood might have given the past new life, but these newcomers are incapable of understanding the ideals which once gave this society its meaning. The accusation of blindness that the Marquis de Chelles flings against Undine in her invasion of European aristocracy can be made also against the plutocrats in their invasion of fashionable New York: " 'You come among us speaking our language, and not knowing what we mean; wanting the things we want, and not knowing why we want them; aping our weakness, exaggerating our follies, ignoring or ridiculing all we care about. . . .' "[27] The difference between the ideals of the insider and the insensibility of the outsider is summarized in the differences between Lily and Undine, both beautiful, full of desire for admiration and luxury, but the one sensitive and intelligent, caught between her desire and her sense of honor and dignity, the other merely grasping and obtuse. Lily is destroyed because of what is best in her; Undine is blindly and recklessly destructive of everything fine that stands in the way of her gratification.

This contrast between insider and outsider is offset by the contrast between the culture of fashionable New York and that of the European aristocracy. Henry James regretted the fact that Edith Wharton sketched in only broad sweeping strokes the cultural differences between Undine and her husband, the Marquis. In *The Age of Innocence,* the contrast is developed through the representative values of Ellen and May. Ellen symbolizes to Archer the richness of Europe in the totality of its culture and art, while May comes to symbolize in turn the arid convention and narrowness of America. These women evoke the sense of a culture less by what they say than by what they are, and particularly by the interiors in which they live. Taste, in Edith Wharton's novels, is a criterion of cultural and moral, as well as purely aesthetic, sensibility; and the furnishings of Ellen's rooms and of the Wellands' home

[27] Edith Wharton, *The Custom of the Country* (New York, Charles Scribner's Sons, 1914), 545.

are revelations of personality, character, and a manner of life. (This implicatory use of details of interior decorating and architecture, the method of suggesting a total culture through a revelation of personal taste, Edith Wharton may well have learned from James.) Archer achieves a comprehensive insight into the difference between American and European culture by sitting in Ellen's rooms for a little while. Everything in the room seems to him an expression of an individual taste educated to the subtleties of beauty and the suggestive charm of things. The "slender tables of dark wood," the "Italian-looking pictures in old frames," the "two Jacqueminot roses" in the "slender vase," the "vague pervading perfume"— these give the room a "faded shadowy charm" as they suggest "old romantic scenes and sentiments."[28] Archer finds Ellen's room "unlike any room he had known." But the Wellands' home has the familiar fixtures that convention demands. It is not only furnished in bad taste, with "its sham Buhl tables" and "purple satin and yellow tuftings"; it is, like everything else about the Wellands, a repudiation of taste insofar as taste is the expression of an individual, sincere, and original response to the world. Thinking of the home that the Wellands are to give him as a wedding present, Archer feels that "his fate is sealed";[29] his future home is to be a replica of the Wellands', just as his future life will be a re-enactment, with only slight variations, of theirs. While Ellen's room opens up to Archer a vision of a life quickened by a sense of art and beauty and enriched by contacts with people of sensibility, the Wellands' home makes him realize the cultural flatness and sterility of his New York.

Once Edith Wharton has revealed the cultural void in which upper New York society is suspended, she completes a picture of what is actually social inanition. With a kind of

[28] *The Age of Innocence,* 68f.
[29] *Ibid.,* 69.

feminine delight in disclosing intimate and petty details, she breaks every possible illusion an outsider might have had about the world of fashionable New York. Whatever sturdy and admirable qualities one might have assumed, in his ignorance, to be implicit in the way of life of this exclusive world she virtually denies by her insistence upon the corruption of these qualities. Good breeding which makes it vulgar to talk about money and unpleasant things turns easily into hypocrisy and moral cowardice. The play of manners can easily conceal indifference, and even cruelty. The rounds of visiting and dining out can become mere monotonous pleasure-seeking; the social duties dwindle away to triviality. The insistence upon tradition becomes a narrow observance of convention, in time stifling real or intense emotion; the past perpetuates itself only as a stagnating influence. Art, politics, and business, the foundations of the state as well as of its culture, are deplored as ungentlemanly and vulgar; the young men remain dilettantes, finding only a shadowy reality in their quiet libraries. Against the aristocracy of Europe, which created and contributed to a tremendously rich cultural heritage, this aristocracy is sterile. It is without social purpose, and for this reason it is disintegrating. The disintegrating forces of the invading plutocrats are only reinforcing the effects of the disintegrating forces within. The compunctions that keep the gentleman from playing any role in modern life and that keep the class from evincing any new interest in the state or in art have ultimately deprived high society of its chance to function in the modern world. These compunctions have, however, a virulent power to destroy: they destroy Lily; they destroy Marvell's chance of self-fulfillment in literary activity; they destroy Archer's will to make a richer and more meaningful life for himself. What they manage to preserve is the sense, if not the reality, of some ideal of social conduct—conduct in the interest of social solidarity; and it is to this ideal that Ellen and

Lily respond. But their response can be only an act of renunciation. The only way to achieve self-fulfillment is through denial of one's self. What chance is there for an intelligent and sensitive person to find personal happiness and at the same time to keep his integrity? Presumably none. In this city, as in Dreiser's Chicago, the promise for personal self-fulfillment is illusory. What is real about Edith Wharton's New York is what condemns it, for its essential reality lies in its broken traditions and in its virulent power to destroy.

The City as Symbol

In DEFENDING himself against the charge that he was merely an autobiographer, Thomas Wolfe was led to consider the relationship between the actuality of life and the reality of art—that is, between literal fact and its literary re-creation. No matter how literally true to life the novelist may try to be, Wolfe pointed out, his reality must be different from actuality, for "everything in a work of art is changed and transfigured by the personality of the artist."[30] Perhaps the most striking example of how Wolfe's own unique personality changed and transfigured his material can be seen in his literary treatment of New York. New York overwhelmed Wolfe with its multifarious forms, changing scenes, and strange dark polyglot people. But while it held this intrinsic interest for him as a place, it never functioned in his novels merely as physical setting or atmosphere. For Wolfe found in its various and changing scenes the objective correlative to his own volatile emotions as well as to what he held to be timeless and impersonal truths. As he re-created the city, he imposed upon it his personal meanings, so that he moved always from literal transcription to symbolic statement. Consequently, the city that emerges in his novels is a unique imaginative conception,

[30] *The Story of a Novel,* 22.

119

for it is a city "changed and transfigured" by the creative processes of art.

As a symbol, the city has an organic place in the pattern of quest that underlies Wolfe's life and work. "Man's search to find a father," Wolfe said, was "the deepest search in life ... central to all living."[31] The quest for a father, for certitude and wisdom, led Wolfe, as it led his heroes, to wandering; and their first destination was a great city of the North. The city—New York in particular, but also the city as generic— came to be equated with every object of youth's quest; and in time it was equated also with all that youth achieved and with all that frustrated him. Youth's journey to the city is, of course, a traditional theme. In America, it had particular historical relevance to the period of industrialization and rapid urban growth. It is also a timeless theme, for youth is ever in quest. And for each person who undertakes the journey, the theme has personal implications. All city writers reveal in their art the personal meanings that the city holds for them, but some (like Dreiser, for example) try to achieve a typicality which is, in effect, an emphasis upon historical truth. Wolfe emphasized the timeless and the personal elements of youth's quest—indeed he equated the two. Eugene Gant is the modern Telemachus in search of a father. Wolfe attempted to give the quest epic proportions, and the city enters the epic as Proteus, god of ever-changing forms. For as Wolfe's violent moods changed, as his insights deepened, and his attitudes took mature definition, the meaning of the city also evolved and changed.

Because of Wolfe's peculiar way of putting together his novels, a certain awkwardness enters any discussion of his use of the city as symbol. In the George Webber novels, New York often has the same symbolic significance that it had had in the earlier novels of Eugene Gant. Thus, there are times when

[31] *Ibid.*, 39.

we can speak of what the city means to Eugene Gant–George Webber. On the other hand, however, the George Webber novels extend the symbolic meaning of the city, so that there are times when we must differentiate between the heroes and indicate the special meanings that the city holds for each. Finally, there are times when the identification between Wolfe and his heroes (or perhaps only between Wolfe and Webber) is so close that we must speak of the city as part of Wolfe's life, and not merely as part of his novels. For all three, the two protagonists and Wolfe, the pattern of quest is basically the same: there is the cycle of desire and frustration, of hope and disillusionment, that initiates them into manhood and the world of art.

In *Of Time and the River* and *The Web and the Rock,* the heroes' longing towards the "golden city" of New York is, on one level, the perennial longing of youth for fame, fortune, and adventure—particularly amorous adventure. Thus, George's vision of the city is "adolescent, fleshly, erotic." But it is more than this. It is a vision both of escape from dark, life-sapping forces and of movement towards creative self-fulfillment. The desire for a creative life is implicated in the antithesis between the South, the haunted region of darkness, and the North, place of golden light; and furthermore in the antithesis between mother and father. The fathers of Wolfe's heroes are, significantly, Northern men; and because they are also men of passion and vitality, in their own way builders and artists, they represent the principle of life as it is expressed in the creative act. The Northern city symbolizes the spiritual fatherland that the heroes seek. It is the place where they are to be reunited with their fathers, as well as with themselves, by a rediscovery of "the lost but unforgotten half of . . . [their] soul[s]."[32] Thus, as Wolfe's heroes dream of

[32] Thomas Wolfe, *Of Time and the River* (New York, Charles Scribner's Sons, 1937), 24.

the North, with the "intolerable and wordless joy of longing which only a Southerner can feel,"[33] they dramatize Wolfe's deepest desires for certitude, fame, and creative self-fulfillment. In adolescent fantasies, they project an image that is common and yet intensely personal of a glowing city that holds promise of adventure, love, fame, and riches, of escape from the "world-lost resignation" and "hill-haunted sorrow" of the South, and of reunion with a spiritual father and fulfillment in the creative life.

"There is no truer legend in the world," Wolfe wrote in *The Web and the Rock,* "than the one about the country boy, the provincial innocent, in his first contact with the city."[34] In *Of Time and the River,* this first moment of arrival is dramatized in one of Wolfe's most stirring rhapsodic passages. His description of the racing trains, which both embody and evoke Eugene Gant's reactions, recapitulates the thrill of a moment of tremendous realization that comes to almost all heroes of the portrait novel, as it comes to almost all arrivals in real life. The city seems to Eugene Gant "something fabulous and enchanted"; even the "common, weary, driven brutal faces" of the city people and their "sterile scrabble of harsh words" seem to possess a "strange and legendary quality."[35] As the concrete realization of a legend, the city thus immediately assumes symbolic stature; for as a legend is timeless, so the city, as generic, is permanent and immutable, embodying "the fixity of time." It is, in other symbolic terms, the "enfabled rock" that endures forever. But in its urgent, streaming movements, the city also epitomizes passing time—the fleeting of the moment. Thus, it suggests both transience and im-

[33] *Ibid.,* 24.

[34] Thomas Wolfe, *The Web and the Rock* (New York, Sun Dial, 1940 reprint), 222. Originally published by Harper and Brothers in 1939.

[35] *Of Time and the River,* 416.

mutability, and as a time symbol, it is central to Wolfe's poetic statement of man's relationship to the moment and eternity.

George Webber's arrival is again the occasion for speculation on the symbolic meaning of the cityscape. But here, as Wolfe himself is more removed from the experience of arrival, as he sees the city with new and sobered insight, and as he tries consciously for artistic restraint, the occasion leads to a rather disillusioned speculation on the meaning of reality. The city as Eugene had dreamed of it had become real through the validating experience of his first thrilling contact with it. But George's first glimpses of the city, which confirm for him the dream he held, are to Wolfe merely the projections of the mind. What is the reality of the city? Wolfe asks. Is it in the external scene or is it in the inner image that one projects outward to shape and color the actuality? In the description of George's arrival, the excitement and wonder have reality only in the mind; for, Wolfe implies, only the dream exists. And time not only leaves it invalidated by experience but it proves it to be false.

The discovery of the realities of New York is for the hero also a process of self-discovery. As he gains insight into the economic, social, and spiritual nature of city life, he comes to formulate his mature attitudes and declare his moral and personal commitments. At first, however, Eugene Gant— George Webber is too much bedazzled by New York's surface glamour to understand its implications. Typically, both heroes identify the spectacle of fashion and wealth with their own secret adolescent image. When Eugene Gant visits his friend's wealthy upstate home, it seems to him "that all he had dreamed was but a poor and shabby counterfeit of this reality—all he had imaged as a boy in his unceasing vision of the shining city, and of the glamorous men and women, the fortunate, good, and happy life that he would find there, seemed nothing but a shadowy and dim prefiguration of the

radiant miracle of this actuality."[36] Because Eugene is still
naïve and socially unconscious, he does not realize the implications of this way of life, "how many nameless lives had
labored, grieved, and come to naught in order that . . . [it]
could come to light."[37]

Eugene's disillusionment with this "radiant" world of
wealth comes suddenly; and his reversal in attitude cannot be
entirely accounted for by the incidents that apparently produce it. Two slight acts of Joel Pierce—his aesthetic appreciation of the play of sunlight and his request that Eugene put
on his jacket when they pass within sight of Joel's grand-
father—suddenly destroy Eugene's illusions not only about
his friend but also about the apparently beautiful way of life
of the rich. These acts seem to Eugene symptomatic of a barrenness ("barren interest . . . in the blind opacity of light . . .
and . . . barren joyless reverence to old age")[38] which is the
antithesis of his hope for a creative, a really rich, life. His disillusionment with Joel is the beginning of his discovery of
the real city and of his self-discovery: "It seemed to him that
here began that . . . painful recognition that the enchanted
world of wealth and love and beauty . . . which he had vis-
ioned as a child . . . did not exist."[39] In his disillusionment,
Eugene turns to another image of the city, this time as "be-
fouled and smutted with the rust and grime of its vast works
and factories, warped and scarred and twisted, stunned, bewildered by the huge multitude of all its errors and blind
gropings, yet still fierce with life."[40] This is the image, to
which Wolfe constantly returns, of the urban jungle; but significantly, the jungle is alive, fierce, and energetic, offering
to the artist its sustaining vitality. The acceptance of the violence and "brutal stupefaction of the streets" is a return also
to the spirit of the father—of fury, lust, and joy—and is there-

[36] *Ibid.*, 539.   [37] *Ibid.*
[38] *Ibid.*, 570.   [39] *Ibid.*   [40] *Ibid.*, 571.

fore related to primal creative instincts. It is at the same time a return to a democratic belief in the common people. Thus Eugene realizes, as he turns away from the Pierces and what they represent, that "goodness and truth [exist] in the mean hearts of common men."[41]

Like Eugene, George Webber had identified wealth with his vision of a "golden city." But his reactions, both of joy in the city and disillusionment with it, follow upon experiences that involve him more personally, and that make his reactions more convincing. Central to all his reactions to the city is his love for his mistress, Esther Jack. When he finds love at its height, Esther and her world represent to him the beauty and fulfillment that the city had promised. When, however, he repudiates love, he announces his enmity towards her world, and like Eugene, sees that his sympathies as an artist must be with the common people. The symbolic equation between love and the city is linear. Any variation in George's feelings evokes a change in his attitude towards the city. In the glory of his love, he is transported by a "golden and exultant vision" of a city in opulence, triumph, and beauty; in the torment of jealousy, he is haunted by a lurid picture of the city, "drawn in lines of lust and cruelty." The evening of Esther Jack's spectacular party brings him to a climactic recognition of the insufficiency of love and, consequently, of the inanity of the frivolous rich. George's repudiation of Esther implies a new understanding of the social and economic structure of the city, of its inequalities and injustices, and also a new dedication to his art. This is summarized in his realization that "love is not enough":

For he had learned tonight that love was not enough. There had to be a higher devotion than all the devotions of this fond imprisonment. There had to be a larger world than this glittering fragment of a world with all its wealth and privilege. Throughout

[41] *Ibid.*

his whole youth and early manhood, this very world of beauty, ease, and luxury, of power, glory, and security, had seemed the ultimate end of human ambition, the furthermost limit to which the aspirations of any man could reach. But tonight, in a hundred separate moments of intense reality, it had revealed to him its very core. He had seen it naked, with its guards down. He had sensed how the hollow pyramid of a false social structure had been erected and sustained upon a base of common mankind's blood and sweat and agony. So now he knew that if he was ever to succeed in writing the books he felt were in him, he must turn about and lift his face up to some nobler height.[42]

In separating himself from Esther, George goes into a period of isolation. Alone in Brooklyn, he explores his inner resources as a writer, as well as Brooklyn's sordid night-world. George's experiences are a dramatic re-creation of Wolfe's own period of exploration as he describes it in *The Story of a Novel*. Days of feverish writing, when Wolfe spilled out all that he had known and experienced (in this way discovering the materials of his art), ended in nights of restless wandering through Brooklyn's streets and back alleys. ". . . For three years I prowled the streets," Wolfe recalled, "explored the swarming web of the million-footed city and came to know it as I had never done before."[43] Essentially, he came to know the consequences of the great depression. They were alive in "the haggard faces of the homeless men, the wanderers, the disinherited of America, the aged workers who had worked and now could work no more, the callow boys who had never worked and now could find no work to do, and who, both together, had been cast loose by a society that had no need of them and left to shift in any way they could—to find their

[42] Thomas Wolfe, *You Can't Go Home Again* (New York, Sun Dial, 1942 reprint), 320. Originally published by Harper and Brothers in 1940.
[43] *The Story of a Novel*, 58.

food in garbage cans, to seek for warmth and fellowship in foul latrines like the one near New York's City Hall, to sleep wrapped up in old newspapers on the concrete floors of subway corridors."[44] As Webber—Wolfe thus "lived, felt, and experienced the full weight of that horrible calamity,"[45] the depression, he became at last fully aware of a world outside of, and separate from, himself. All along, he had seen the city as the projection of his inner image. But now, at last, the city imposed upon his mind its own reality. It was a thing in itself, and not merely the protean counterpart of his thoughts and moods. And because it became an objective reality, the city symbol reflects Wolfe's orientation towards a more objective view of life. The jungle image of the city, which expresses George Webber's sobered view at the end of *You Can't Go Home Again* (as well as Wolfe's own in *The Story of a Novel*) is far removed from the golden vision of the dreaming young Southern boy. The hopes of a magic city are brought face to face with the horrible reality of half-human men prowling the streets of Brooklyn and sleeping in filthy latrines. This is the image of a desperate reality. One's response to it, George Webber says in *You Can't Go Home Again,* must not be, however, resignation or despair, but courage. Wolfe himself took courage from the fact of man's endurance, which helped him survive even this "horrible calamity." He affirmed, directly and through his protagonist, his faith in the common people. But this faith was expressed only as an explicit affirmation, for its dramatic potentialities for his art remained unrealized as death cut short his career.

This pattern of social awakening is particularly characteristic of the literature of the thirties, understandably so, since that was the decade of the depression. But there were other expressions of disillusionment with the city that bore the

[44] Wolfe, *You Can't Go Home Again,* 729.
[45] Wolfe, *The Story of a Novel,* 59.

more unique stamp of Wolfe's personality. What Wolfe had to say about the awful desolation of city life was not individual, but his impassioned denunciations, his rantings, and his often brilliant and essential impressions of city people were in his own definitive idiom. He saw the desolation of city life concretized in the "emptiness of city youth" and in the "new look" of the subway riders. The city youth, "poor, sallow, dark, swarthy creatures . . . with rasping tongues, loose mouths and ugly jeering eyes," became Wolfe's representation of a modern kind of "death-in-life."[46] His objection to the appearance of these polyglot people reflects his own prejudices and snobbishness; but also it reveals his feeling that the city deprived youth of the "grand dreams and the music of the fleeting and impossible reveries—all that makes youth lovely and desirable, and keeps man's faith."[47] Passages in *Of Time and the River,* recapitulated in *You Can't Go Home Again,* summarize the sociological thesis that Farrell dramatizes in at least eight novels—that a spiritual poverty in the city deprives youth of its grand potentialities. Wolfe saw also in the defenseless, weary faces of the city's subway-riders the same "new look" of desolation, a "horrible, indefinable, and abominably desolate and anonymous look"[48] of men separated from nature and submitted to the violence of subterranean machines.

Wolfe's prowlings in Brooklyn and his observations of the beaten faces of the common people of the city seemed to him to verify his belief that modern man was dislocated and homeless. The city became again his key symbol for expressing his central theme of man's homelessness, aloneness, and alienation; and in expressing this, it became also symbolic of the ironies of time. The pathetic attempts of people to establish a home in the "great No Home of the earth" are revealed to

[46] *Of Time and the River,* 498.
[47] *Ibid.*
[48] *Ibid.,* 594.

Eugene Gant when he visits a young couple in their small rented apartment. The transience of city life and the essential homelessness of man are also epitomized by the Leopold Hotel: here the pretence at making a home and taking roots is pathetic as well as ironic. The real condition of man, suggested in the refrain in *Of Time and the River,* is that of the homeless and isolated wanderer in the city: ". . . we walk the streets, we walk the streets forever, we walk the streets of life alone."[49]

This homeless wandering represented also the condition of alienation of the American artist. His quest for a certitude and a spiritual fatherland was doomed to failure in a city that was "the most homeless home in the world." In *The Web and the Rock,* Wolfe stated the futility of the search for a stone, a leaf, a door: "the city is the place where men are constantly seeking to find their door and where they are doomed to wandering forever."[50] The defeat of the quest for certitude, which left the artist alone and homeless, was on one level related to the sociological conditions of life in the city, to instability, anonymity, rootlessness, and impermanence. But it was also related to the inexorableness of time itself. Time defeated the artist in his quest as much as particular social and spiritual conditions. And once again, the city became a symbol of Wolfe's frustrations over the brevity of man's time and his recognition of a separate immutable time. The city stands as the rock of immutability: time flows past it, just as the Hudson River flows past Manhattan. Man is caught and carried away in its flowing stream. Though he makes his gestures and thinks he has achieved his ends, he discovers, when his brief time is past, that he has left no mark upon the immutable rock; there is no permanence to his identity.

Wolfe's contest with time was represented in part by his

[49] *Ibid.,* 155.
[50] *The Web and the Rock,* 229.

obsession with "Amount and Number," his desire to devour all knowledge, to remember all facts, to experience all places and forms of life. This was what he saw as the legendary hunger of youth, and again the city became the counterpart to his compulsive desire. The city was big enough and varied enough both to stir and to feed this hunger. The metaphor of eating the city expresses this: Youth comes "to eat you [Wolfe writes in *Of Time and the River*], branch and root and tree; to devour you . . . to consume you to your sources, river and spire and rock, down to your iron roots; to entomb within our flesh forever the huge substance of your billion-footed pavements, the intolerable web and memory of dark million-visaged time."[51]

The desire to incorporate the city, also a desire to become part of permanence and immutable time, is, Wolfe believed, doomed to frustration. To youth and to the artist, the city "promises all" but "offers nothing." Actually, however, both Wolfe and his heroes found in the city certain objects of their quest, but they rejected all of them except artistic fulfillment as empty and futile. George Webber, for example, found that love, as he experienced it most intensely with Esther Jack, was "not enough." Fame, as personified by Lloyd McHarg (Sinclair Lewis) was depleting and as barren as the empty pleasures of the rich. Ties with one's spiritual father—Foxhall Edwards (Maxwell Perkins)—were constricting and had finally to be denied. What remained, then, of one's youthful dreams? What was accomplished by man's frenzied activities? What lasted of his turbulent passions? While on the one hand, Wolfe's thought moved in the direction of certain social affirmations, and he pronounced his belief both in his own creative work and in the democratic ideals of America, on the other hand, he saw the frustration of all hopes as time caught man in its stream. This frustration is overtly declared in Wolfe's

[51] *Of Time and the River,* 508.

130

outburst against the immutable city upon which youth, for all his heartbreaking efforts, cannot make any lasting impression: "What have we taken from you, protean and phantasmal shape of time? What have we remembered of your million images, of your billion weavings out of accident and number, of the mindless fury of your dateless days, the brutal stupefaction of your thousand streets and pavements? What have we seen and known that is ours forever? Gigantic city, we have taken nothing—not even a handful of your trampled dust—we have made no image on your iron breast and left not even the print of a heel upon your stony-hearted pavements."[52]

Thus, in creating a modern and personal version of the legend of youth's quest and frustrations, Wolfe used the city as his key symbol. As Proteus, the city underwent constant change. It was the correlative to both dream and reality, to hope and realization, and to every disturbed and turbulent emotion, every awakening idea, every obsession and affirmation that was part of Wolfe's inner life. It was his knowledge and his language, always "changed and transfigured" by his personality. Yet despite the many literary uses Wolfe made of the city, there were certain things he did not do, and to some extent these measure his deficiencies as an artist. He could not bring order to his use of this symbol, just as he could not give order to all the materials of his art. His response to the city was emotionally dictated, so that his symbolic use of it depended upon vacillating moods and irrational changing emotions. He contradicted himself, mainly because he lacked control enough to direct his materials. He moved always in a world of extremes: New York was a "golden legend" or else a brutal, violent jungle thick with stunned and stupefied man-swarms. He could summarize sociological truths about the everyday life of the city-dweller and his hurt-

[52] *Ibid.*, 509.

131

lings through subterranean pathways; but he seldom gave a concrete dramatization of urban manners. He tried to epitomize the city in a single City-Voice or in one inclusive image; but he often did little more than give a gross travesty of Brooklyn speech or create an image which was distorted by his own intemperate way of viewing life. He remained, for all his prowlings and his intimate knowledge of the jungle qualities of the city, a giant stranger and somewhat of a snob, proud, in this world of polyglot peoples, of his pure American background. Only in the end, when the objective facts of low urban life overwhelmed him, did the external reality impose itself upon his mind more strongly than his subjective emotions imposed themselves upon the scene. For "Faustian" as was his mood and his hunger, the city was yet more immense than he, and finally it impressed upon him its own truths concerning a sociological and spiritual situation in modern America. Wolfe's recognition of man's homelessness and frustrations in the city and of the social injustices implicated in the gross inequalities of wealth places him in the main tradition of twentieth-century city fiction. But his unique distinction as a city novelist lies in his personalization of the city as he "changed and transfigured" it and made it his central, protean symbol.

CHAPTER 5

John Dos Passos:

THE SYNOPTIC NOVEL

The Novelist as "Architect of History"

JOHN DOS PASSOS' *Manhattan Transfer*, first hailed by Sinclair Lewis as a germinal work and called by Joseph Warren Beach "one of the most brilliant and original American novels of the century,"[1] holds a unique place in American city fiction. The finest example of the synoptic form of the city novel, it is one of the most ambitious experiments in the use of urban materials. Perhaps no other city novel reveals such sheer virtuosity in the handling of urban imagery and symbolism, such skill in creating the city as an entity in itself, and such ingenuity in making a complex form the vehicle of implicatory social commentary. In its search for techniques to project the city immediately, in all its dazzling and stupefacient variety, in its sensuous shapes and aesthetic moments, its pace, rhythms, and atmosphere, *Manhattan Transfer* becomes a kind of text on the art of the city novel. Yet the achievement of *Manhattan Transfer* is not only its brilliant and imaginative creation of modern New York as an immediate place: its achievement is also its serious social and moral interpretation of a twentieth-century way of life. Un-

[1] Joseph Warren Beach, *The Twentieth-Century Novel: Studies in Technique* (New York, The Century Company, 1932), 437.

133

derlying the aesthetics of the novel is a concept of the novelist as an "architect of history"—a shaper of moral opinion who influences the group mind of his times by compelling and revealing works of art. The total achievement of *Manhattan Transfer* as city fiction must be evaluated in terms of Dos Passos' peculiar concept of the novelist's function, a concept that determined the historical sweep of the novel, the direct focusing upon the city rather than upon its people, and the underlying interpretation of Manhattan as a huge symbol of twentieth-century historical tendencies.

In various essays, prefaces, and letters (almost all written in the thirties), Dos Passos expressed his views on the relationship between social history and literature, between the writer's moral responsibility to his times and his search for a technique. Underlying these views was an urgent sense of the dynamics of social change—specifically, a feeling that America was standing at a historical crossroad. As he expressed it in one essay (the idea is also stated in *U.S.A.* in the biographical sketch of Veblen): "This is an epoch of sudden and dangerous transition. Industrial life is turning a corner and is either going to make the curve or smash up in the ditch."[2]

The sense that he was living through a crucial period of deep-reaching historical change was given theoretical validity by the dialectical formula of Marx. Marxian theory defined history as a dynamic process in which one social system and its forms gave way to another. But abstract theory stood confirmed for Dos Passos by his personal observations of social change in America and "in all countries"—in Spain, Russia, South America, Mexico, and the Orient. These observations are recorded in his early travel books, *Rosinante to the Road Again* and *In All Countries*. It is a mistake to consider these

[2] John Dos Passos, "Why Write for the Theatre Anyway?" Introduction to *Three Plays* (New York, Harcourt, Brace and Company, 1934), xx.

134

books wistful expressions of Dos Passos' early escapism, for they reveal him actually as a concerned and alerted social observer, sensitive to symptoms of social evolution everywhere and particularly interested in the mechanisms of revolution. While revolution brought violent and abrupt social change to Russia and Mexico, a slow evolutionary process was bringing it to Spain. Dos Passos evaluated the change in Spain (as industrialism encroached upon an ancient agricultural way of life) in terms of the past. Always he brought to bear upon the present a keen nostalgic sense of the past. Perhaps the past as he envisioned it was idealized, never having been really as generous to the individual nor as culturally rich as he liked to think. But the awareness of the past as an idealistic point of reference influenced his judgment of the contemporary scene.

When he looked upon America of the twenties and thirties, he evoked an image of a Jeffersonian past in which democratic ideals had been instituted as a way of life. These ideals seemed to him under deliberate assault in twentieth-century America. They were attacked directly during and by World War I. He said himself that he had been unable to reconcile the "brutalities" and "oppressions" of the war with the ideals of progress he had been led to believe in.[3] The war seemed to him a "horrible monstrosity."[4] He shared the general disillusionment of his generation which had come to regard the war as (to use his character Joe William's phrase) "a plot of the big interests."[5] The basis for the war was industrial greed and mass deception: it had been made possible (as another character says) only by "oceans of lies" that had deceived

[3] John Dos Passos, "A Preface Twenty-Five Years Later," Preface to *First Encounter* (New York, Philosophical Library, 1945), n.p. *First Encounter* was published originally in 1920 as *One Man's Initiation—1917* (London, George Allen and Unwin, Ltd.).
[4] *Ibid.*
[5] John Dos Passos, "The 42nd Parallel," *U.S.A.* (New York, Harcourt, Brace and Company, 1938), 412.

"honest, liberal, kindly people."[6] These people, the common people, were deprived of their fundamental liberties not only in the army, but worse, in a "counter-revolutionary" movement taking place in postwar America. Concerted attacks against labor (the lynching of Wobblies and the shooting down of strikers), race riots, Ku Klux Klan raids, and governmentally instituted anti-Bolshevist purges seemed to Dos Passos the overt signs of a deliberate movement to suppress the people while securing the economic supremacy of the big moneyed interests. Perhaps no one incident seemed to him so clearly a violation of America's fundamental ideals as the execution of Sacco and Vanzetti. His character Mary French undoubtedly expresses his own view at the time of the trials when she says, "If the state of Massachusetts can kill these two innocent men in the face of the protest of the whole world it'll mean that there never will be any justice in America ever again."[7] In his essay "The Wrong Set of Words" he notes that during demonstrations against the Sacco-Vanzetti trials people were being "arrested for distributing the Declaration of Independence."[8] He saw a significant relationship between the war and the execution. The war had "exalted hatred to a virtue"; after the war, the persecution of anarchists and foreigners offered a means for people to release their "pentup hatred and suspicion."[9] His bitterness against the "rightthinking Puritan born Americans" who wanted these men to die arose not only out of his sense of immediate injustice: it grew out of his vision of a past when America had been heroic—at Lexington, Bunker Hill, and Gettysburg—in a continuous historical struggle for human liberty.

Thus, theory and observation directed Dos Passos to the

[6] *One Man's Initiation—1917*, 25.

[7] "The Big Money," *U.S.A.*, 451.

[8] John Dos Passos, *In All Countries* (New York, Harcourt, Brace and Company, 1934), 177.

[9] See *Ibid.*, 173–89.

fact of social change. The Marxian dynamic view of history and the actual signs of evolution, revolution, and counter-revolution gave him the sense that these were critical times. For America, repudiating through violence and injustice its democratic ideals, it was indeed a "tragic moment." In a letter to F. Scott Fitzgerald, written in 1936, he says, "We're living in one of the damnedest tragic moments in history";[10] and he goes on to tell Fitzgerald that it is his (Fitzgerald's) moral obligation (as well as, presumably, his own) to write "a first rate novel" about the social tragedy of the times. This was the writer's responsibility—to reveal, and exercise moral judgment upon, the social tendencies of his times. "American writers who want to do the most valuable kind of work [he says in another place] will find themselves trying to discover the deep currents of historical change under the surface of opinions, orthodoxies, heresies, gossip and journalistic garbage of the day."[11] Again when he speaks of the need for a revitalized American theatre, he defines the function of literature, specifically here of the drama, to be that of a "transformer for the deep high tension currents of history."[12] The relationship of literature to its historical times is summarized in his praise of Fitzgerald's unfinished novel, *The Last Tycoon.* This he considered a "good work" because it had the "quality of detaching itself from its period while embodying its period"[13] and because in it the author had "managed to

[10] John Dos Passos, "A Letter from Dos Passos to Fitzgerald," in F. Scott Fitzgerald, *The Crack-Up* (ed. by Edmund Wilson, New York, New Directions, 1945), 311. The letter is dated 1936.

[11] John Dos Passos, "The Writer as Technician," *American Writers' Congress* (ed. by Henry Hart, New York, International Publishers, 1935), 82.

[12] Dos Passos, "Why Write for the Theatre Anyway?" *Three Plays,* xxii.

[13] Dos Passos, "A Note on Fitzgerald," in Fitzgerald, *The Crack-Up,* 343.

establish that unshakable moral attitude towards the world we live in and towards its temporary standards that is the basic essential of a powerful work of imagination."[14] In other words, a good novel objectified and interpreted contemporary life from a detached or nonpersonal—that is, a historical—point of view, and at the same time it passed moral judgment upon the social life it depicted. Underlying this concept of the novel was a conviction in the power of art to influence the pattern of social change. "Important" and "compelling" works of art, Dos Passos believed, could affect the course of social history, for they could "mold and influence ways of thinking to the point of changing and rebuilding . . . the mind of the group."[15] Thus, as the serious novelist helped shape contemporary opinion, he became in effect an "architect of history."[16]

Technique as Social Commentary in Manhattan Transfer

IT IS AS an architect of history that Dos Passos wrote *Manhattan Transfer* and *U.S.A.* Both novels dramatize a process of social change. Their implicit intention is to press upon the public mind an awareness of a historical drift away from the American ideals of democracy, individuality, and liberty. This intention explains the scope and fluidity of these novels, the necessity of showing the passage of years, and of re-creating the essential, if not the total, features of society. While these so-called "collectivist" novels have been criticized by such discerning readers as Malcolm Cowley and Edmund

[14] *Ibid.,* 339.

[15] "The Writer as Technician," *American Writers' Congress,* 79.

[16] John Dos Passos, Introduction, *Three Soldiers* (New York, Modern Library, 1932), viii. *Three Soldiers* was published originally in 1921.

138

Wilson[17] for not giving full representation to all aspects of American life, to the moral and beautiful as well as the demoralized and sordid, the relevant question is not whether they "tell the whole truth" (to use Delmore Schwartz's phrase[18]): it is whether they discern essential and underlying historical movements. In focusing upon the historical direction of American life, Dos Passos necessarily *abstracted* elements from the American scene. He wanted to show the drift towards monopoly capitalism, and his intention committed him to exclusion as much as to inclusion.

The technical problem inherent in Dos Passos' subject was to find a formal framework to express an interpretation and a moral judgment of the times. His own concept of the novel as a work that detaches itself from the historical period and embodies it committed him to an art of implication. He could not state his judgment of the times explicitly: it had to be inherent in the picture of the times. Moreover, his technique for creating the essential characteristics of the present as a historical period had also to evoke a picture of the past; historical change could be assessed only if the past stood forward as an emotional and social point of reference.

Dos Passos' early novels, *One Man's Initiation, Three Soldiers,* and *Streets of Night,* reveal him groping for a technique. These are the novels of his apprenticeship, and he was not entirely successful in them. With extreme virtuosity, he transformed each impression of the outer world into an aesthetic experience; each slight movement (for example, the

[17] See Malcolm Cowley, "Dos Passos: Poet Against the World," *After the Genteel Tradition* (ed. by Malcolm Cowley, New York, Norton and Company, 1937), 168–85; Edmund Wilson, "Dos Passos and the Social Revolution," *New Republic,* Vol. LVIII (April 17, 1929), 256–59; and Joseph Warren Beach, *American Fiction: 1920–1940* (New York, The Macmillan Company, 1941), 41.

[18] See Delmore Schwartz, "John Dos Passos and the Whole Truth," *Southern Review,* Vol. IV (Autumn, 1938), 351–67.

pouring of wine into a glass) into a perfect moment of harmoniously balanced shape and color; each feeling into a dramatic awareness. But meanwhile the total structure of his novel, which was to be the form that would "set the mind of tomorrow's generation,"[19] fell apart. Consequently, *One Man's Initiation* displays Dos Passos' craftsmanship in striking imagery, but the social theme is expressed through the device of the apprentice, exposition. Martin Howe must make an explicit condemnation of the war, for neither his view nor the moral attitude of the individualist, the Catholic, the Communist, and the Anarchist is dramatized—they are all flatly stated. *Three Soldiers* evidently had an elaborate aesthetic plan (indicated in the symbolism of the chapter headings), but it broke down as John Andrews, the only character through whose sensibility the outer world took on aesthetic meaning, and the only one who could verbalize a moral attitude towards war, became Dos Passos' direct spokesman. In *Streets of Night,* as in the two earlier novels, the theme of cultural disintegration is expressed through a contrast between the present and the golden past of the Renaissance. But again the theme is developed mainly through direct statement rather than dramatic action; and again Dos Passos is the meticulous master of aesthetic detail. Individual images are arresting but unintegrated with the underlying social theme. The fact that the characters are always talking about their inner sterility may be considered a dramatic device for expressing a view of modern life; more likely it reflects, like the intrusive lush imagery, a failure to make form itself a statement of meaning.

Because these early novels achieved startling aesthetic effects with imagery and because they recalled a romantic past as a judgment upon the present, critics have said that the predominant strain in the early Dos Passos is aesthetic escapism.

[19] Dos Passos, Introduction, *Three Soldiers,* viii.

Malcolm Cowley was the first to suggest that Dos Passos began his career as a "late-Romantic, a tender individualist, an aesthete traveling about the world in an ivory tower" and that he later developed into a "hard-minded realist, a collectivist, a radical historian of the class struggle."[20] But while Cowley cautioned against drawing too fine a distinction between romantic and realistic strains in Dos Passos, later critics have insisted upon an apparently clear-cut discontinuity between Dos Passos the aesthete and the realist. Yet the novels leading up to *Manhattan Transfer* were already thematically concerned with immediate problems of the times, even if they were not completely successful in finding a formal framework to dramatize the times. Their aestheticism exists superficially in manner, rather than inherently in material. The key scene in *One Man's Initiation,* for example, is that in which the soldiers realistically face the present and discuss possible moral attitudes towards the war as well as plans for social action after the war. In *Three Soldiers,* John Andrews deserts the army in "a gesture" for individual freedom, just as in *Streets of Night,* Wenny chooses suicide as an act of social condemnation. But it is in *Manhattan Transfer* that Dos Passos the "hard-headed realist . . . radical historian of the class struggle" most clearly expresses himself—not because he has arrived at a new realistic stand as a novelist, but because he has achieved, through his apprenticeship, a firmer grasp of his art. *Manhattan Transfer* establishes Dos Passos' control over the techniques of implicatory statement. Here he finally avoids the structural division between dramatic action and expository statement, which in his earlier novels had left his theme unincorporated in form. Here theme and form become an aesthetic integer. The techniques that create the dramatic world of the novel establish toward it a firm social and moral atti-

[20] Cowley, "Dos Passos: Poet Against the World," *After the Genteel Tradition,* 168.

141

tude. Thus technique becomes the vehicle of social commentary. The stream of modern history is captured in the novel's dramatic action, structure, pace, mood, symbols, and characters. And as these formal elements create a dramatic world in the dynamic process of social change, they implicitly judge and condemn the historical tendencies of the times.

Since technique is clearly Dos Passos' means of statement, analysis of his technique reveals his social and moral interpretations of city life. His is a technique of abstraction which proceeds through an impressionistic method. The result of his technique is not a realistic scene or character in the sense that Dreiser's hotel lobby or restaurant—or a character like Drouet, so consciously modelled after a flesh and blood type —was real. Dos Passos' realism consists in striking essential details abstracted from their total context. Whereas Dreiser accumulates details in order to reproduce the actuality as closely as possible, Dos Passos selects a few evocative details that are to suggest the essential quality of the whole. Thus his realism involves a considerable distortion of actuality, but it is a realism to which the imagination can give assent. If a restaurant is not merely a succession of odors or an East Side street is not merely a succession of colors (of glaring sunlight, patch quilts hanging on fire escapes, pushcarts of fruit), the total scene is suggested by these abstract sensory appeals. Dos Passos' method, then, is to give an impression of reality, rather than to give, like Dreiser, a total cataloguing of actual details. The method of abstraction is fundamental to his creation of the city as a place, an atmosphere, a way of life, and a historical expression of the times. It is fundamental too to his creation of character and of social relationships. The selective process is severely imposed upon all the material of urban life —necessarily so, not only because he was giving a synoptic view of the city (embracing its variety and complexity) but even more important, because he was giving an interpretation of an underlying historical trend. Thus his cityscapes are only fleeting sensuous impressions of scene. His people are only representatives of a human state of mind intrinsic to the city —they are not fully realized flesh and blood people, but abstract states of being. And his total city is not a faithful reproduction of complementary and balancing details: it is an expression of a historical trend. Twentieth-century Manhattan, as Dos Passos portrays it in an abstract literary picture, embodies the trend away from formulated American ideals of a social system that would allow the individual fullest opportunity for equality and personal self-fulfillment as a human being. It symbolizes rather the trend towards a mechanized kind of life that is expressed, in economic terms, in monopoly capitalism and, in human terms, in the loss of man's human capacities for love and self-realization. The abstract qualities that are presented as urban scenes, characters, atmosphere, social patterns, and historical tendencies are implicit commentaries upon the moral significance of modern American city life. Dos Passos' judgment is inherent in his selective process and in the results of this selective process as a unique and personally envisioned city emerges in the novel as twentieth-century Manhattan.

The brilliant and changing cityscapes are made immediate in brief sensuous impressions, each evocative and incisive, and each giving way to the next in syncopated cinematic movement. As the smallest unit of structure, the fleeting aesthetic impression is ideally suited to the synoptic form, for while it allows for range and flexibility, the rapid transition from one impression to another accelerates the novel's pace to suggest the incessant restless movement within the city itself. The peculiar beauty of the urban scene is created primarily through abstract and kinetic color arrangements. An East Side street, for example, is created as a patterned succession of colors— "a sunstriped tunnel hung with skyblue and smokedsalmon and mustardyellow quilts littered with second hand ginger-bread-colored furniture."[21] On the first page of his first novel, Dos Passos had used the technique of dramatizing color, that is, of giving it the quality of movement, so that abstracted colors "agitate," "flutter," and "slide together." In *Manhattan Transfer,* static scenes become dynamic relationships of color and of light and shadow. Here, for example, in an impression of the Mall at Central Park, colors move and exert pressure: "great rosy and purple and pistachiogreen bubbles of twilight . . . *swell out* of the grass and trees and ponds, *bulge* against the tall houses sharp gray as dead teeth *round* the southern end of the park, *melt* into the indigo zenith."[22] The epigraph on dusk devolving on the city illustrates too that Dos Passos was treating light and shadow, as well as color, as a painter would. Houses, objects, signs, and people appear as chunks of brilliance or shadow, and again the visual appeal is translated into tactile sensations of pressure and into kinetic qualities of movement:

Dusk gently smooths crispangled streets. Dark presses tight the steaming asphalt city, crushes the fretwork of windows and lettered signs and chimneys and watertanks and ventilators and fire-escapes and moldings and patterns and corrugations and eyes and hands and neckties into blue chunks, into black enormous blocks. Under the rolling heavier heavier pressure windows blurt light. Night crushes bright milk out of arclights, squeezes the sullen blocks until they drip red, yellow, green into streets resounding with feet. All the asphalt oozes light. Light spurts from lettering on roofs, mills dizzily among wheels, stains rolling tons of sky.[23]

The beauty of the city lies in its color formations, sometimes brilliant and gaudy, sometimes muted and subdued. All other sensory details, those of sound, weather, and odor,

[21] Dos Passos, *Manhattan Transfer,* 10.
[22] *Ibid.,* 202.   [23] *Ibid.,* 112.

are oppressively ugly. The cacophony of the city streets swells from a jumbling of incessant noises—the "growing rumble of traffic," "the frenzied bell of a fire engine," "the long moan of a steamboat whistle," and the "children's voices screeching." The people "grope continually through a tangle of gritty sawedged brittle noise."[24] Grit is palpable on their lips.[25] The weather oppresses them: in winter a "razor wind" cuts the ear and makes the forehead ache;[26] in summer a hot afternoon sun lies on the back like a heavy hand, and "sunlight squirms in bright worms of heat on [one's] face and hands."[27]

Most offensive of all, and perhaps most brilliantly used for thematic implications, are the odors of New York. A stench seems to rise from the massing humanity herded in tenements or crowded in "pigeonhole rooms," "jiggling subways," and jammed busses. Beneath the "goldplated exterior" of the city lies the brutal fact of man's indignity in a crowded, sweaty world where there is no room. Ellen's momentary awareness of the "unwashed smell" of a man's body evokes an image of closeness and fetor: "Under all the nickleplated, goldplated streets enameled with May, uneasily she could feel the huddling smell, spreading in dark slow crouching masses like corruption oozing from broken sewers."[28] To Jimmy the smell suggests the mass frustration in the city, the "huddling stuffiness of pigeonhole rooms where men and women's bodies writhed alone tortured by the night and the young summer."[29]

From such sharp and kaleidoscopic sensuous impressions of urban scenes, the city is registered immediately in its color, odor, din, and gaudy brilliance. And as it comes to life, it is its own indictment. Under its changing and variegated aspects is the unchanging fact of its oppressiveness: it is a world that grates the nerves and assails the senses with ugliness, clatter,

[24] *Ibid.*, 136.   [25] *Ibid.*, 263, 266.   [26] *Ibid.*, 344.
[27] *Ibid.*, 177.   [28] *Ibid.*, 395.   [29] *Ibid.*, 194.

and stench. While these sensuous impressions record the outer scene from the point of view of a disengaged but sensitive observer (Dos Passos himself), the scene is also registered specifically through the eyes of the characters. As they move through the city they perceive people and objects as dissociated images—that is, they do not receive unified and total impressions of entities but only fragmentary impressions of parts of the whole. From a bus, a character sees the street as a succession of "sunshades, summer dresses, straw hats";[30] in the subway he sees people as "elbows, packages, shoulders, buttocks"[31] or as "faces, hats, hands, newspapers jiggling like corn in a popper";[32] and in the street he sees children as "dirty torn shirts, slobbering mouths."[33]

In *Streets of Night,* the dissociated image had been mainly ornamental, expressing Dos Passos' own pleasure in aesthetic moments, rather than related intrinsically to the material of the novel. For example, a series of startling images suggest the impressions received by the three main characters as they walk the streets; but these impressions do not contribute to any larger formal purpose within the novel. Here is sheer indulgence in metaphor by a young writer delighting in his virtuosity:

Faces bloomed and faded through a jumbled luminous mist, white as plaster casts, red as raw steak, yellow and warted like summer squashes, smooth and expressionless like cantaloupes. Occasionally a door yawned black and real in the spinning flicker of the snow and the lights, or a wall seemed to bulge to splitting with its denseness.[34]

[30] *Ibid.,* 136. [31] *Ibid.,* 148.
[32] *Ibid.,* 356. [33] *Ibid.,* 241.
[34] John Dos Passos, *Streets of Night* (New York, George Doran Company, 1923), 192f.

In *Manhattan Transfer,* the dissociated image has integral thematic significance. As it hastens the pace of the novel, it contributes to the evocation of urban moods and rhythms. As it makes constant reference to the external scene (even when character or action is momentarily the center of interest), it underscores the synoptic intention to create the city as protagonist. Most important, as it records objects of perception as the characters experience them, it implies a certain quality in the relationship between the character and other people about him. For example, as Ellen walks along with Stan, her *manner* of seeing, as reflected in the dissociated image, is quite different from, say, Carrie's small-town kind of reaction in *Sister Carrie.* Carrie responds to people as human beings; one reason she so deeply envies the well-dressed strangers about her is that she perceives them as individuals. Ellen, however, sees people in the same impersonal way she sees objects: "Aloof, as if looking through thick glass into an aquarium, she watched faces, fruit in storewindows, cans of vegetables, jars of olives, redhotpokerplants . . . newspapers, electric signs . . . sudden jetbright glances of eyes under straw hats, attitudes of chins, thin lips pouting lips, Cupid's bows, hungry shadows under cheekbones."[35]

The fact that one's perception of people is on the same level as the perception of things suggests not only the impersonality in the city's crowds but also the loneliness within the crowd. In the last scene of *Manhattan Transfer,* as Jimmy Herf wanders through the city streets, he too catches dissociated glimpses of faces and disjointed sounds of human footsteps and conversation; but he knows himself to be essentially alone. In a mood of alienation and loneliness, he realizes the barriers of indifference and impersonality that keep people apart—and this forlorn realization contributes to his decision to leave the city.

[35] *Manhattan Transfer,* 153.

Just as the external scene is created and assessed by a selective method of impressionism, so is urban time. Time in the sense of tempo runs at the same hectic pace in the personal lives of the characters as in the separate life of the city as a social entity. The quick jagged transition from impression to impression sets the tempo to a rapid nervous beat. As odd moments in the lives of the characters receive stress and time intervals are chosen in an irregular pattern, the movement within the novel becomes syncopated; the novel beats with a jazz tempo that epitomizes the hectic, brassy quality of modern city life. In the same way that Dos Passos had handled color like a painter, he handles variations in time like a jazz musician.

Time in another sense, as crucial moments and as spanning years, is distinct for the characters and for the city. In Jimmy Herf's personal history, the moment when he marries Ellen may be crucial, but in the history of twentieth-century Manhattan this moment is inconsequential. What is important in time for the city is historical sweep that reveals social tendencies. The novel shows Manhattan changing through the decades from an ideal of a modern metropolis (that moves Ed Thatcher and the architects Specker and Sandbourne to a glorious vision of the future) to a disordered world of vice and destruction that sets the mad tramp raving at the end of the novel with a vision of urban doom.

The consequences of the passage of chronological time are revealed in the structure of the novel, which in its circular movement—in the return at the end to the very point of the beginning—expresses the futility of the years. As a unifying element within the synoptic novel, this circular structure imposes a formal pattern, as well as a thematic significance on the numerous and apparently unrelated and inconsequential incidents in the novel. The ferry slip, described in the opening epigraph, is the defining point in the circular movement: at the beginning of the novel it is a place of entry into the city, and at the end, as Jimmy repudiates New York, it becomes a place of departure. Chapter I develops the theme of coming to the city by showing the various ways people arrive at New York. (Ellen is born into urban life; Bud Korpenning migrates from upstate country; and the anonymous Jew of the last scene has immigrated.) Once people have found their way into Manhattan, they are absorbed into its whirling life. The action of the novel moves them away from the ferry slip towards "the center of things," while a counteraction directs Jimmy gradually but with growing impetus back to the ferry slip as a point of escape. Encompassed within the movement away from and back to the original defining point is the ironic pattern of action without progress. Action is ceaseless: the people engage in frenetic affairs of love, business, marriage, and careers; the seasons change; the years pass—but in the end, actions have cancelled each other, decisions have remained abortive and plans inchoate, and time has defeated one's hopes in the city. Whatever progress certain characters may seem to have made is more apparent than real. Congo Jake has been transformed from a ragamuffin to Armand Duval, millionaire bootlegger, but he faces jail;[36] George Baldwin seems to have achieved success, but his final position is precarious, his inner life void, and his future with Ellen (who has become emptied of feeling and hopeless) is inauspicious.

The imagery and mood in which entry to the city is expressed already foreshadow the ugly futility that each character is to face. Although in the first chapter, the people are yet untouched by city life, they are described in disagreeable or derogatory images. In the opening epigraph, the crowds flocking through the ferry slip into Manhattan are described as pressing "through the manuresmelling wooden tunnel of

[36] *Ibid.*, 382.

the ferryhouse, crushed and jostling like apples fed down a chute into a press."[37] The newborn baby Ellen is "a knot of earthworms" squirming in a basket which the nurse holds away from herself, as though it were a "bedpan"; "the nurse, holding the basket . . . as if it were a bedpan, opened the door to a big hot dry room with greenish distempered walls where in the air tinctured with smells of alcohol and iodoform hung writhing a faint sourish squalling from other baskets . . . ."[38]

After this squeamish and offensive picture of birth comes the derogatory image of the country boy's entry. Bud Korpenning is a caricature of the bumpkin: he has red wrists "that stuck out from the frayed sleeves of his coat," a "skinny turkey's throat," blistered "roadswelled feet," sweated temples, and of course, a stock naïve manner.[39] In the last scene of the chapter, the immigrant Jew, inspired by the billboard American, shaves off his beard in a gesture of assimilation. Though the scene is short, the ugliness of New York's East Side is made prominent in the "annihilating clatter of the L trains" and the "rancid sweet huddled smell of packed tenements."[40] Thus, the introductory imagery establishes an attitude towards Manhattan and a prevailing mood that is to function as a unifying element in the novel.

The circular movement into, within, and away from the city is broken into three sections, each of which ends climactically with an act of moral defeat. Section I closes with Bud's suicide after he has failed to get "into the center of things." His melodramatic end adumbrates in a small way the larger pattern of failure in which all of the characters are involved. Except for the fact that his dead body annoys the captain near whose boat it falls, his death passes unnoticed; and even the one reaction of annoyance has thematic implications, for it shows to what extent the nexus of human sympathy has been

[37] *Ibid.,* 3. [38] *Ibid.*
[39] *Ibid.,* 4. [40] *Ibid.,* 10.

broken by the urgencies and methods of city life. Bud's failure
to make any warm human contacts in the city, his constant
sense of aloneness, and his unmourned solitary death are part
of, and intrinsic to, the larger pattern of impersonal relationships that exists in the great city. An indifferent world remains unmoved by either his struggles to live or his bitter
decision to die.

Section II ends with Ellen's abortion, also an act of death
and defeat. Her earlier impulse to bear Stan's child is swept
away in the frenetic but sterile activities that make up her life.
By this act of abortion she embraces sterility as her destiny.
Abortion is symbolic of an inner emptiness, a loss of humanity,
as the normal cycle of human life is shattered within an en-
compassing cycle of modern city life which robs woman of
her womanhood and man of his purpose.

Section III ends with Jimmy Herf's indecisive recognition
of this destructive effect of city life. He knows that he must
escape from Manhattan, but this is a negative kind of knowledge, for he does not know where he must go nor what destiny
he must or can create. The development of his pattern of rejection is the one progressive movement within the circle of
futile and self-vitiating acts. As he rejects the business world
and its goal of success, the impassioned but futile world of
Greenwich Village (inhabited by radicals too far lost in an
alcoholic haze and too deeply demoralized to act), and finally
the entire urban world of overpowering, jutting skyscrapers,
he feels his accomplishment to be that he is at least "beginning
to learn a few of the things I dont want."[41]

Dos Passos' method for dramatizing Jimmy's final awareness, the awareness that leads him to the ferry slip in an act
that closes the circle of futility, brings attention to one of the
most important aesthetic elements in the novel—the intricate
and patterned use of urban symbolism. In a drunken halluci-

[41] *Ibid.*, 360.

151

nation, Jimmy sees a skyscraper falling on him, a skyscraper whose window holds a beckoning gold foil figure of Ellen, but whose door he cannot find. The skyscraper symbolizes his frustration in the city and its destructive power over man; and his nightmare vision of the skyscraper determines him to get out of Manhattan as fast as he can. The skyscraper is only one symbol in a complex pattern of urban symbolism which functions both to create the city as a place and atmosphere and to define its underlying social implications as a way of life. Dos Passos' handling of the symbols of *Manhattan Transfer* shows what he had learned from his early works *Three Soldiers* and *Streets of Night*. In *Three Soldiers,* the key symbol of the machine, which represents the soldier, is introduced as section headings: "Making the Mold"; "The Metal Cools"; "Machines"; and "Rust." The implication is that war sets the soldier into a mold that deprives him of his individuality; war uses him as if he were a machine and discards him when his usefulness is over. While the symbol is rich in meaning, it remains unincorporated into the narrative structure; introduced in the section headings, its symbolic value is unexploited within the novel. In *Streets of Night,* the symbolism is a more integral part of the form. The long narrow streets of Boston where the characters walk and deplore the sterility of their lives become the ominous representation of that sterility. In these streets, Fanshaw's dreams of the rich full life of the Renaissance or Wenny's dreams of love and fulfillment are revealed in ironic contrast with the narrow, conventional background of Boston. Before Wenny kills himself, he has realized that there is "no place for love in the city of Boston."[42] Only death—or the counterpart of death in life, sterility—fills the "empty darkness" of "the long streets of night,"[43] "the terrible, throbbing streets."[44] Although Dos Passos is rather

---

[42] Dos Passos, *Streets of Night,* 200.
[43] *Ibid.,* 158.   [44] *Ibid.,* 311.

melodramatic here, he succeeds for the first time in integrating symbol, theme, and form: the streets function in the narrative structure as physical setting, while they also are given thematic significance as symbol.

In *Manhattan Transfer,* as in *Three Soldiers,* the urban symbols serve as chapter headings and as subjects of the epigraphs. And, as in *Streets of Night,* they function within the narrative structure as physical properties of the scene. Commonplace phrases heard on the city streets, buildings, machines, snatches from songs and jingles, and occasional biblical allusions all take on symbolic meaning—and almost all, significantly, are suggestive of destruction. Thus, the selection of the symbols involves an implicit criticism of twentieth-century Manhattan: of its tawdriness (Great Lady on a White Horse, Nine Days' Wonder, Nickelodeon); its materialism (Dollars); its futile excitement (Animals' Fair, Rollercoaster); its deadening routine (Revolving Doors); its terrifying modern beauty (Skyscraper); and its destructiveness (Steamroller, Fire Engine, One More River to Jordan, Longlegged Jack of the Isthmus, The Burthen of Nineveh).

These symbols appear within the narrative as apparently innocent expressions or as commonplace urban structures or sights. But gradually, as they reappear and weave into a complex pattern, they take on an ominous meaning; and almost all of them are brought together as symbols of doom in Stan Emery's hallucinatory death scene. Great Lady on a White Horse, for example, appears first as the Danderine Lady, a woman riding through the streets like a modern Godiva, advertising a cure for dandruff. In contrast to Godiva she is the embodiment of the cheap spirit of commercialism that finds expression in the bad taste of modern advertising. Later she reappears as the figure in a nursery rhyme referred to by Stan and Ellen; and finally, like the other symbols, she represents death in Stan's last drunken nightmare.

Another symbol, the Animals' Fair, is mentioned first in an innocent jingle, but as it appears in different contexts, its destructive implications also become clear: the giant Animals' Fair is Manhattan itself. Here people are cooped in prison-like cages. As George Baldwin says, "All we can do is go round and round in a squirrel cage."[45] When Jimmy Herf characterizes his life in his typical small and crowded New York apartment, he too sees this image: "If we only had more space . . . . We live cramped in our squirrelcage."[46] Gradually, then, the innocent rhyme takes on broader significance as the vision of a huge animals' fair in which caged hopeless creatures run about frantically in small closed rooms becomes the imaginative presentation of urban life.

Nickelodeon, the machine in lowly form, is suggestive of a complete mechanization of a way of life, in which a nickel buys a canned moment of music, an automatic cup of coffee, or forgetfulness at the stereopticon, where "you can peep at yellowed yesterdays."[47] Nine Days' Wonder, which applies to Ellen's sudden rise to stardom, calls to mind the irrational pattern of success on Broadway, where fame may be sudden and fleeting. Rollercoaster and Revolving Doors, stand in opposition as symbols, one representing the restlessness, the other the monotony, of modern life. The Rollercoaster comments on the quality of pleasure in the city; here is a machine designed to satisfy bored excitement-seekers with an artificial thrill of danger, a meaningless gyration that passes for real experience. Again the symbol leads to a comprehensive vision of the city, this time as a giant rollercoaster (just as it is also a giant animals' fair) in which people climb to dizzy heights only to lurch violently down into emptiness in an action devoid of meaning or consequence.[48] The Revolving Doors, on

---

[45] *Manhattan Transfer,* 220. [46] *Ibid.,* 329. [47] *Ibid.,* 291.
[48] See the impressionistic description of the Rollercoaster, *Ibid.,* 237.

the other hand, epitomize the dull routine of the business world in which the time clock establishes man's pace, while revolving doors feed him "in a tape and out ... noon and night and morning, ... grinding out ... years like sausage meat."[49] The doors exist physically as the entrance to an office building in which Jimmy Herf's uncle has offered him the opportunity of a business career. As Jimmy watches people stream through the revolving doors, he suddenly sees his destiny as a seeker of material success: he will be fed through these doors all his life in a monotony of days devoted to making money. In this moment of awareness, he rejects a scale of values that makes business and success man's highest ideal and insidiously leads people to become automatons. The symbolism of the doors reveals in one short paragraph Jimmy's vision of the business world and the motives for his decision:

For a moment not knowing which way to go, he stands back against the wall . . . watching people elbow their way through the perpetually revolving doors; softcheeked girls chewing gum, hatchetfaced girls with bangs, creamfaced boys his own age, young toughs with their hats on one side ... flat bodies of young men and women, paunched bodies of elderly men, all elbowing, shoving, shuffling, fed in two endless tapes through the revolving doors out into Broadway, in off Broadway. Jimmy fed in a tape in and out the revolving doors, noon and night and morning, the revolving doors grinding out his years like sausage meat. All of a sudden his muscles stiffen. Uncle Jeff and his office can go plumb to hell. . . . He squares his shoulders and shoves his way to the revolving doors ... walks down towards the Battery ... turns and stares long up the deep gash of Broadway, facing the wind squarely. Uncle Jeff and his office can go plumb to hell.[50]

The symbolic meaning of Skyscraper is ambivalent, for the skyscraper represents both the beauty and the terror of

[49] *Ibid.*, 120. [50] *Ibid.*, 120f.

155

the twentieth-century giant city. Standing strong and clean, it is the central image in the idealistic dreams of Specker and Sandbourne, the architects who envision a magnificent modern city of steel and glass. To Stan Emery it also appears as the symbol of something certain, enduring, and good: in his muddled drunken reverie, he experiences a sudden irrational desire to be a skyscraper. As an expression of modern beauty, the Skyscraper seems at times separate from the other symbols of a frenetic age, from the Rollercoaster, Fire Engine, or Nickelodeon. Yet, in its very strength, it too becomes ominous, for as it towers above the individual it dwarfs him by its own magnificence. To Jimmy Herf, the Skyscraper appears as a frightening representation of the city's power to destroy man. He dreams of a skyscraper falling upon him: "All these April nights combing the streets alone a skyscraper has obsessed him, a grooved building jutting up with uncountable bright windows falling onto him out of a scudding sky."[51] In its windows he seems to see glorified beckoning faces of Follies girls and a beckoning gold foil figure of Ellen; but in his frustrating nightmare he cannot find the door to the falling skyscraper—just as in real life he cannot find the way to Ellen's love. Thus, the building that is a familiar property of the scene becomes transmuted into the symbol of all the obstacles in the city which keep Jimmy from attaining happiness and fulfillment. The strength that has made the Skyscraper an object of beauty makes it also an object of dread.

The symbol that comprehends all the others and firmly establishes their thematic significance is "Metropolis." At the opening of *Manhattan Transfer,* New York is in a period of growth and development; an influx of immigrants is swelling the population and free land speculation is producing fortunes. The pervasive atmosphere is one of excitement and hope. The symbol of Metropolis, as it appears in the early

[51] *Ibid.,* 365.

156

part of the novel, suggests the hope inspired by the growing city. When Ed Thatcher sees a newspaper account describing New York as the "world's second metropolis," he has a momentary vision of a glorious destiny: the sounds from the street seem to merge into an overwhelming sound of marching feet that move in a vast parade "through long streets towards something tall white full of colonnades and stately. Metropolis."[52] But hope in the future of the city is already negated by a long history of other cities which like New York also held early promise, but which destroyed themselves by their own inner weaknesses. The epigraph on Metropolis[53] establishes a historical continuity between New York and cities of the biblical and historical past, Babylon, Nineveh, Athens, Rome, and Constantinople. References to the destruction of ancient cities, expressed through the symbols of Long-legged Jack of the Isthmus (a figure recalling the great flood) and the Burthen of Nineveh, are balanced by symbols of death in the modern city—Fire Engine (Stan and Anna die by fire) and Steamroller. These symbols present and reiterate the embracing theme of social disintegration and doom. In the last chapter this theme is stated explicitly in the ranting of a crazy tramp: " 'Do you know how long God took to destroy the tower of Babel, folks? Seven minutes. Do you know how long the Lord God took to destroy Babylon and Nineveh? Seven minutes. There's more wickedness in one block in New York City than there was in a square mile in Nineveh, and how long do you think the Lord God of Sabbaoth will take to destroy New York City an Brooklyn an the Bronx? Seven seconds. Seven seconds.' "[54] The wild babbling of the tramp states explicitly the underlying theme of the destruction of modern society. The expression is of course exaggerated, but the irony is that only a madman has recognized the destiny of this mad world.

[52] *Ibid.,* 13.   [53] *Ibid.,* 12.   [54] *Ibid.,* 380f.

157

In his use of urban symbols as a means of expressing social criticism, Dos Passos made an important contribution to the city novel. He showed that ordinary and typical physical properties of the milieu could be raised effectively to a symbolic level; and by his range, he suggested the unlimited possibility of the locale as a source of symbols. More important, his own imaginative processes revealed how profoundly the writer's way of thinking could be affected by the nature of his material. Urban material had become so thoroughly absorbed into his creative imagination that he seemed naturally to express himself in terms of urban images and symbols. (For example, he uses the Rollercoaster as symbol and also metaphorically as image: Ellen "had started to drop with a lurching drop like a rollercoaster's into shuddering pits of misery.")[55] Finally, Dos Passos' symbolism pointed the way to one solution of the city novelist's aesthetic problem of establishing an attitude towards the city without becoming an outright moralist. Dos Passos shows how urban symbols can be used as a technique of implicit social commentary.

Yet for all their brilliance, the symbols in *Manhattan Transfer* may be more important for the possibilities they open to the city novelist than for their unequivocal success within the novel. The very fact that Dos Passos was a conscious innovator may account for the fault in his handling of the symbolism, namely, his overemphasis upon symbolic pattern which makes it overshadow the characters. Because the symbols express the social motifs of the novel, Dos Passos seemed to consider it necessary to bring them to the foreground in order to reinforce the thematic significance of his characters' actions. For example, in the scene of Stan Emery's early and terrible death, Dos Passos introduces an elaborate symbolic phantasy to reinforce the implication that this waste of life is not merely a personal tragedy but that it fits into and is sym-

[55] *Ibid.*, 153.

bolic of a larger pattern of social decay. But the symbolism overshadows the human element. While the phantasy is rather spectacular, in a nightmarish way, Stan himself, as a wasted, tragic figure to arouse compassion and indignation, hardly emerges. Moreover, there is an essential falseness to this crucial scene, for Dos Passos is passing off his own nightmare vision of the city as that of a character who has never been shown to have the awareness that would lead him to see urban properties as symbols or to weave them into a complex hallucinatory pattern expressive of a total vision of city life. In other words, the symbolic phantasy is imposed upon Stan. Apparently Dos Passos recognized how much he was emphasizing symbolism at the expense of characterization, for in *U.S.A.* his characters are self-sustained people. Their imaginative processes—the terms in which their phantasies are conceived—are expressions of the quality of their own minds and experiences; and this is one reason why they impress us as individuals. When they fail to be individuals, it is not because the author has made them incongruously express his ideas rather than their own but because individuality has gone out of modern man.

The characters of *Manhattan Transfer* are human counterparts of the symbols; and they also are made to fit into the comprehensive aesthetic design of the novel. Like the symbols, they are taken from the social context and given wider meaning as a reflection of the moral temper of the times. Like the structure, they move in a circular pattern that is expressive of the futility of their acts. Like the physical city, the scenes, tempo, and atmosphere, they are created through a technique of impressionism that abstracts only their essential qualities. And like all the formal elements within the novel, they fit into a complex aesthetic design that is in itself Dos Passos' moral condemnation of the social tendencies in twentieth-century America.

The impressionistic method of creating character involves a strict selection of isolated moments for dramatization. The characters of *Manhattan Transfer* are thus revealed in flash-shots of apparently disconnected actions rather than in a steady process of continuous and progressive development. The particular incidents in their lives that are dramatized often seem inconsequential and unrelated. Ellen, for example, appears in disjointed images that show her at various moments in her life, but these images do not imply causal relationships nor show how or why one image comes to supersede another. The connection between Ellen the squalling infant and Ellen the child or the mature woman depends upon the mechanics of physical resemblance. For example, the way she sleeps as a child, her chin between her knees, is also the way she sleeps as a woman. But beyond such superficial resemblances the character who appears in various moments and gestures as Ellen lacks a continuous identity. And not only does there not seem to be a unifying principle in the selection of incidents from the characters' lives: even within an incident, emphasis often seems displaced. An inconsequential fact will be described in detail while a crucial one will be slurred over. For example, there is an elaborate description of how Jimmy Herf, still a child, watches and then kills a fly. This isolated act has no particular significance to Jimmy's character, for he is neither cruel nor capricious. Its real function is rather to deflect attention from a crucial event (Jimmy's mother has suffered an invaliding stroke) in order that the reader may discover it for himself and so be more deeply affected by it. Dos Passos' method here involves a kind of literary feinting, as well as a deliberate withdrawal of the author as direct commentator. Whereas a novelist like Dreiser always evaluates his characters' experiences for the reader by techniques of carefully placed stress (as well as by explicit statement), Dos Passos forces his reader, through indirection, to his own evaluations.

One effect of this impressionistic method of character portrayal is the subordination of individuals' lives to the life-pattern of the city. The dominating continuous personality that emerges may not be that of any person: but it is that of New York itself. Thus the synoptic intention to create the city as protagonist is fulfilled. The significant inference to be drawn from the fact that separate moments in a personal history do not go to form a coherent personality is that Manhattan fosters a human state of dissociation. In a milieu of confusion and disorder, people may respond to isolated stimuli, experience isolated feelings, and engage in isolated actions—but they do not achieve inner unity. The pattern of their inner lives is one of jagged discontinuity. Just as the story of their actions is told in isolated and apparently unconnected episodes so the meaning of their existence is inherent in their failure to achieve self-realization through a process of progressive development. Thus there is thematic significance to Dos Passos' technique of characterization. As Joseph Warren Beach has pointed out, the method of discontinuous narration "underlines the discontinuity in the psychic life of the characters."[56]

But when we consider the bare skeletal nature of the characters, that they exist for us only in abstracted, disengaged, and usually trivial moments of experience, we begin to feel that they are not really fictional people at all. That is, they are not so much *people* who are suffering an inner discontinuity as they are merely *discontinuous states of mind and feeling*. As they fit into the total picture of Manhattan, they lose human identity, and they are absorbed into an aesthetic design as abstract states of dissociation representative of a widespread human condition. Edmund Wilson's objection that even in the social milieu of the novel "human beings are still capable of affection, enthusiasm and enjoyment—even of in-

[56] Beach, *American Fiction: 1920–1940*, 43.

tegrity and courage"[57] is based on the false assumption that Dos Passos intended to give realistic and representative samples of all kinds of people. But the concern is not really with people: it is with an essential state of being. While there are always individual human variations (just as there are moments of beauty in the chaotic gaudy urban scene), the characteristic human condition is that of self-division and moral failure. The basic effect of industrial urbanism, as Dos Passos interprets it, is to destroy human integrity and man's capacity for wholesome and fullhearted emotions. The disorganized characters of *Manhattan Transfer* are created in terms of a startling vision of human disintegration—of man rushing frenetically after false or elusive ideals, confounded by his inabilities and inner emptiness, lost in a search for an identity, self-divided and confused. And as this vision grows sharper it reveals that these are not really men at all but jigging marionettes engaged in a perpetual motion that brings them actually or spiritually nowhere.

Perhaps the most serious objection to Dos Passos' people is not that they are unrepresentative of all types but rather that as discontinuous states of mind they cannot evoke the fullest emotional response from the reader. We respond in literature to people whose humanity we recognize, even as we may recognize their weaknesses, cruelty, or foolishness; but we can hardly become distressed over the fate of an abstract state of mind. The success of *U.S.A.,* in contrast to a basic failure in *Manhattan Transfer,* is that the characters emerge as recognizable, if not entirely sympathetic, human beings to whom we can respond, while at the same time they are striking representatives of a state of mind and of an entire historical epoch.

While all the characters embody some aspect of modern

[57] Wilson, "Dos Passos and the Social Revolution," *New Republic,* Vol. LVIII (April 17, 1929), 257.

human defeat, there are differences that divide them roughly into three groups. Some are helpless victims of an economic system; some are reflections of the consequences of material success; and some are personifications of the psychic state of self-division. The peripheral characters struggling for subsistence are perhaps most sympathetically portrayed. There is the exploited Anna, trying to make a living in a sweatshop, and Francie and her lover Dutch, the desperate jobless veteran, trying to survive through crime. They have genuine and wholesome impulses, but they are doomed: Anna is horribly mutilated in a fire in the backroom of Madame Soubrine's dress shop (where Ellen selects a trousseau for a loveless marriage); and Francie and Dutch face twenty years in prison.

Those who achieve material success are as much immersed in a destructive element as those who fail, although the struggle for success seems to be the one organizing principle that can give unity to an individual's actions. (Thus as Stan rejects this goal—" 'Why the hell does everyone want to succeed?' " he cries; " '. . . what can you do with success when you get it?' "[58]—he leaves himself without a centralizing purpose. In random acts of dissipation he loses his identity and destroys himself.) But the characters who achieve success pay heavily for it: Gus McNiel loses his simple dream of family life and happiness as he becomes a corrupt and corrupting politician; and George Baldwin compromises himself in his private as well as his public affairs. When Baldwin reflects upon the state of his existence, he sees himself caught in a hopeless moil. "Good God," he cries to himself, "how am I going to get my existence straightened out? . . . Proportion, that's it. To lay out your life like a prudent gardener, plowing and sowing."[59] He turns for self-delivery to marriage with Ellen. " 'Life's going to mean something to me now . . . ,' " he tells her;

[58] Dos Passos, *Manhattan Transfer*, 175.
[59] *Ibid.*, 279.

" 'God if you knew how empty life had been for so many years. I've been like a tin mechanical toy, all hollow inside.' "[60]

Baldwin's description mortifies Ellen because it expresses her own feelings as she commits herself to him in a loveless marriage. The scene in which human warmth drains out of her as she makes a definitive and petrifying gesture is brilliantly conceived in imagistic terms. Before Ellen makes her final commitment, she sees herself as a "hypothetical dollself" capable of "various positions" and "gestures." But her acceptance of a marriage of convenience leaves her "frozen in a single gesture" as her fate is determined: she is to become a useless leisured woman forever "haunting beauty parlors, packed in boncilla, having your face raised."[61] The description of the process of dehumanization is worth quoting not only for its imagery but also for its summary of what happens inwardly to almost all the people of *Manhattan Transfer:*

Through dinner she felt a gradual icy coldness stealing through her like novocaine. She had made up her mind. It seemed as if she had set the photograph of herself in her own place, forever frozen into a single gesture. An invisible silk band of bitterness was tightening round her throat, strangling. Beyond the plates, the ivory pink lamp, the broken pieces of bread, his [Baldwin's] face above the blank shirtfront jerked and nodded; . . . Ellen felt herself sitting with her ankles crossed, rigid as a porcelain figure under her clothes, everything about her seemed to be growing hard and enameled, the air bluestreaked with cigarettesmoke, was turning to glass. His wooden face of a marionette waggled senselessly in front of her. She shuddered and hunched up her shoulders.[62]

While Ellen articulates her sense of failure by the general statement that she's "messed things up," Jimmy Herf gives a more precise statement of his feeling of dissociation. He sees that " 'the trouble with me is I cant decide what I want most,

[60] *Ibid.,* 375.　[61] *Ibid.,* 397.　[62] *Ibid.,* 375.

so my motion is circular, helpless and confoundedly discouraging.' "[63] He reviews his life as a history of waste: "In Yonkers I buried my boyhood, in Marseilles with the wind in my face I dumped my calf years into the harbor. Where in New York shall I bury my twenties?"[64] His final resolution is to leave the city which he vaguely sees as the cause of his failure and frustration and the obstacle to his happiness. But even his last act lacks positive direction. He is escaping from the frightening world of scudding skyscrapers, but he does not know where he is headed nor how far is the journey to self-discovery.

Dos Passos' dissociated, frustrated, and emotionally drained people are reflections of a social milieu. They live in, and incorporate into their lives, the disorder about them—the economic disorder that fosters inequality and exploitation of man by man; the political disorder that fosters corruption; the social disorder that allows for tenuous and shallow human relationships; and the moral disorder that submerges the people in an atmosphere of irresponsibility, drunkenness, infidelity, and confusion. Having never known the restrictions of a binding moral code, these people simply assume an attitude of amorality; and by their nonchalant acceptance of all irregularities, they reinforce this attitude in each other. Ellen, for example, assures Cassandra that certainly "abortion is the only thing to do."[65] Against a setting of social disorganization, marriage lacks meaning or enduring qualities. Nellie McNiel is faithless after little more than a year of marriage, and Ellen moves through marriage and divorce almost casually and with selfish or confused motives. That these people lack lovable or admirable qualities is not merely an oversight. It is in their lack of warm human appeal that they impress upon us the moral consequences of a manner of life and of an underlying historical tendency towards social disintegration. Charmless, inept, confused, demoralized, they are Dos Passos' stern in-

[63] *Ibid.*, 176.   [64] *Ibid.*, 353.   [65] *Ibid.*, 189.

dictment of the times. As fictional people they are not memorable; as abstract representations of a human state of being they are appalling. But as part of the complex aesthetic design of *Manhattan Transfer,* the design that embodies and expresses a social vision, they are implicit commentaries on the moral structure of the times. They represent, like the chaotic setting, the din, stench, and cacophony of the city, the nerve-racking pace, the jagged tempo, the symbols of doom, and the structure of futility, an undercurrent of social tensions that Dos Passos interpreted to be creating the most tragic moment in American history.

The Fulfillment of Form in U.S.A.

BEHIND *U.S.A.* is the same emotional impetus, the same burning vision of modern decadence, and the same sense of urgency that underlie *Manhattan Transfer.* But Dos Passos wrote *U.S.A.* with the experience of *Manhattan Transfer* behind him. And he had learned from this experience. Whether or not he realized it, *Manhattan Transfer* was the preliminary apprentice-piece for his masterwork, *U.S.A.* The earlier novel helped bring his creative faculties to the point of their fullest development, and the fruition of his talents, the fulfillment of the form he was seeking to embody and assess the times, is displayed in the trilogy. Strictly speaking, *U.S.A.* is not a city novel: it is a unique work that should not be confined to a limited category. But because it reveals Dos Passos' broad synoptic intention, and because it is, within a larger framework, one of the best revelations of urbanism as a way of life, it can legitimately be discussed here, even if only suggestively. The main purpose will be to show how Dos Passos carried over to *U.S.A.* the same ideas and intentions he had in *Manhattan Transfer,* while he transmuted, rather than changed, his literary methods.

166

Although *Manhattan Transfer* clearly reflected Dos Passos' aesthetic sensibility and social conscience, it was obvious that Dos Passos was trying to establish an impersonal relationship between himself and his work. He tried to make himself a sensitive camera lens that registered and reflected a complex scene; his purpose was to record a picture in its details and as it existed independent of himself as interpreter. The assumption was that if the picture was faithful to the essentials of reality, an intelligent observer could draw from it certain inevitable inferences. In *U.S.A.*, Dos Passos introduced the Camera Eye sections in order to permit himself a direct expression of personal views and emotions, while at the same time he maintained the separation between himself as recorder and the picture he was recording. Technically, the Camera Eye shows the perfection of his impressionistic method. These fleeting impressions that capture objective acts as well as the inner stream of consciousness have been reduced to essentials in order to achieve the heightened effect of concentration. We have only to compare the way the same scene is treated in *Manhattan Transfer* and in *U.S.A.*[66] to realize how fully Dos Passos was now able to exploit the impressionistic method both for its economy and its effect of intensity. Thematically, the Camera Eye sections provide a keystone upon which the entire structure of the trilogy rests. Far from being the residual product of Dos Passos' poetic talents, as some critics claim, they are the immediate expression of his social and moral conscience. They contain the story of his growth to an awareness of the social tragedy overtaking the country. Here he reveals the quality of his own mind and experiences as well as the observations that led him to see

[66] Compare, for example, the way Dos Passos handles the raid on Cassandra's soiree in *Manhattan Transfer* with the Camera Eye section in "1919," *U.S.A.*, called "a mattress covered with something from Vantine's."

that America was becoming self-divided, that its ideals of justice and freedom were being trampled underfoot.

It is in the Camera Eye section that he states explicitly his view that "America our nation has been beaten by strangers who have bought the laws and fenced off the meadows and cut down the woods for pulp and turned our pleasant cities into slums and sweated the wealth out of our people and when they want to they hire the executioner to throw the switch."[67] The contrast between an idealistic past and the present, which is always implicit in his works, is clearly defined in these passages. The Camera Eye shows him standing at the historic spot where the immigrants, "the kingkillers haters of oppression," landed. He recalls the "threehundred years the immigrants toiled into the west," and then turns to the present to see "another immigrant . . . hater of oppression," Bartolomeo Vanzetti, hounded and killed.[68]

The Camera Eye shows too the growth of his determination to speak out in the language of the artist in protest against this degradation of American ideals. As he leaves Boston, the scene of past acts of historic greatness and of the present injustice, he asks: "How can I make them feel how our fathers our uncles haters of oppression came to this coast how say Don't let them scare you   how make them feel who are your oppressors America."[69] It is the task of the artist to reconstitute the glorious phrases of the past that expressed our hopes and ideals—"to rebuild the ruined words worn slimy in the mouths of lawyers districtattorneys collegepresidents judges."[70] This is what he has tried to do in *U.S.A.* by a kind of reverse process: he re-creates a shattered America in order to recall a past made great by an integrity of ideals. The artist himself does not belong within this picture of a society in decay, for he is the instrument through which the picture is

[67] "The Big Money," *U.S.A.*, 462 f.
[68] *Ibid.*, 436.   [69] *Ibid.*, 437.   [70] *Ibid.*

projected. Moreover, although he has emerged from this society, he cannot be identified with it or considered part of it, for he has rejected it by his disapproval and his refusal to conform to its pattern. The difference between the artist who has become a Camera Eye that reflects and judges the social scene and the people who are part of the scene is, then, an essential one; and it is maintained by an actual division with the trilogy.

Just as Dos Passos used urban symbols in *Manhattan Transfer* to represent the destructive forces in modern society, he uses here prominent twentieth-century men to symbolize the two opposing factions of a self-divided America. The particular aspect of American life these people represent is clearly secondary in importance to the social ideal and historical tendency they stand for. According to Dos Passos, America has become self-divided because of an inner conflict between social ideals. The resolution of this conflict will determine the destiny of the country, whether it will harden into a monopolistic society which crushes the common man and uses him as fodder for imperialistic war or into a true democracy which carries out our traditional ideals of justice and equality. Thorstein Veblen is Dos Passos' key figure not only because he represents specific social ideals that Dos Passos finds admirable but more important, because he describes with rare perspicuity the alternative forms American society can take. On the one hand, it can become "a warlike society strangled by the bureaucracies of the monopolies forced by the law of diminishing returns to grind down more and more the common man for profits"; or, on the other hand, it might become "a new matteroffact commonsense society dominated by the needs of the men and woman who did the work and the incredibly vast possibilities for peace and plenty offered by the progress of technology."[71]

[71] *Ibid.*, 101f.

Each person Dos Passos has selected for a biographical sketch in some way represents one of these alternatives and the ideals upon which it rests. Men like Minor Keith, Carnegie, Wilson, Morgan, Ford, Hearst, and Samuel Insull have impelled society in the direction of monopolism; wittingly or unwittingly, selfishly or misguidedly, they have fostered wars in foreign countries and hatred and oppression at home. They have guarded the interests of big business at the expense of the common man's liberty. They are the motive powers behind the lynchings, witch-hunts, and night-raids that were America's tragedy and disgrace. Opposed to them in principle and act are Dos Passos' defeated heroes: Eugene V. Debs, Big Bill Haywood, Bob La Follette, Jack Reed, Randolph Bourne, Paxton Hibben, Joe Hill, Wesley Everest, Frank Lloyd Wright, and Thorstein Veblen. Dos Passos interprets even such a nonpolitical figure as Isadora Duncan as a symbol of the force that resists oppression and reaction. Like each of the men named above, she maintained integrity as an individual. Her integrity lay in being a free artist, in resisting not only the "philistines" who would not let her dance in America, but also the warmakers who would have her give up Wagner and support their "butchery." The test that Dos Passos has applied to each of his symbolic figures is whether or not they supported the war: if they did, they represent the historic force of oppression, and if they did not, they stand for the common cause of the people who are the force behind the progress towards democracy. Thus, Isadora Duncan represents not simply Art but the artist's love for the people, which makes him abhor oppression and its attendant evil, war: "She was an American like Walt Whitman; the murdering rulers of the world were not her people; the marchers were her people; artists were not on the side of the machineguns; she was an American in a Greek tunic; she was for the people."[72]

[72] *Ibid.*, 157.

The biographical sketches contain Dos Passos' most trench-
ant writing; and as we understand the profound symbolic
meaning these people had for him, we can see why he was
moved to the intenseness that makes his irony so brutally effective. In *Manhattan Transfer,* he had exerted the full force
of his inventive and imaginative powers upon the urban symbols which stood for a manner of life and a process of social
decay—both of which he deplored. But he was making symbols out of impersonal, and hence unmoral, elements; and he
could not possibly feel towards them either the bitterness or
the sympathy he felt towards the people in his sketches. He
could respond to his contemporaries not merely as aesthetic
elements but also as people who had moral responsibility and
were therefore to be despised for their moral guilt or admired
for their integrity. The emotions these people could evoke and
focalize, and that a Skyscraper or a Rollercoaster could not,
vitalize them as symbols. In *Manhattan Transfer,* Dos Passos
was obviously fascinated by the possibilities for creating aesthetic patterns with the symbols, while here in *U.S.A.* the
representative men are much more to him than aesthetic material. They are the very expression of his essential social
beliefs, and as he portrays them, he is able finally to make his
ideas, emotions, and expression one aesthetic integer.

The Newsreel sections re-create the newspaper of the times
as a scanning reader might see them. They have both factual
and atmospheric value: they tell us what is happening, and
they also give us a sense of the social milieu. Their most serious shortcoming is not that they force an artificial separation
between the narrative and its social background but that as
an aesthetic unit in themselves, they are relatively uninterest-
ing. While the subway-rider may flick through his newspaper
with genuine interest, the novel-reader does not look for bare
and undigested information, no matter how pertinent it may
be to the fictitious action. Rather he anticipates the aesthetic

171

pleasure which comes from finding artistic order in the material he reads. There can be no doubt that Dos Passos has carefully selected and arranged the newspaper excerpts, but both his objective in the Newsreel sections and the technique used to achieve it make it impossible for him to rise above the aesthetic limitations inherent in newspaper scanning. In *Manhattan Transfer,* he had made brief references to newspaper articles mainly for their factual value, while the atmosphere and tensions of the scene were re-created by the very movement and pace of the novel. The organization of *U.S.A.* into large narrative units dealing with one person prevents Dos Passos from attaining the atmospheric effects he achieved in *Manhattan Transfer* by handling the narrative in an irregular and discontinuous manner. Nevertheless, the narrative sections of *U.S.A.* succeed so well in capturing the quality of the mood of the milieu, as well as of the characters, that one really does not need to supplement them with Newsreel passages that give a sense of the times.

Perhaps the most brilliant achievement of the Newsreel sections is that as they provide a historical counterpart to the fictional sections, they make fiction more acceptable as truth than the accounts from real life. The Newsreels record such inanities, falsehoods, and ironic perversities that by contrast the inanities and ironies that are fictional begin to seem more true to life. The quality of the mass mentality revealed by the Newsreels would make us more willing to accept Dos Passos' characters not because they have the same quality of mind but because, if anything, they are on a higher level. No matter how sordid or selfish they are, they have managed at least not to sink to such acts of madness as the newspapers report nor to subscribe to such self-deceptions as the American leaders preach. Some of the remarks of Wilson, Taft, or Hoover that Dos Passos quotes here are beyond the talents of his characters most skilled in verbal legerdemain, Dick Savage and Ward

Moorehouse. By placing fact and fiction in juxtaposition, Dos Passos has succeeded curiously in gaining for his fiction an assent which we are unwilling to give to facts.

Although in *U.S.A.* Dos Passos shows his people suffering from the same inner confusions and spiritual emptiness that had typified the characters of his earlier novel *Manhattan Transfer,* he is much more successful in capturing their essential humanity as well as their individual manners. The larger narrative unit allows him to create a continuous identity for his characters, so that they are no longer merely vivid but fragmentary states of mind; and because he deals with them as continuous personalities, he succeeds better in showing their inner disintegration. The dramatic effectiveness of Dick Savage's moral collapse, for example, derives from the effectiveness with which Dos Passos has built him up as a character. His life appears to us as more than a series of unrelated moments; it is a patterned sequence in which we can trace the dissolutive process that transforms Dick from a rather idealistic youth into a hack and libertine. Dos Passos brings us into an immediate contact with his characters by adapting for each one of them a language directly expressive of the quality of his mind and sensibility. He writes the narrative in the idiom of the characters, thus creating them for us by the very style in which he describes them. His sheer mastery of the language of the people has never been demonstrated so impressively as in these narrative sections in which he has made successfully high aesthetic demands upon even the coarsest vulgate speech. Style can no longer be separated as a vehicle of expression: it has become character. His purpose is to achieve the highest degree of objectivity by withdrawing himself as narrator and allowing the characters to be the medium through which their stories receive expression. The effect of this is that each character exists as an almost completely self-sustained element, for the evidence of the outside personality

173

of the creator, which might be contained in the style, has been obliterated.

Yet Dos Passos' highest achievement with his characters is not the vivid and immediate projection of their personalities. Rather, it is the perfect identification of the state of the human spirit with the spirit of the times. Charley Anderson is the age of "The Big Money," as is Ward Moorehouse, or Dick Savage at the end of the trilogy. Joe Williams and "Nineteen-Nineteen" are conterminous—we cannot tell at what point the identity of one is separate from that of the other. The people are the human correlatives of the historical moment. That helps to explain why we find them, for the most part, so offensive. The tragedy of their inner emptiness and ineffectuality is the social tragedy of what seemed to Dos Passos mad years of war and ignominious money-making. The hope we find in Mary French is the hope that the historic moment still offers us a chance to make a better society and a finer people. Dos Passos has created his characters, then, with a multiple consciousness; he is conscious of them as individual human beings, mainly worthy of our irony and disdain; he is conscious of them as being the social and historic times; he is conscious of them, also, as the part and the whole of the social tragedy of twentieth-century America.

CHAPTER 6

James T. Farrell:

THE ECOLOGICAL NOVEL

Theory and Form

THE CITY of James T. Farrell's novels is the South Side Chicago of his childhood. It was a drab world, lacking in variety, color, beauty, or surprise—but it provided Farrell with the substance of his art and his purpose as a city novelist. Perhaps the most outstanding fact about the South Side was its insularity. Although its boundaries were physical, the barriers between it and the outside world were social and emotional. Poverty kept the people at home, bigotry and prejudice isolated them from neighbors of different religion or background, and suspicion of secular education prevented them from reaching out towards a broadening knowledge. The consequence of social isolation was that one's vision of life, of the variety and complexity of the human experience, was narrowed to what one found in the South Side. Even the physical surroundings imposed emotional limitations: the "gravel playgrounds and artificially pretty parks" could hardly inspire a sense of wonder or lift one to spiritual heights. "We city-dwellers," Farrell has written, "have been educated without the lyric emotions."[1] Thus, the phrase that Joseph Warren Beach has applied to Farrell's art can be applied to the South Side: it suffered from "the lack of any principle of

[1] James T. Farrell, "Thirty and Under," *The League of Frightened Philistines*, 150.

175

relief."[2] And in the vision of life projected in Farrell's novels this lack of relief is an essential and fundamental quality. Days follow days in a monotonous round: the essence of life is sameness, and unrelieved sameness constitutes impoverishment. Moments of relief as they are pictured in the Danny O'Neill novels are more apparent than real. For a few hours, the family may seem drawn together in harmony, spiritually united in conquest over the spiritual vacuity that surrounds them like a noxious element. But the inner resources of the people are not strong enough to counterbalance the effects of their impoverished world; and the mellow Christmas dinner ends in another family row.

The very insularity of the South Side meant, however, that its values went unchallenged, and, consequently, that its system of manners remained distinctive and intact. The collective assumptions of the South Side were expressed in a pattern of behavior and speech that established its way of life. As one who had experienced this way of life and known no other during all his formative years, Farrell could present with extraordinary precision its language and manners. Few city writers are as much the insider as he; and of the writers who have the same kind of inmost knowledge of manners, none has exploited his material to such powerful effect. Novels like Isidor Schneider's *From the Kingdom of Necessity* and Joseph Gollomb's *Unquiet,* also studies in neighborhood life, are meager beside Farrell's works; Michael Gold's *Jews Without Money* is abortive fiction; and such a recent work as Alfred Kazin's *A Walker in the City* remains a personal reminiscence. One of the few novels of city manners that can approach Farrell's early work in artistic achievement is Meyer Levin's *The Old Bunch,* which re-creates the intimate way of life within a Jewish neighborhood in Chicago.

As Farrell began to make a mature evaluation of his world,

[2] Joseph Warren Beach, *American Fiction: 1920–1940,* 303.

as he began to appreciate its effects upon the people who struggled within it for meager livings and small satisfactions, he developed the motives and emotions fundamental to his art. He realized, first of all, that he must find an escape from the South Side. His survival, as a person and a writer, seemed to depend upon his breaking with a past that lived on in his mind as painful and humiliating memories. The need for purgation, so common an impulse behind literary creation, gave Farrell his impetus. He turned to writing as a means of self-deliverance, for he felt that if he could objectify the world of his childhood by giving it independent life within the novel, he could "purge himself completely from the world he [had] known."[3]

The emotional drive behind Farrell's art was anger. Anger led him to seek literary expression: it determined his motifs and called forth his irony. In his own life, as in the lives of his characters, anger marked a climactic point in the development of a social awareness. It was a sign of recognition—of a coming into awareness of the destructive forces in the environment. Thus, as Danny O'Neill begins to understand the implications and effects of his confinement to the South Side, he begins to live his "days of anger." In the Bernard Carr[4] novels, anger is an emotional point of reference to which are related all of Bernard's present activities, trivial and boring as often they are. Bernard's struggles in New York are significant mainly in terms of his past in Chicago when his vision of city

[3] James T. Farrell, "The Young Manhood of Studs Lonigan," *Studs Lonigan* (New York, Modern Library, 1938), 371.

[4] In 1946, Farrell published *Bernard Clare* (New York, Vanguard Press). Because of a libel suit by a man who had this name (the suit was dismissed) he changed his hero's name to Bernard Carr in the sequel to this novel, *The Road Between* (New York, Vanguard Press, 1949). References in this chapter to the 'Bernard Carr novels' signify both these works. *Yet Other Waters* (New York, Vanguard Press, 1952) continues Bernard's story.

life crystallized and his anger was born. The growth of anger in Farrell, as well as in characters who are his spokesmen, reveals also an instinct or desire for self-preservation. Before Studs Lonigan is destroyed, he has experienced frustration and bafflement, but not the anger of awareness. He has not really understood the implications of his environment, and because he is not alerted to their dangers, he cannot fight or flee or in any way protect himself.

Farrell's personal anger takes formal expression as irony. As with Dreiser, irony is implicit in the "grim contrasts [between] vision and reality"[5]—between the glorious promise in American life and bitter unfulfillment. The promises are made explicit in speeches delivered by the priests to their charges and in platitudes handed down by fathers to their sons. Set against the promises are the realities of American life—Studs Lonigan wasted to death before he is thirty, Jim O'Neill paralyzed and helpless after a lifetime of work, the "go-getter" Al O'Flaherty, a failure, betrayed by the system he had extolled. But Farrell does more than give individual examples of unfulfillment. He creates an entire world which in itself constitutes one of the most unforgivable "broken promises of American life."[6] The South Side of his childhood, re-created in the novels, is his evidence of hopes betrayed, as well as of social irony. Out of the dreams of America has come a fulfillment such as this which is their mockery.

Thus, Farrell's material implicated him in social criticism. Other writers might perhaps have responded to his background with despair, cynicism, indifference, or an escapist desire to retreat from reality into romance. But Farrell, like many of his contemporaries, committed himself to a militant art. His judgment condemned the South Side; his conscience

[5] Farrell, *The Road Between*, 105. Although Bernard uses this phrase in describing his writing, he is clearly speaking for Farrell, too.
[6] *Ibid.*, 105.

told him that for the sake of the people whose lives it blighted it must be reconstructed. And his literary theory pointed the way towards an art of social consequence. In his theory of literature, Farrell faced a question that arises out of an interest divided between art and social reform: What has the desire to create novels to do with the desire to renovate society? Both motives had emerged concurrently from the same matrix of experience and social observation; but could they both be satisfied by the single act of literary creation?

Unlike the left-wing critics, Farrell was not to make a simple equation between art and propaganda. He distinguished between the two by defining literature as a form of revelation, and propaganda as a form of political action. In the 1930's he was defending the autonomy of art, pointing out that its "functions" were "not exhausted or even well performed if it seeks to limit itself to usurping functions better served by direct political agitation, by political slogans, and by political pamphlets."[7] In the 1940's, he answered such left-wing writers and critics as Isidor Schneider and Albert Maltz, who were writing in the *New Masses,* with his "Notes for a New Literary Controversy," in which he stated that the propagandist and the creative literary artist had distinctly different functions, purposes, and methods. Farrell's definition of literature as an "instrument of social control,"[8] makes clear his belief that fiction could not be directly a "means of solving problems" within society. Rather it was "a means of helping people to discover more about themselves and about the condition of life about them."[9] As literature brought the reader to a sharper awareness, it was, however, instrumental in social

[7] James T. Farrell, "A Note On Literary Criticism," *Nation,* Vol. CXLII (March 11, 1936), 315. For an elaboration of the ideas presented here, see his *A Note on Literary Criticism.*

[8] *Ibid.,* 315.

[9] James T. Farrell, "Social Themes in American Realism," *Literature and Morality* (New York, Vanguard Press, 1947), 24.

reform, for it is awareness that produces the pressing sense of concern that moves man finally to act. In order to make the reader more sensitive to his world, literature must exploit fully its aesthetic potentialities. As art, it could make a unique and powerful claim upon the human mind and emotions: it could broaden man's understanding, extend his sympathies, and sharpen his perceptions. It could make his experience of contemporary life more meaningful by giving artistic order to its apparently chaotic realities. "The main effect," and also the "more lasting effect," of literature, Farrell wrote, is "the result of making men understand their world more clearly, of making them feel life more keenly, more sensitively, more imaginatively. In this way it plays its role in changing the world."[10]

The implicit assumption underlying Farrell's theory is that knowledge will make us free. Whatever the artist has to add to our experience and understanding of the world about us, of any part of it, can be of social consequence. The corollary of this is that the writer himself must be free to "describe and reveal the discoveries which come from an honest and relentless effort to explore to the bitter end the nature of experience."[11] Farrell's objection to both the humanistic and the Marxist critics was not merely that they apply false criteria to literature; it was that they try to shackle the creative talent to dogma by predetermining for the artist the kind of material he should use and the kind of response he should make to it. Only as the writer remains free to discover and define his own meaning of life will art be effective; and only then, too, will it "contribute toward ... the liberation ... of men."[12]

Thus, Farrell's critical views, as well as his narrow experi-

[10] "A Note on Literary Criticism," *Nation,* Vol. CXLII (March 11, 1936), 315.
[11] Preface, *Literature and Morality,* xi.
[12] *Ibid.,* 14.

ence, limited the scope of his fiction to the materials of his own immediate past. According to his theory, the novelist should explore to the bitter end the reality of his time; and as we have seen, the realities he knew most intimately were of the everyday life in South Side Chicago. While the commonplaceness of the materials at his command might have dismayed another writer, it seemed to Farrell a positive virtue. He felt that he had a "true and representative story to tell of how people have lived, suffered and enjoyed, striven and forged ideals, loved and hated, died in my time."[13] Moreover, the very conditions that the realistic urban novel had to reveal gave such a novel its function. "It is especially the fact of modern urban life," Farrell argued, "that individuals are isolated and estranged. This phenomenon is, in itself, a sufficient justification of the effort to present a realism of everyday life, a realism involving the continuity of everyday life, a realism dealing with the conduct of urban childhood and youth."[14]

Man's spiritual isolation in the modern world was not a mere sociological fact to Farrell; it was a cutting personal experience. He recalled the times in his own youth when "I felt that I was alone in facing the problems that were troubling me; so often I seemed lost in an inner state of bewildered loneliness."[15] He thought that the novel could establish communication between people who in real life had become lost in their private inner worlds and were no longer able to reach out towards each other. "By objectifying the problems, the doubts, the moods, the patterns of language, of action and of relationships of youth,"[16] literature could show man that his inner experience of alienation, far from being peculiar, was

[13] James T. Farrell, "James Farrell on James Farrell," *New Republic,* Vol. CIII (October 28, 1940), 596.

[14] James T. Farrell, Foreword, *Short Stories* (New York, Penguin Books, Inc., 1946), n.p.

[15] *Ibid.,* n.p. [16] *Ibid.,* n.p.

181

common and widespread and symptomatic of the chronic social problems of our age. Thus, Farrell developed in his critical writings a systematic rationale for the city writer. He went beyond general statements in defense of the realistic treatment of urban life to draw a specific relationship between the characteristics of urbanism and the city novelists' intentions and functions.

Both personal and social factors led Farrell to concentrate upon "the condition of childhood and youth in urban twentieth-century America."[17] His own childhood always remained extraordinarily vivid and meaningful to him; and he was the kind of novelist who created his most powerful works out of the memories of childhood. In addition to the intrinsic appeal of the past as literary material, the subject of urban youth allowed him the fullest exploitation of his theme of spiritual isolation and of the urban background. Childhood and adolescence, the periods of self-discovery, were especially periods of isolation and estrangement. The problems inherent in the process of growing up kept one withdrawn from others and focused one's interest about one's self. And since youth was malleable and responsive to outer influences, the study of youth allowed for an exploration of the social world in which human character and destiny are shaped. Farrell was never concerned with environmental facts as such; unlike Dreiser, he did not pause to examine peculiar and interesting aspects of the locale. The meaning of the environment was defined in its effects upon the inner man. He dealt mainly with "boys growing up" because "the exploration of the psychology of boyhood affords me a better opportunity to reveal ... the concrete processes whereby society, through the instrumentality of social institutions, forms and molds character, giving to the individual the very content of his consciousness."[18]

[17] *Ibid.*, n.p.

When he started his first novel, Farrell had already decided that his "task was . . . to try and recreate a sense of what life meant to Studs Lonigan."[19] In subsequent novels, he still tried to give a sense of what life meant to his characters. By showing the city neighborhood as his people saw it and as it acted upon them, Farrell broke down the distinction between environment and character, the outer world and the interior life, and revealed them as complementary aspects of the same thing. Mark Schorer, in his article "Technique as Discovery," has complained that "in a realist like Farrell we have the environment only, which we know from the newspapers."[20] Whether it is legitimate, or even meaningful, to speak of "the environment only" is of course open to question: the term refers to surrounding conditions or influences, and the idea of a thing or person being surrounded is implicit in it. More pertinent, however, is the question Schorer's criticism raises of the difference between the kind of knowledge offered by newspapers and that offered by realistic fiction. A newspaper *tells* us about an experience; fiction makes us *live through* it. The difference in the kind of knowledge we get is not merely qualitative; it is a difference in kind. In Farrell's novels we know the environment not because we were told about it but because we were submitted to the imaginative experience of "living through" it. The environment is not reported as sociological fact. It is translated into character and human destiny. Studs Lonigan *is* his environment; and as we enter into his consciousness we achieve a knowledge of the environment that is experiential. We feel the environment from within, in the way it impresses itself upon the mind and makes us what

[18] "James Farrell on James Farrell," *New Republic,* Vol. CIII (October 28, 1940), 596.

[19] Introduction, *Studs Lonigan,* xi.

[20] Mark Schorer, "Technique as Discovery," *Forms of Modern Fiction,* (ed. by William Van O'Connor, Minneapolis, University of Minnesota Press, 1948), 28.

we are. This is not an external knowledge gleaned from a newspaper report. It is an experience of imaginative literature.

Farrell's concern with urban youth makes his novels a kind of aesthetic correlative to the case history. Like the case history, they collect data about an individual's past that show by reference to the influences that have acted upon him why he has become what he is. While Farrell's data are the dramatic facts of fiction, which have truth as imaginative rather than sociological realities, they are compiled, as in the case history, by an additive process; fact is piled on fact. Although selection and arrangement are the essence of any art, Farrell is relatively more interested in the addition of details than in their omission. His subject is the daily passage of time in the city and the slow formation of character in response to the pressures of time. Like the case history, his novels reveal that man's character and fate are shaped through a slow and accumulative process. As the individual makes his responses to the outer world, he discovers within himself certain motives, potentialities, and desires, and thus achieves his identity. The pace of Farrell's novels becomes a dramatic realization of an assumption that is implicit in them and in the case history— that character is shaped not by isolated or sporadic influences, but by influences that are recurrent and persistent. This assumption explains also why Farrell gives equal treatment to both apparently trivial and climactic incidents. In this way he suggests that dramatic or sensational moments in one's life are organic with duller ones; they come as the climax to a sequence of apparently ordinary events which are as significant as the sensational outcome they produce. The outbursts of violence in his novels (the orgiastic football game in *Studs Lonigan* and the shocks of the sudden death of Studs and his pals or of little Arty O'Neill) are the *consequences* of a long series of small incidents. Because Farrell was concerned with *causes* as well as with consequences, he gives the same treatment to dramatic episodes and to the commonplace ones that lead to them.

Like the case history, the novels depict events in the order of their occurrence. Commentary is reduced to a minimum. The concern of both forms is primarily with the revelation of facts whose meaning a qualified reader must discern for himself. While a novel such as Willard Motley's *Knock On Any Door,* which comes close to being an actual case history, introduces a sociological commentator and interpreter, Farrell's novels rely upon the implicatory meanings of dramatic action and character. Farrell believed, like Dreiser, that if he created his characters and situations realistically and vividly, they would convey their own tragic implications.

This analogy of the novel with the case history calls attention to the general characteristics of Farrell's art—his objective method of presentation, his comprehensive treatment of social backgrounds, his fidelity to chronological time, and the uniformity in his manner of portraying trivial and climactic episodes. The total effect of his art was fundamentally different from that towards which Dos Passos had worked in *Manhattan Transfer.* Although *Manhattan Transfer* apparently suggested to Farrell methods he used in *Gas-House McGinty,* and to a lesser extent in *Studs Lonigan,* for expressing man's elaborate reveries and dreams, it could not provide him with a technique for exploring his peculiar urban world. Dos Passos had evolved a form for revealing an entire city in both its outer brilliance and inner decay; Farrell needed a form that would reveal only a small part of the vast and complex urban scene. Dos Passos' Manhattan was a world of dramatic contrasts and fast, syncopated rhythms. To convey the essence of this world, Dos Passos gave brilliant and fleeting impressions of city life rather than exact reproductions of details and daily events; and he covered long sweeps of time in order to dramatize the historical process of social change. Farrell moved at a pedestrian pace in order to suggest the monotony of city life and to show the effects of the slow attrition of time. Thus, his method required elaboration of detail, while Dos Passos' required condensation.

Although Farrell shared certain of Dreiser's social views and worked within his realistic tradition, his specific formal problems were also different from those Dreiser had faced; for both his materials and his intention were different. Farrell's Chicago was a stagnant city, not at all like the vital, growing Chicago of Dreiser's novels. It did not inspire in youth wild hopes and ambitions, nor was there in it that dramatic contrast between a surface glamour and an undercurrent of struggle which Dreiser's form had been created to express. Farrell's characters were commonplace people whose sensibilities had become blunted, people of lesser talents and smaller desires than Dreiser's egocentric, yearning heroes. Most important, Farrell was concerned with the minute details of a way of life characteristic of a small and distinctive social group, while Dreiser dealt with broad social facts about the city, with its underlying economic structure and its system of values.

This last difference points to the fact that as a city novelist Farrell was moving in a direction quite different from that taken by Dreiser earlier in the century; for in his portrayal of the distinctive ways of a social group, he became essentially a novelist of manners. Indeed, Lionel Trilling, who defined the novel of manners in its current broad sense,[21] has said that the "very essence" of *Studs Lonigan* is its "serious concern with manners."[22] It is in the light of his problems and achievements as a city novelist of manners that Farrell's contributions to urban literature should be assessed; for as he sought for

[21] Lionel Trilling, "Manners, Morals, and the Novel," *The Liberal Imagination* (New York, Viking Press, 1950), 205–22.
[22] Trilling, "Art and Fortune," *The Liberal Imagination,* 259.

the techniques that would enable him to exploit urban manners, he departed from a formal tradition Dreiser had helped to establish and that in his own way Dos Passos carried on. Both writers were interested in presenting social generalizations about city life; but Farrell developed methods that would reveal city life in its small and particular details.

Because Farrell and Dreiser have often been linked together as naturalists, the artistic differences between them as city novelists should be pointed out. By contrasting the two we begin to arrive at what is individual—and also significant —in Farrell's art. Briefly, their differences might be summarized this way:

(1) Dreiser never developed a keen sensitivity to the presence and implications of urban manners, except those of fashion and housefurnishings. Perhaps this was because of a temperamental way of seeing things, but more likely it was because as a newcomer to the city, Dreiser found his attention focusing upon gross social facts new to him, such as the economic discrepancies among city people and the common drive towards material success. Farrell, born and reared in the city, was never far enough away from it to lose sight of the minute details that were an integral part of his everyday life.

(2) Dreiser's realism consisted in an exact registering of the objective details of the setting and in the creation of type-characters who exhibited type-reactions. Farrell did not distinguish as sharply between place and character; he revealed the setting as it had become incorporated into the character's subjective world and had affected his manners and feelings.

(3) The structure of Dreiser's novels, a parallel structure created by the symmetrical arrangement of contrasting situations and characters, gave formal expression to his concept of urban society as a fretwork of contrasts between rich and poor. Farrell's structure was based upon a consciousness of time in the city, upon a sense of the day as a unit, and of days

187

in succession filled with monotony and emptiness. His structural units were consequently smaller and more precisely defined than Dreiser's, just as his technique for noting details was finer and more precise.

As a form of urban literature, Farrell's works are the best example of the ecological city novel. The ecological novel is distinguished from both the portrait and the synoptic novels by its restriction to a small spatial unit within the city. Dreiser's protagonist was a single person, and Dos Passos' was Manhattan itself: Farrell's is a specific neighborhood. His people are rooted in South Side Chicago, and the South Side shapes their character and destiny, just as in Ann Petry's *The Street,* Harlem determines Lutie Johnson's fate, or in Nelson Algren's *The Man with the Golden Arm,* Chicago's 'Skid Row' determines Frankie Machine's way of life and ultimate destiny. The characters of the ecological novel are essentially properties of the scene. And yet, curiously enough, it is precisely because they belong to a particularized locale—because they have absorbed the outer world into their consciousness and are making constant responses to what is immediately outside them—that these characters come to life as the most real and individualized human beings in city fiction.

Because the ecological novel imposes certain limitations upon the writer, confining him to a small cultural entity within a vast city, it was ideally suited to Farrell's talents and purposes. It turned to advantage his narrow experience of city life: he was confined by a formal structure to the one neighborhood he knew intimately and could portray with authority. He could depict in smallest detail the manners of this narrow world, for the limitation in scope allowed for a concentration upon detail. Moreover, since the world of the city's children and youth is the small, circumscribed area of their immediate neighborhood, the ecological novel was the ideal form for revealing the way young people lived and grew up in the city.

188

Character and Milieu

FARRELL's characters fall into three main categories. There are the 'dramatic' characters, those who suffer the effects of the South Side as a social and moral environment; the 'reflective' characters, those who are scarred by the environment but become aware of its effects, hate them, and determine to fight against them; and the 'background' characters, those who *are* the environment, the personification of the narrowness, spiritual poverty, and brutality inherent in the South Side as a way of life.

All the young people in *Studs Lonigan,* except Danny O'Neill, are 'dramatic' characters. In his introduction to *Studs Lonigan,* Farrell had spoken of his desire "to reveal the concrete effects of spiritual poverty."[23] These effects are revealed in what the children are becoming and in what finally they have become. As Fran Lonigan becomes a hard, empty woman, as Martin Lonigan becomes a brutal, hard-drinking young man, as Red Kelly turns into a petty, self-seeking politician, the implications of the environment become dramatic realities. The concrete effects of the environment are revealed also in the early death of the young boys who had stood in front of poolrooms or on street corners waiting for adventure. "Judgment Day," the last book of the *Studs Lonigan* trilogy, opens on the theme of early death, as Studs and some of his old gang return from their friend's wake. The realization that death has overtaken many of the young men leaves them awed and depressed: " 'You know, boys, [Red says] speaking straight from the shoulder, it does kind of get you the way so many of our old gang passed away. Arnold Sheehan, the Haggertys and Tommy, Hink Weber who killed himself in the nut house, Slug Mason beating the Federal Government Prohibition rap by dying of pneumonia, all our old pals. Lord

[23] Introduction, *Studs Lonigan,* xii.

have mercy on their souls. Here today and gone tomorrow, nobody ever spoke truer words.' "[24]

These young people, who are "here today and gone tomorrow," act out a pattern of destiny that is determined by their environment. Whether they incorporate themselves into their narrow and petty world or whether they die after wild and fatal attempts to break out of their dull routines, they represent dramatically the stultifying effects of South Side Chicago.

Why is their world deprived of spiritual vitality? Through his 'background' characters Farrell answers this question in dramatic terms. As parents and priests, the background characters have individual personalities, but they are also representative of a moral and social environment. The characteristics of South Side Chicago are essentially those of the older generation. The sterility of the neighborhood inheres in the sterile love of Mrs. Lonigan for her son, in the empty ideals of success of Paddy Lonigan, or in the now meaningless rituals of the priests. Its crassness is in the sentiments of the parents who admire the cheap, strutting politicians and hold them examples of success. Its brutality is the brutality of Margaret and Mother O'Flaherty, striking each other blindly in drunken rage; of Al O'Flaherty, beating the children in sudden violent temper; of pious Lizz O'Neill, spitting upon her neighbors; and of all the older men, expressing their deepest frustrations in curses upon Negro and Jew.

Farrell is invariably successful with these background characters, for while he made them personifications of social characteristics, he saw them also as distinctive and thoroughly human people. He understood that in their own way they suffered and paid for what they were, even as they made their children suffer. Though he sympathized with them, he was

[24] "Judgment Day," *Studs Lonigan,* 9.

190

alienated from them; and this tension within his emotion provides a dramatic tension within his fictional portraits. Farrell understood their struggles to become self-made men; he could appreciate their pride in the fact that they had more to offer their children than they had been offered. But he realized too that in their struggles they had lost a spiritual vitality, and now they created a social and spiritual void in which their children must stifle and be destroyed.

Their early years of poverty have made the parents ardent subscribers to the ideal of material success. They want to give their sons something better than they had had. For example, at the beginning of "Young Lonigan," Paddy Lonigan is shown musing over his "grim battle" to win economic security and give his children a decent and comfortable home. His own memories are of "poverty, the cold house in winter with the wind breaking through the cracks. Days without food. His father, a big strong man, worrying, coming home drunk . . . his mother working and slaving, washing, scrubbing, cooking in their crowded little home."[25]

In contrast to this, Paddy thinks of what he and his wife have done for their children:

. . . given the kids a good home, fed and clothed them, set the right example for them, sent them to Catholic schools to be educated, seen that they performed their religious duties, hustled them off to confession regularly, given them money for the collection, never allowed them to miss mass, even in winter, let them play properly so they'd be healthy, given them money for good clean amusements like the movies because they were also educational, done everything a parent can do for a child.[26]

[25] *Ibid.*, 431.
[26] "Young Lonigan," *Studs Lonigan,* 21. Paddy's interior monologue at the beginning of the trilogy is balanced by another bitter one at the end.

191

Jim O'Neill does less for his family not because he is less devoted or less hard-working but only because he earns less
money. Al O'Flaherty is willing to support his nephew and
niece and foster their cultural development.

Yet despite the good intentions of the older generation,
the children suffer. The parents are misguided in their efforts
and blind to the consequences of their own inadequacies; and
they are victimized along with the children by social forces
beyond their control. The depression ruins Paddy as well as
Studs. Prohibition has the boys drinking liquor that blinds
them or eats away their minds, while the parents stand by
powerless. Working conditions keep the parents away from
the home (Al O'Flaherty is usually on the road) or else make
them so weary that they come home at night irritable and
impatient, unable to give their children the companionship
they need.

Moreover, the parents' personal conduct sets the younger
generation an example of violence and bigotry. Although they
want to be good fathers and mothers, they never appreciate
the harmful effects of their fits of drunkenness and sudden
temper. The ideals they hold out to the children are essentially
materialistic ones which turn a growing girl like Fran Lonigan into a hard young materialist or else so fail to inspire the
young men that they are left groping for a life goal. Because
the immigrant parents remember their struggles against poverty, they set high value upon money, a secure job, a little
home; but to their children, who have never known terrible
poverty, these goals seem dull and commonplace; the young
boys want excitement and adventure.

Perhaps most important is the fact that the parents' spiritual resources are spent. They retain their intense prejudices
and hatreds, but they have lost a certain vigor of imagination
and love. In his introductions to *Studs Lonigan* Farrell explains what has happened to the older generation:

192

The fathers, grandfathers, great grandfathers of boys like Studs Lonigan came to America as to a new world. They came from the shores of that island whose history is one of the most bitter of all nations. Most of them were poor immigrants. Some of them could not read or write. They belonged at the bottom of the American social and economic ladder. Many of them did menial work, and the lives which they led were hard. They struggled upward in American society just as have other immigrant groups and races before and after them. Their lives constituted a process in which they were assimilated into the American petty bourgeoisie and the American labor aristocracy. Their lives were dedicated to work, to advancing themselves, to saving and thrift, to raising their families. They rose socially and economically. Ultimately many of them owned buildings and conducted their own small business enterprises. They became politicians, straw bosses, salesmen, boss craftsmen and the like. And they became tired. Their spiritual resources were meager. They believed in the American myth of success and advancement. They believed in the teachings and dogma of their faith. They believed that with homilies, platitudes about faith and work, and little fables about good example, they could educate their children. They believed that thus their children would start off in the race of life with greater advantages than they had had, and that their children would advance so much the farther, so many more rungs on the economic and social ladder.[27]

Whenever the fathers try to communicate with their sons they fall into platitudes. Perhaps the best example of this is Al Flaherty's pathetic and sometimes comic attempts to 'be a pal' to Danny O'Neill. As Danny grows older he becomes more and more removed from his uncle, until at the end, while he sympathizes with and pities him, he breaks from him completely. The love of the women for their children also fails to unite the younger and older generations. Although Mother O'Flaherty loves Danny jealously, she lives in a world so different from his that she cannot help him with the real and

[27] Introduction, *Studs Lonigan,* xiif.

193

immediate problems of growing up. Mrs. Lonigan's love for Studs is a selfish emotion: she wants him to remain her baby even though he is constantly squirming out of her possessive and stifling embrace. She has her own dreams about his future and never realizes that he faces inner problems and is impelled by private needs which do not fit into her picture of him.

Family life degenerates into a relationship of bickering and nagging, the parents striking at the children, the children fighting among themselves. A plague falls on each household. In the O'Flaherty home, Margaret's drunken bouts leave the children trembling and insecure. In the O'Neill home, Lizz's slatternly ways breed dirt and disorder. In the Lonigan's home, Mrs. Lonigan's shallowness and Paddy's sheer inadequacy are reflected in constant squabbles and in the prevailing atmosphere of sterility. The older people are touchy and irritable, dissatisfied with their personal lives and annoyed by the noise and closeness of their apartments. The children are emotionally insecure, afraid of an unexpected blow, a sudden flare of temper, or another drunken row.

This failure within the home is part of a larger collapse of institutional life. It is not merely the family which is collapsing, no longer fulfilling a positive function, but also the church and the school. As Farrell has pointed out in his introduction to *Studs Lonigan*, "the important institutions in the education of Studs Lonigan were the home and the family, the church, the school, and the playground. These institutions broke down and did not serve their desired function."[28] In the home there was bickering and conflict. In the church there was bigotry and worldliness. And in the streets there was the gang practicing minor brutalities, speaking a language of obscenity, and brooding over the lack of excitement.

Studs Lonigan shows the priests concerned with worldly, rather than spiritual, problems. Father Gilhooley, carried

[28] *Ibid.,* xiii.

away by his plans for a new and glorious church, is so busy collecting money for his project that he forgets his first duty, to give spiritual guidance. At the end, he has his church, but, ironically, his people have left it as the Negroes have advanced into the white neighborhood. Under such guidance it is understandable that the people themselves have lost hold of the essence of their religion. The church-going Lonigans are bigoted and proud, spurning those who hold religious beliefs different from their own. As they distort their religion into a means of self-aggrandizement, they fail to comprehend or carry out the principles they profess to hold. They show neither charity nor forgiveness, justifying their own hardness of heart by pointing to another's sins. Every action of Mrs. Lonigan towards the pregnant Catherine is contrary to the teachings of her religion: in the moment that is a test of her charity she fails, just as she has failed in her daily life to make her religion a living thing. Lizz O'Neill is another who has perverted her religion. Although the church gives her comfort, she fails to put into practice its fundamental teachings. She turns to Mary for protection, but she does not realize that Mary should also be her example of motherhood and Christianity.

This religion which has become sterile in the hands of worldly-minded priests and bigoted parishioners closes the minds of the children to the one secular influence that might help them—education. When the children attend parochial school, the nuns fail to inspire them with a love of learning. Rather the children associate education with the drabness of the parochial school and with the ineffectuality or violence of their teachers. The real accomplishment of this early education is to make the children lose their awe of nuns and priests, whose suppressed rages they despise and whose punishments they fear. Yet there is little likelihood that the young people will go on to higher education; for though they cannot respect their parochial schools, they have been taught that the University of Chicago breeds atheists, and in a vague, superstitious way they fear the loss of faith. Danny is the only one who breaks away and attends the University. And there he finally finds a way of escape from the dead world about him. But for the others, there is no broadening influence, no hope for new knowledge or inspiring visions of life.

The failure of social institutions to play a constructive part in the individual's spiritual life has serious personal consequences. It throws the individual back upon himself, and his inner experience becomes one of loneliness, alienation, and unfulfillment. In critical writings, Farrell has stated explicitly a view of modern man to which the novels give dramatic expression: "The conditions of American life," he has said, "create alienated and truncated personalities, a fact which has already engaged the attention of more than one generation of sociologists, political scientists, psychologists, judges, social workers, and others."[29] All of his novels are concerned with the "self-estranged modern man." Studs, for example, goes through life essentially alone. Even when he is about to propose marriage to Catherine, he feels that they are strangers to each other, that she does not really know him, just as all his life no one has known him. As he is going to ask her to marry him, he thinks: "Suppose he should make a fool of himself? After all, he was really a stranger to her. He was really a stranger to everyone else in the world also, and they really did not know what went on inside of him, and how he felt about many, many things."[30]

Like Studs, Danny O'Neill finds himself a stranger among the people close to him. As a child and adolescent, he had felt lost and confused, but he had not understood the meaning

[29] "The Language of Hollywood," *The League of Frightened Philistines,* 177.
[30] "Judgment Day," *Studs Lonigan,* 26.

and implications of his state of mind. As he comes into maturity, however, he realizes that social circumstances have estranged him from his people and that now his own deliberate act of will must separate him from them completely. The title of the first novel of the tetralogy, a line from A. E. Housman which Farrell said "concentrated, for me, the significance of the book,"[31] states the stranger-motif. While the title applies specifically to Danny, it has general appropriateness to the rest of the characters who are also strangers in a world they never made. Farrell's comment on the significance of his title *A World I Never Made* is illuminating:

[Danny] is living in a world that he has not made, and he is an anxious little boy who has many fears. Living with his grandmother, he is something of a stranger. For despite the fact that he is doted on, he is, nonetheless, a stranger. He is not in his own home. At the age of seven, these conditions of his life contribute toward creating, in early years, those feelings, anxieties and emotions which contribute to that feeling of homelessness so noticeable in our whole modern period. Danny, seen here first at the age of seven, is being prepared, educated in the day by day patterns of urban life. He begins with a feeling of homelessness, and he is a child with many anxieties as he experiences his first confrontations with the world that he never made.[32]

Father and Son deals more specifically with the estrangement between Jim O'Neill and Danny. Each needs the love of the other, but their attempts to communicate end usually in misunderstandings, mutual irritations, and regrets. In *My Days of Anger,* Danny recognizes the fact that he has always been estranged from his family. As a child he had found himself caught in a crosscurrent of antipathies between the

[31] James T. Farrell, Introduction, *A World I Never Made* (Cleveland, World Publishing Company, 1947), x. This novel was published originally in 1936.
[32] *Ibid.,* x.

197

O'Neill's and the O'Flaherty's, and he had belonged to neither family. Economic pressures first separated him from his parents, while tensions within the home, differences in attitudes and ideals, and a growing awareness of his own individuality estranged him from the O'Flaherty's. He finally comes to understand the fact of his alienation: "He had escaped from uncle's influence. Yesterday at mass he had realized he was growing away from the life of the neighborhood. With the family, he had seen himself more or less a stranger looking on at them."[33] Mother O'Flaherty's death symbolizes his final separation and release from the past. When she dies, the cohesive force which had kept the family together, if only in token unity, is gone; and the tension within him, which had come from living closely among people who remain essentially strangers, is also broken. He expresses his alienation now by an overt act as he determines to leave Chicago altogether and create for himself a new and productive life in New York.

The situation which Farrell explores is a pathological one. A society is sick if the people within it live among themselves as strangers. Farrell presents this situation in its totality by showing that there has been a collapse within both the private inner world and the broader social world. He suggests, too, that there is a cyclical pattern of interaction between the individual and society: social pressures destroy the individual, and the individual in turn creates social chaos. This cycle can be broken only by a deliberate exercise of human will. While Studs Lonigan reflects the pathological elements within an urban society which destroy the individual unconscious of them, Danny O'Neill reveals how the socially conscious individual can set about to rebuild his own private inner world, as well as the world about him.

[33] James T. Farrell, *My Days of Anger* (Cleveland, World Publishing Company, 1947), 193. This novel was originally published in 1943.

Studs Lonigan's days are filled with emptiness. His most vital experiences are his own daydreams of himself. As Farrell points out, Studs dreams first of what he will be, and then as he attains maturity without achieving self-fulfillment, he dreams of what he has been. His entire life reveals a basic dissociation—that is, he cannot organize his activities towards a progressive and continuous realization of his fundamental wishes. He has only a vague sense of what he wants and no clear vision of how to get it. His attempts to satisfy an immediate need for excitement bring him momentary pleasures but no lasting satisfactions. There are only two passing occasions when he feels himself completely fulfilled: the first, when he sits with Lucy in Washington Park; the second, when he beats up Weary Reilley. Each moment marks the end of something. With Lucy, a pure and deeply romantic feeling comes to a climax and is never recovered: when Studs finds their names chalked on the sidewalk streets by his leering friends, he proves he is not a sissy by spurning Lucy, and this act loses her to him forever. His fight with Weary proves him the "tough guy" of his day-dreams—but drink is to dissipate his young strength. Perhaps the most humiliating scene in the trilogy is the one that balances the victory over Reilley, the scene in which Studs fights with his younger brother and is thoroughly thrashed. When it is already too late for him, Studs tries to face the fact that the years have been frittered away without purpose or design. He turns to Catherine in hopes that marriage will give meaning to his life. But deep within him, he knows that it is not she but Lucy he wants, a Lucy of his own romantic dreams; and the truth comes home to him that dreams and realities are infinitely apart. He has the growing conviction that he is nobody, for he cannot discover or objectify his real self either in his acts or in his personal relationships. He begins to hear "a . . . voice that wasn't his voice, and that perhaps might have been the voice of his conscience" which tells him: "You're nothing but a slob. You're getting to be a great big fat slob. Nothing on the ball anymore. Slob! Slob! Fat slob! Double slob!"[34] This is an accusation that he cannot deny and cannot live with. Indeed, this fear that he is not really the tough and invincible Studs Lonigan of his daydreams has always haunted him and made him uncertain.

In his adolescence, Studs turns for assurance to the gang. On the surface the gang seems merely a commonplace and innocent union of boys, but it is, actually, a kind of outlaw institution which sets up values opposed to those of the parents. Once Studs joins the Fifty-Eighth Street boys, he commits himself to the code of the "tough-guy." Since only sissies go to school, he turns truant. Since tough-guys drink and smoke, he forces himself to swallow the corroding bootleg liquor. And since sexual exploits are a mark of virility, he gets his manly dose of the "clap." One critic has stated that "the tragedy of Studs Lonigan is that he is not a rebel."[35] The fact is, however, that Studs lives in constant rebellion against his family and his priest, for gangdom is in itself a form of rebellion against established social institutions. It provides a picture of the ideal young man that thrills the boys as their fathers' commonplace ideals never do, and it gives them in activities of violence release for their energies and an opportunity to prove their virility. In his study of the urban gang, Professor Thrasher has said: "The fundamental fact about the gang is that it finds in the boys who become its members a fund of energy that is undirected, undisciplined, and uncontrolled by any socially desirable patterns, and it gives to that energy an opportunity for expression in the first, the most spontaneous, and elemental manner possible, and at the same

[34] "The Young Manhood," *Studs Lonigan,* 393.
[35] Robert Lovett, "James T. Farrell," *English Journal,* Vol. XXVI (May, 1937), 352.

time intensifies all the natural impulses by the process of cumulative stimulation."[36]

The far-reaching personal effects of Studs' conformity to gang ideals is that he destroys himself. Bootleg whisky and wild parties ruin his health, while the constant search for excitement prevents him from engaging in constructive activities. The outlets which the gang provides for pent-up energies are destructive—not only to the boys themselves but to the well-being of society as a whole. In placing exaggerated value upon sexual exploits and violence, it encourages the boys to become seducers and bullies. It provides a pernicious form of amusement in open attacks upon minority groups. The boys find relief from boredom and a thrill of power in thrashing a Jewish child who happens to pass their street or in going "to the park to look for Jews and throw pepper in their eyes."[37] The brutal Weary Reilley is master of the techniques of aggression. He describes to admiring listeners how he sent home a victim "with a handful of teeth and a puss full of blood." The moral of this story as he sees it is this: "Anyway, I learned something. Instead of breaking my dukes any more on some rat's face, I'm getting me a nice pair of brass knucks."[38] The crippling of Jewboy Schwartz in a football game is the ultimate realization of the latent impulses of the gang, and to the boys it seems a consummation: they have asserted their physical superiority and given violent expression to their repressed hatreds.

The Negro is also subject to attack. He is routed out of the "white man's park" and beaten when he approaches the white man's neighborhood. In their prejudices, the gang and the parents are in accord; both release their own frustrations

[36] Frederick Thrasher, *The Gang: A Study of 1313 Gangs in Chicago* (Chicago, University of Chicago Press, 1927), 101.

[37] "Young Lonigan," *Studs Lonigan,* 155.

[38] *Ibid.,* 47.

by attacking weaker groups. The interracial tensions come into prominence in "Judgment Day" as the neighborhood deteriorates with the slow invasion of the Negroes. Studs hears the Negro cursed and reviled at home; but while the family gives him a powerful example of blind race hatred, it is the gang that teaches him how to find excitement and gratification in attacks upon minority groups.

These violent feelings towards minority groups have serious social implications, for the young people are learning to look for a scapegoat on whom to blame their personal failures. In their tirades against the Jews, Paddy Lonigan and Al O'Flaherty give the boys a lesson in fascistic thinking. Paddy says: " 'Well, that's what we get for letting the Jew international bankers get control of our country. You know what we need? We need a man like Mussolini here in America. A strong man to take things out of the hands of the Jew international bankers and the gangsters. If we had a man like Mussolini over here for two months, he'd straighten out a lot of people and put them where they belong, behind the bars or against a wall.' "[39] This kind of talk reveals an effect of personal failure and frustration more dangerous even than the random attacks upon Jews and Negroes. It betrays a latent tendency towards an American fascism.

Tommy Gallagher's Crusade, a work of much lesser artistic merit than *Studs Lonigan,* picks up this theme of latent fascism and develops it more fully by showing how the personal dissatisfactions of a young man lead him to join a fascistic organization. The "Association" offers Tommy an outlet for his energies and baffled anger. Like Studs, Tommy has a secret feeling of his own inadequacy; yet he is also convinced in an adolescent way that "something big was going to happen to him."[40] He becomes active in an organization whose pur-

[39] "Judgment Day," *Studs Lonigan,* 307.
[40] James T. Farrell, "Tommy Gallagher's Crusade," *Short Stories,*

pose is to wipe out Jews and Communists in America. Only when he participates in the group's activities does he have a sense of belonging. Then life holds something real and exciting for him: "Since he'd gotten interested in Father Moylan and joined the Association for Christian Freedom, this feeling had gotten stronger in him . . . life had gotten more exciting. He had things to do that gave him a feeling of his own place in the world that he'd never had before."[41] In his everyday life Tommy has failed as a son and a wage earner, but he can blame his failure upon someone else; and this relieves the pressing sense of his own inadequacy. He has learned to direct an anger against himself towards someone outside him and weaker than he. When he saw "foreign or Semitic faces" in the street, "hatred flared in his soul. They were the kind whom he blamed for his plight."[42] Tommy Gallagher's crusade is, then, a crusade against an innocent people. His ideal is to find some leader like Hitler—or to become himself another Hitler[43]—and wipe out an entire minority group. But he is also on a crusade to find himself as a person, for, like Studs, he has never been able to discover or objectify his real identity. He has found that in himself he has no reality, but that he can achieve an identity through destroying someone else.

This, then, is the destructive cycle: a society which does not give its young people a real chance to achieve fulfillment will become self-divided as they turn upon each other in frustration and bitterness. The people implicated in this cycle are blind to its meaning; they feel only their confusion and anger. Unless they become aware of the implications of their acts, the cycle will follow its insidious course; personal frustrations will grow stronger, hatreds more intense, and the conflicts more open and violent. The one hope we have is that we will begin to understand what is happening within us and see what we

190. *Tommy Gallagher's Crusade* was published originally in 1939.
[41] *Ibid.,* 190. [42] *Ibid.,* 212. [43] *Ibid.,* 213.

are doing to each other. If this happens, we have the chance to cease being victims of destiny, like Studs, and to become masters of our fate, as Danny hopes to be.

As Danny comes finally to recognize the destructive elements that have brought Studs to early death, he sets up a pattern of awareness, repudiation, and social action. While the process of recognition is gradual, a sudden vision of the world about him crystallizes when he attends his cousin's wake. Here are gathered people he has known all his life, and here are uttered again the pious, false sentiments and the platitudes Danny has always heard. These people express the gospel of material success even while their own spiritual poverty is revealed. It is fitting, Farrell says, that Danny's moment of illumination should come at a wake; for Danny sees that his people are "dead, dead in their souls, dead in spirit. And they were the men who helped ruin Chicago."[44]

Renunciation follows upon Danny's awareness. He decides to give up a sterile religion and to break meaningless family ties:

He looked at the stones, the buildings. These stones belonged to something he had escaped. These stones were the physical aspects of a world in which another Danny O'Neill had lived. His heart was heavy. He had finally taken off a way of life, a world in itself, as if it were a worn-out suit of clothes. He was making a last break with his past. Nothing remained with him of that past now but scars and wounds, agonies, frustrations, lacerations, sufferings, death. These he would always carry with him, just as he would his own weaknesses and his own follies. But his anger had now cooled to irony; his hatred was not against people, but against a world which destroyed people. And in that world the last compromise had been eradicated. He remembered the night when he had cursed a non-existent God on his way home from the gas station. He recalled the morning last January when he had stood in the center

[44] *My Days of Anger*, 322.

of the campus and vowed that no power on earth would stop him. Then he had been without his weapons. Now he had his weapons. Now he was leaving and he was fully armed. With what weapons he had, he would break a world, or that world would break him. He was prepared for battle.[45]

When he decides to leave Chicago, he is not simply running away from the city, as Jimmy Herf ran away from New York. He is running away from his enemy in order to be able to advance upon him in open attack. His enemy he clearly sees as a way of life which has destroyed his people:

His people had not been fulfilled. He had not understood them all these years. He would do no penance now for these; he would do something surpassing penance. There was a loyalty to the dead, a loyalty beyond penance and regret. He would do battle so that others did not remain unfulfilled as he and his family had been. For what he had seen, for what he had been, for what he had learned of these agonies, these failures, these frustrations, these lacerations, there would never be forgiveness in his heart. *Everything that created these was his enemy.*[46]

The weapon he has forged for himself is his art, through which he hopes to bring others to social awareness. His novels are to re-create the sorrows and sufferings he has seen and experienced and reveal the elements in our way of life which destroy people. That he would meet with resistance he knew. He had already seen what effect his realistic stories had upon his writing professor, who had expressed the essential criticism of his work:

"You want to be a realist [he had said]. But is it realism to say that all life is unhappy? Isn't there balance? Isn't there a contrast of joy to sorrow? It seems to me that the true realist is the one who

[45] *Ibid.,* 400f.
[46] *Ibid.,* 401. Italics mine.

205

tells us there is good and bad in life, that happiness and unhappiness balance one another. Your writing is too mordant. You're too bitter. You know your material, but you go at it with two feet, kicking and punching. Your irony is always overstressed. Unless you change your tone, I don't think the public will ever bother to read you. . . ."[47]

But if there is truth in writing, the public can never afford *not* to read it, and Danny's plea is for the truth of what he has said. "I didn't make unhappiness," he cries out. "I didn't invent Chicago. I'm only trying to describe Chicago as I know it."[48] He has faith in man's desire for truth; and in this faith his art takes root. He believes that man could create a better life for himself if once he saw clearly the everyday realities of our common way of living. He answers the protests against his realism with an impassioned question: "To make the world better, don't you have to make people know what it's like, make people know what they're like?"[49]

As Danny thus describes his world as an objective reality outside of him and determines upon a course of action as a militant writer, he becomes a 'reflective' character, one no longer being acted upon by the environment but fully conscious of its nature and implications. As a reflective character, he is Farrell's direct spokesman, making explicit Farrell's own view of the city and his motives as an artist. The question Danny raises here—"To make the world better, don't you have to make people know what it's like?"—is one that illuminates Farrell's work as a city novelist. Farrell's immediate goal also was to "make people know" a way of life as it was experienced by the people who were caught up in it and destroyed. The way of life was essentially a dreary and cheerless one; yet out of the unpromising materials it offered to the writer, Farrell hoped to create an art that would stir men's hearts and awaken their social conscience.

[47] *Ibid.*, 303. [48] *Ibid.* [49] *Ibid.*, 304.

Structure and Style

FARRELL'S success in re-creating the South Side arises out of a technical skill for which most critics do not give him credit. His novels have come under attack for structural deficiencies and most violently for their style. But if we approach Farrell as a city novelist who was seeking to re-create a particular urban world by using the materials it offered—its characters, settings, and language—we can see that both structurally and stylistically *Studs Lonigan* and the Danny O'Neill series are significant artistic achievements. Specifically, Farrell's use of the restricted point of view, of urban speech patterns, and of an episodic structure reveals him as a careful and deliberate artist who knew what effects he wanted to achieve and the techniques appropriate to them.

Modern fiction has adopted the restricted point of view as a strategy of psychological revelation and as a means of achieving formal discipline. In Farrell, the restricted point of view has also thematic implications. Since character and environment are organic—since environment *is* its effects upon character—the study of South Side Chicago becomes an exploration of the inner life. As we see the outer world reflected within the narrow consciousness of the characters, we come to understand the limitations and deficiencies of the environment and their implications for the city man. In *Studs Lonigan,* Farrell projected the scene mainly from within the mind of Studs, although he also moved into the minds of other characters. Separate italicized passages explored the point of view of minor characters such as Mrs. Lonigan, Davey Cohn, Danny O'Neill, and Martin Lonigan, while also within the text, lesser figures come into prominence occasionally as point-of-view characters. The point-of-view character shifts frequently in the Danny O'Neill novels from Danny himself to members of

207

his family. *Father and Son* brings Jim O'Neill into prominence, while *My Days of Anger* is written mostly from within the mind of Danny, now no longer an uncertain child but a young man coming into mature self-knowledge and social awareness.

Farrell's characters are most distinctively themselves in their emotions rather than in action. Indeed the commonplace routine of their lives leaves little opportunity for any but routine activities. In their reveries and musings, their recollections, angers, bafflements, and prejudices, they give expression to their inmost selves. As each in his turn becomes the point-of-view character, we gain entry into his inner world in which the stream of emotions and half-formed ideas flows continuously with the motion of life. The effectiveness of Farrell's use of the restricted point of view is revealed in the vividness and immediacy of his characters. Their "living reality" (to use Bernard De Voto's phrase)[50] cannot be denied, even by Farrell's severest critics. His people spring to life as vital, idiosyncratic, and fully believable human beings. One thinks not only of Studs and Danny, but of all the O'Flaherty's: the inimitable Grandmother; Al, the prim bachelor, full of platitudes and good intentions, but of uncontrollable temper; Margaret, womanly and maternal, and lost. One thinks of hardworking, doomed Jim O'Neill and his slatternly Lizz with her belly swollen with child and a dirty rag around her jaw to comfort her toothaches. There is a crowded stream of lesser figures, each distinctively himself, each alive with his own reality: Paddy Lonigan, Mrs. Carr, little Arty, Ed Lanson.

Because his point-of-view characters are commonplace and narrow people, Farrell has been accused either of giving a one-sided and distorted vision of life or of not fully exploiting his material. But the restricted point of view limits the experi-

[50] Bernard De Voto, Review of *A World I Never Made*, The Saturday Review of Literature, Vol. XIV (October 24, 1936), 5.

ence within the novel to what is in the characters' minds and to the responses to life of which they are capable. To live momentarily within the mind of Lizz O'Neill is to see life in a one-sided and distorted way. Through other characters, Danny O'Neill and Bernard Carr, Farrell sought to balance the narrow vision of such people as Lizz or the Lonigans. These young men have dreams of a better and larger world than the one they live in. For the most part, however, Farrell wanted the reader to live through the experience of narrow and ignorant characters, for they revealed the essential aridity of the South Side. From their point of view, life is a succession of cares and petty annoyances, of frustrations, anxieties, work, sickness, and death. A critic who argues like Mark Schorer[51] that Farrell's techniques do not permit him fully to exploit his material is, actually, finding fault with the content and the limitations of the personal view of life formed by the characters. This is Farrell's point exactly: that when you go into the desolate minds of these people, you discover the effects of a way of life that has confined their thoughts and cramped their spirit.

Although Farrell's style has been severely criticized, it is an effective medium through which milieu and character come to life. As a city novelist, Farrell was keenly aware of the inappropriateness of a lyrical manner to the materials of everyday urban life.[52] He adopted the language of his characters as his aesthetic medium, and his versatility as a stylist is revealed in the variety of distinctive speech patterns he recreated. Although a vulgar street language was the natural expression of his characters, there is a variety of styles that range from the balanced and flatulent speech of the priests, a

[51] Schorer, "Technique as Discovery," *Forms of Modern Fiction,* 9–29.

[52] See "In Search of an Image," *The League of Frightened Philistines,* 154–60.

speech "fat with superlatives," to the pedantic speech of Al O'Flaherty or the lyrical rhythms of Mother O'Flaherty.

Any particular style is a revelation of character. This fact apparently escaped Mark Schorer when he said of Farrell that "in sheer clumsiness of style, no living writer exceeds him, for his prose is asked to perform no service beyond communication of the most rudimentary kind of fact."[53] While in general the language gives an immediate sense of an urban atmosphere, specifically it reveals the characters' quality of mind. The triteness and fatuity of some of the characters' speech is expressive of a blunted sensibility. Their rhythms and intonations recall occasionally their Irish love of rhetoric. Perhaps most important, the language of obscenity and violence reveals significant inner hostilities and frustrations. Schorer's statements on Farrell's style must be contradicted by an assertion that Farrell has made style "a technique of discovery"; but what it discovers is a terrible state of human limitation. For example, Al O'Flaherty's simple and unqualified declarative sentences reveal his inadequacy to deal with the complexities of literature and philosophy. He wants to be profound, but the very manner of his speech reflects the fatuity of what he is saying. This is Al carrying on "intellectual conversation":

[Pickwick is] a very civilized man, and he is interested in life. He is always going around to learn. He has great curiosity. And he has friends. One of them is named Winkle. . . . Mike, you want to read this book, *Pickwick Papers*. Pickwick is a real gentleman, and he's always getting into trouble. . . .[54]

---

[53] Schorer, "Technique as Discovery," *Forms of Modern Fiction*, 24.

[54] James T. Farrell, *No Star Is Lost*, 492. This novel was published originally in 1938.

[Priests] study theology and philosophy, and philosophy is the queen of the sciences. . . . Heard about an American philosopher named William James. His brother is a fine writer. Wrote a book called *Daisy Miller*. The story is laid in Rome. A wonderful book. He writes with a beautiful style.[55]

In contrast to her son's flat and platitudinous talk, Mother O'Flaherty's speech is lyrical and poetic; it is a speech modulated to her character and frame of mind. An old woman, she muses upon the past in a language that is evocative and rhythmic:

Lo and behold, when I was a girl running the bush in the old country I did hear tell of stories and stories of America. And didn't the people say how rich it was and there was money to be had in America, and some there were that did hear tell that the streets were paved with gold in New York. They were killing and fighting in the old country, and they're killing and fighting in America. And look at me now, here in America, an old woman in the latter end of me days. It's a queer world, indeed it is. All of them are going straight to the Devil himself. Ah, Tom, it was a black day, a black day when we came out to America. Didn't I know that there'd be no luck when I sailed away on a Friday?[56]

The scene of Lizz at prayer, quoted below, shows that Farrell could achieve an effect of richness even when he was limited to the language of an almost illiterate woman. Although the sentences here are short, simple, and direct—such sentences as Lizz herself would be capable of constructing—they produce the rhythm of religious prayer and the mood of devotion. The diction is for the most part commonplace; but through a poetic use of repetition, the language achieves emotional impact. The feeling of trust that Farrell dramatizes has been expressed in the Litany of the Blessed Virgin; but in

[55] *Ibid.*, 493.
[56] *My Days of Anger*, 366.

211

the litany the metaphors are complex and elaborate and the
symbols are beyond the apprehensions of an ignorant woman.
As in the prayer by Alphonsus Liguori (the prayer on the
Sacred Name of Mary), the name of the Virgin Mother is
repeated and emphasized, and each repetition contributes to
the total effect of the scene; but again, the language of Alphonsus Liguori was textured and beautiful, while Farrell's
was the simple language of his character. First a few sentences describe the church; then Lizz is seen in her devotion;
and by the end, there is created before us a verbal genre painting of an ignorant woman, heavy with child, kneeling before
a shadowy Virgin in the still, empty church:

The church was quiet, deserted, and as yet unlighted. The
altar light hanging in front of the Blessed Sacrament was a small
gleam of red in the shadows. Lizz was alone in the church. She
knelt before the altar of the Blessed Virgin. The statue before her
was half lost in the shadows. The blue robe of Mary seemed less
bright than usual. The color on her cheeks was diminished. There
was not a sound in the church. Lizz raised her hands beseech-
ingly to the statue of Mary. She came to Mary. She placed herself
in Mary's hands. Who, if not the Mother of God, would look
down on the mothers of the poor? Her trust was in Mary. No
matter what happened to her, no matter what befell her family,
Lizz felt that she had Mary. She felt close to the Blessed Virgin,
closer to her than to any human being on earth. She said a Hail
Mary, and then she knelt at the altar of the Blessed Virgin, gazing
up at the statue which was not clearly visible. . . . She gazed
enrapt at the statue of the Blessed Virgin. Mary had gone through
labor and given birth. Mary had seen her Son die on the cross.
Mary Herself had been a suffering mother. She was now the comfort of suffering mothers. . . . She wanted to feel herself close to
Mary. And alone in the church, without another soul in it, without
a sound, she was close to Mary. Everything in her heart, Mary
knew. Mary knew of her worry. Mary knew that she was afraid.

212

She was a child of Mary and she placed her trust in Mary's hands. If she lived or died, she was Mary's child. She beseeched Mary's help and comfort. . . . She prayed. Again she knelt, gazing in rapture with shining eyes at the statue while the candlelight played on it. Lizz got up reluctantly. She blessed herself. She cast a last glance at the statue. She turned and walked slowly down the aisle. She genuflected awkwardly in the rear of the church, blessed herself with holy water and left. She walked home slowly because of the cumbersomeness of her body.[57]

In *Studs Lonigan,* vulgar speech becomes an aesthetic medium for revealing character. Except when Farrell is giving expression in his own terms to Studs' vivid reveries, he adopts Studs' idiom. This Armistice Day scene, for example, is described in Studs' city slang:

The Chicago loop was like a nuthouse on fire. . . .

Studs followed a guy playing a clarinet. A bag of water dropped on the guy's bean. He played on, and a fellow clamped him on the dome with a banana stalk. . . .[58]

[Studs] fought his way into a store in a jam, copped a horn, crushed out, and blew the horn for all he was worth. A funny-looking egg pushed a wheel-barrow along. . . . Studs got behind the guy, blowing his horn, feeling swell . . . hoping that Lucy Scanlan would see him and think that he was pretty much the real stuff.

. . . a girl's dress . . . got torn off, and Studs fought to get a look at her. But she flung herself into the arms of a sailor and yelled for him to hurry up and take her with him where she wouldn't need the damn rags. Jesus, it made him hot.[59]

Farrell dramatizes Studs' character here in two ways— through the use of the restricted point of view and through the use of the vulgar idiom. What does he accomplish by his

[57] *No Star Is Lost,* 596f.
[58] "The Young Manhood," *Studs Lonigan,* 35.
[59] *Ibid.,* 37.

methods? First of all, he has registered a total impression of a scene: he has captured the mood of the action while recording also its details—this is the lowest order of his achievement, the direct communication of dramatic facts. Secondly, as he has conveyed the subjective meaning which the scene holds for Studs, he makes this a moment of character revelation. Studs' reactions to this wild celebration reveal not only a present state of mind but also permanent and unsatisfied inner needs. This is an occasion for Studs to escape from a captive sense of aloneness. He is part of the mob, participating in something, and that alone, for one whose days are empty, upon whose hands time hangs heavily, is all the meaning the day need have. As Studs abandons himself to the spirit of the group, he feels "swell." His feeling is something positive that fills an inner void and gives him an awareness of his own reality. Now he can assert himself and be convinced that he is the "real thing." His excitement and pleasure take on sexual meaning, since inevitably, intense emotion leads him to want the only kind of expression he has learned to give his emotion, sexual expression. Studs' response reveals, then, certain personal limitations: a limitation in his ability to apprehend and interpret events of his time; a need (which rises out of inner uncertainty) to make every occasion serve his vanity; and an inability to find release for pleasurable excitement except in acts of violence or in sex. (This last has devastating consequences. Studs spoils an innocent relationship with Catherine, and thus his chance to rehabilitate himself, because he must have this sexual expression in order to validate, as it were, the reality of their relationship.)

All this becomes known as the scene is re-created from Studs' point of view. Farrell's use of Studs' own idiom yields more than a knowledge of Studs; it gives us the living boy himself. Whereas the restricted point of view made him a registering mind, the reality of his speech establishes him as the young, would-be city "tough." His idiom is the slang of the city streets, reproduced here without pedantic attempts at exact enunciations: "funny-looking egg"; "a nuthouse on fire"; "bean" or "dome" for head; "copped" and "crushed out." The statement of Studs' feelings is not refined simply because he is aware of them only in a crude sort of way: he "feels swell," just as he is also capable of feeling "lousy." The texture of his language, which reveals him conditioned to the stereotyped and hackneyed, unable to discriminate finely among his feelings, has thematic significance; for the lack of qualification within his expression rises out of the failure of his sensibility.

There is a further significance to Studs' language. Like the other boys of his gang, he speaks a tongue of violence and brutality. As Farrell has pointed out in his critical writing, insult, vituperation, and obscenity become a means of asserting one's self-importance when other means have been denied:

The class, group, and racial tensions in American society produce frustration and violence when there is a world or society of isolated and more-or-less estranged individuals who express their natures in a savage personal struggle of vanities. When you do not express your vanity through money and social position, you do it by your fists, by your sexual conquests, and by your language of insult and aggression.[60]

Studs and his gang are haunted by the fear that they are really "slobs." They want an objective proof, something they can see or hear, to convince them of their own manhood. By savage attacks upon Negroes and Jews and much vaunted sexual conquests, they try to objectify their toughness and strength. They turn, too, to a language of violence, not only because it is the only familiar idiom heard about them but

[60] Farrell, "Social Themes in American Realism," *Literature and Morality,* 22 f.

215

also because it satisfies this deep-rooted need for self-assertion. Here, for example, is an excerpt from a casual conversation (the boys are discussing their fathers' vain attempts to make them work by refusing them money):

"My old man tried that once, and I blew. He knows better than to try it again. . . . If he cracks wise about it, he knows I'll just tell him all right fellow, and blow. I can get me a gat and pull a stickup when I need the kale," Reilley said. . . .

"You know, boys, sometimes I think it would be a good idea to go on the bum," Doyle said. . . .

"If you did go, you might meet Davey Cohen. Hell, he's been gone three years, ever since that time we gang-shagged that little bitch Iris, and she told him no soap because he was a hebe," said Red.

"If somebody hasn't croaked that kike by this time, they ought to. I don't like kikes," Weary said.[61]

In vocabulary and sentiment this is gangster talk. Yet these are sons of respectable working people who will grow up to be, not outlaws, but salesmen, local politicians, mechanics, housepainters (those of them, that is, who are not dead before they are thirty). Their manner of speech is a reflection of their values. They speak like the stereotyped tough-guy of the films because the gangster, ruthless and self-dependent, personifies their ideal of virility.

When, in *My Days of Anger,* Farrell introduces a more complex and allusive language, the effect is not an increased richness in texture, but irony. Irony lies in the contrast between the language of the past and the reality of the present. The contrast is made in Danny's attempt to apply the beautiful phrases from past literature to people and situations about him. As he reads the great poets of the past, he tries to carry their words into his daily life by finding new applications for

[61] "The Young Manhood," *Studs Lonigan,* 48.

216

them within his own experience. Thus, by indirection only, the idea of beauty enters into the world of the novel. Beauty does not exist here, but one may be reminded of it and its absence by Danny's literary allusions. Words and phrases suggestive of beauty belong to another culture, and when Danny tries to incorporate them into his speech, they become merely incongruous. Danny knows no woman who incarnates the love lines of the Romantic poets; and when he repeats to himself the sentiment "she walked with beauty," he must follow it with: "and she was a hashslinger."[62] Only a few glimpses of the coarse young waitress are necessary to make the poet's words a mockery. In this manner, as the beauty of the past is set against the crass ugliness of the present, Danny's poetic allusions have ironical effect.

Like the language, the episodic structure of the novel is a means through which Farrell makes his reader know the South Side and its people. The novels are built upon short and self-contained episodes which give way to each other in a cinematic movement. While scenes shift and replace each other rapidly as in a motion picture, the action within each scene is fully dramatized. This episodic structure extends the scope of the ecological novel as each small unit allows Farrell to explore an aspect of the neighborhood, from the stuffy interiors (the crowded living rooms, kitchens, basement clubrooms, churches, or dance hall) to the streets, alleys, ball parks, or trash-lots. Thus, the physical locales, which Dreiser had described in expository passages and Dos Passos had recaptured in fleeting sense impressions, are dramatized in the short episode. Whatever contrasts are to be found in the South Side, contrasts, for example, between the O'Flaherty apartment and the O'Neill home, are noted through the detail in the episode. And since the small unit is perfectly suited to contain the small and ordinary activities of daily life, the episodic structure

[62] *My Days of Anger,* 9.

217

allows a minute study of manners. Moreover, the juxtaposition of episodes reveals the irony of situations. Events commonplace enough in themselves take on a new and ironical meaning when placed alongside each other. The address of the priest to his graduation class, for example, becomes charged with irony because what he says about the fine homes and splendid parents of the children must be contrasted with the drunkenness and squabbling revealed in the previous episodes.

Although Farrell stands criticized for diffuseness, his use of the episode shows an ability to compress material and make a single episode not only a dramatic integer but also a form of social commentary. Incidents which on first glance seem merely trivial, even superfluous, prove usually to be significant as a revelation of individual character, as well as of a total way of life. Climactic scenes, such as the New Year's Eve party in *Studs Lonigan,* dramatically realize tendencies within the characters which had already been revealed in slighter episodes. Weary Reilley's brutal behavior has been adumbrated in the early scenes of *Studs Lonigan,* scenes which often seemed to record merely meaningless and repetitious conversations and acts. Their meaning, though, was implicatory; for, as they showed these boys full of energies for which they could find no outlet, they foreshadowed the future. It was perhaps inevitable that the gang's unused vitality and frustration should burst out in this orgiastic party and result in destruction. The meaning of most of the episodes in Studs' life is his early death. This very same party has consequences he can never escape: pneumonia, the weakening of his system, angina, and finally, death.

If we should turn to a lesser character, Jim O'Neill, we find again that every episode in his life is also a commentary upon it. His Sunday mornings at home, when he tries to clean his house of garbage, papers, dirty dishes, and bedbugs, are symbolic of the whole pattern of his life. He has the will; he works and tries; but he cannot overcome or escape the effects of his poverty. His child dies because the doctor will not come to the poor. And even when he earns more money, the house he lives in is still dirty; for his wife can never rise above the slovenly habits of a lifetime. Finally, the futility of his struggle is revealed in his illness: the reward for a lifetime of work is paralysis and death. It is only Danny who can interpret the meaning of the small and the cumulative incidents in his father's life. At first Danny thought that he would follow his father's example and work hard to be a success; but when he realizes that his own struggle would be as futile as his father's endless struggle against dust and bedbugs, he sets out to find a different way of life.

The episodes of Lizz at church, quoted above, is another example of Farrell's ability to compress meaning within a small aesthetic unit. This scene is, first of all, a dramatic realization of Lizz's trust in Mary. Here is an immediate sense of what her feeling is, not reported but created before us. Here, too, is the reason for her devotion; as we are made to see Mary as she does, we realize why Mary is the only one who can give her the comfort she needs. Lizz conceives of Mary only in terms of her own human sufferings and trials. Since Mary has suffered through poverty and motherhood, She can sympathize with Lizz and protect her. Thematically, the episode is very significant; it shows how in a world where people are essentially alone, one character has escaped from her solitude and united herself with some higher source of strength and virtue. But all that Lizz finds in her love for Mary is negated in the world about her, and even her trust in the Virgin contributes to the confusion about her. Her religion shuts her in, away from the rest of her family: she can solace herself for the dirt and poverty she lives in by placing a candle on the altar, but her children are left to play in the garbage on the floor. Her actions raise complicated questions, for as

219

we see what consolation religion offers her we sympathize with her piety. But as we see in what condition her children are left as she takes Jim's hard-earned pennies to buy candles instead of food we must condemn such feelings. This single episode bears an organic relationship to the rest of the action in the Danny O'Neill novels and also to the fundamental themes of man's aloneness and spiritual impoverishment in the modern city.

Because the episodes re-create the minute activities of the day, the novel as a whole is slowly paced. For long spans, little seems to be happening. One day is like the next. Every morning Margaret O'Flaherty is back at her cash register at the hotel; Jim O'Neill is at the Express company; Al is selling shoes—and the young, adventurous boys like Studs are wondering what to do with themselves. Almost always, the characters' attempts to break out of their monotonous routine end disastrously. Since they do not know how to find excitement and self-expression except in drink, violence, or sex, an acceleration in pace is significant of some wild and orgiastic action. Except for the climactic moments of raving and drunkenness or the dramatic fits of depression and self-pity, Margaret's years, for instance, are a dull pattern of routine work at the hotel and of cooking and cleaning at home. Like all of Farrell's characters, she is victimized by the slow passage of time which brings no reward for her labors, but inevitable punishment for her sins. Because the novel is paced slowly, the changes in the characters are sometimes almost imperceptible; but suddenly, when one sees Margaret sink into middle-age, Studs collapse in the street, or Jim O'Neill fall into a paralytic stupor, one realizes with a shock how much they have changed under the pressures of work, boredom, and time. Then one realizes, too, that the pace has thematic significance, for it is by the slow seeping away of strength and courage and hope, by the emptiness of time, that these people are destroyed.

In the novels that followed the Danny O'Neill tetralogy, *Ellen Rogers, Bernard Clare,* and *The Road Between,* Farrell's techniques were much less effective; for in these works he was dealing with settings and people on a different level from those which his techniques had been developed to exploit. He could reveal the inner life and the social implications of 'dramatic' characters like Studs or 'background' characters like Lizz O'Neill and Mother O'Flaherty; but he was inadept at handling a thoughtful 'reflective' character like Bernard Carr. As soon as he removed himself from the lower middle-class milieu and tried to re-create the world of Ellen Rogers or to reveal a way of life in New York, his writing grew weaker. He lacked that profound understanding of the manners of these worlds that he had of the Chicago neighborhood to which his novels have given lasting life.

The greater richness of *The Road Between* as compared to *Bernard Clare* can be explained largely by the fact that half its scenes are laid in the South Side. The most vivid characters are not the young intellectuals of New York but the commonplace family group in Chicago. Farrell was better able to exploit a family squabble in the living room than a mob-action in Union Square; and the difference in his success in creating the milieu of the two cities reveals how essentially he was a novelist of manners. He wrote at his best when he wrote as the insider, and all the years he had spent in New York as a struggling author could not make him know the city in the way he knew his South Side. Within *The Road Between* there is a significant difference in the way the backgrounds of the two cities are projected. When the scene was laid in Chicago, the homes and streets were created; and as in the earlier novels, they became an integral part of a dramatic action. The New York background, however, is summarized and interpreted in expository passages. The fact that Bernard is analyzing the scene in his own mind does not

221

make it dramatic; it is still simply an analysis, even though it is introduced as Bernard's impression. As Bernard is "crystallizing his impression of New York,"[63] we get a rather crude description of the most obvious elements of an urban scene, a description in terms of generalities and formally separated from the action as observation. Through such general and commonplace descriptions, the city can never emerge as immediately as do the streets of Chicago in the earlier novels.

In *Bernard Clare,* the episodic structure used before so strategically becomes at times almost emptied of significance. Farrell often merely duplicated an incident, as though he no longer had the power to transform it into an aesthetic entity. When he records Bernard's "nine hours a day behind a counter,"[64] for example, he puts an absolute minimum into each episodic unit. He simply transcribes incidents in Bernard's day; and though he gives an immediate sense of the tedium and the meaninglessness of Bernard's work, he reduces the episode to such an impossible minimum that the tedium we experience is, unfortunately, our own. Here, then, is the *reductio ad absurdum* of the episodic structure:

V

"Prince Albert," a customer said.
Bernard found the can, took the money, rang up the sale.

VI

"Two Chesterfields."
Bernard made the sale.

VII

"Luckies."
"Thank you," Bernard said, making the sale.

[63] *The Road Between,* 217.
[64] *Bernard Clare,* 53.

VIII

"Can I have two nickels, please?"

Bernard took her dime, rang a no sale, graciously handed her two nickels.[65]

In a review of *Bernard Clare,* Matthiessen stated that Bernard was a "poor register."[66] Perhaps it would be more accurate to say that Farrell simply was not equipped to handle a register like this young, serious-minded writer. His most successful characters had always been children, adolescents, and simple, emotional, unthinking people. When he was faced with a presumably sensitive and intellectual adult, he could deal neither with his ideas nor with his processes of thought. Thus, in *The Road Between,* the thought process is frequently expressed as a series of questions that Bernard poses to himself. Too often, however, these unanswered questions sound like suggested topics for a philosophical inquiry; they touch upon subjects and drop them abruptly, but they do not give a real sense of a character involved in thought. For example, Farrell touches only the very surface of Bernard's mind with a technique of self-questioning such as this:

But what if he did become a success? [Bernard thinks] He was afraid of success. . . . If he became somebody with money, would he change? Would he become another one of these American writers who was a mere flash in the pan, starting in a blaze of promise and then growing fatuous and selling out?

Tapping his bare foot on the piece of oilcloth under him, he resolved that he would never sell out.[67]

Another example suggests that Farrell is trying to show Bernard's mind probing fundamental questions; but again

[65] *Ibid.,* 57.

[66] F. O. Matthiessen, Review of *Bernard Clare, New York Times Book Review,* May 12, 1946, 1.

[67] *The Road Between,* 10.

the questions themselves give us only a general suggestion of what Bernard is like as a personality:

He wanted to tell her that he was lonely, too, intensely lonely. Locked out of the world and trying to touch it with his heart and his mind.... Was he more lonely than she? Was there a common loneliness in all human relationships, and did this exist regardless of how much men and women loved one another? ... And this scene in his own life, was it not a variation of scenes he would describe, a variation of scenes his mother and father had experienced?[68]

If we compare this with any of the passages quoted above from the earlier novels, we can see how seriously Farrell fails here to create his character. The language is flat, the ideas commonplace, and the exploration of the ideas most superficial. Yet, we cannot say, as we did with Studs, that the quality of the language expresses and creates the character's sensibility; for here the essential failure lies not with Bernard (we understood that he is supposed to have a sensitive and perceptive mind) but with Farrell himself. He is often reduced to such unsatisfying, brief glimpses into the mind of his hero as this:

[Bernard] was thinking of values, wondering what was really right and wrong, and telling himself that there was really no solving of the personal problems of human relationships. And yet, did people have to be so ugly to one another? What had made his father so ugly?
They all lapsed into moody silence.[69]

These persistent questions serve as a formal device for revealing Bernard's inner uncertainty. Even though he has determined his purpose in life, he still suffers from doubts

[68] *Ibid.*, 245. [69] *Ibid.*, 313.

about himself. His are the uncertainties and despairs peculiar to the young creative artist who has not yet proved his ability. To indicate that a person is unsure of himself by a direct recording of the questions he constantly asks himself is, however, one of the least subtle or dramatic methods of creating a state of mind. Farrell is simply making Bernard verbalize his doubts. Thus, Bernard wonders if he is doing the right thing by taking leave from his job in order to finish his novel:

But did he have the right to take this chance? The New Era wouldn't hold his place open for so many weeks. . . . Wasn't he selfish? Had he the right to risk Elizabeth and their unborn child to his ambition? But wasn't he risking the very justification of his own life also? He began to doubt his decision, but he knew the decision had been made.[70]

The characters in the earlier novels, who were incapable of articulating so clearly their inner uncertainties, were revealed through other and more successful methods. In *Studs Lonigan,* the inner state of mind is revealed as revery. Unlike Bernard, Studs, who does not have a clear insight into the problems troubling him, cannot verbalize his insecurities. But he can create a dynamic picture of himself as he would like to be; and his daydreams are a dramatic exploration of the inner man. These daydreams become most elaborate and most removed from reality at times when Studs is experiencing a profound sense of helplessness and frustration. He sees himself as 'Dough-boy Lonigan' facing solitary death with bravado; as 'Lonewolf Lonigan,' man against society; or (now he is an adult remembering past dreams of strength) as 'the old Studs Lonigan,' sneering at a world which has hurt him but which he will smash back at and destroy. There is a vital difference in the kind of uncertainty Bernard and Studs feel. Bernard knows his objective, but he has yet to prove to him-

[70] *Ibid.,* 231.

225

self that he can find the effective means to his goal. Studs, on the other hand, has never clearly visualized his purpose in life. As his daydreams reveal, he can see only an exaggerated and distorted picture of some make-believe person from the movies; but this is an impossible person. Who he is and of what he is capable he does not know; therefore, his uncertainty is more devastating than Bernard's. He is uncertain of his own reality. He knows that there is a tremendous discrepancy between his imagined self and his real self; yet the image appeals to him even though he realizes that it shows him a false picture of himself.

The closing scenes of Section One of "Judgment Day" are among the most powerful in Farrell's novels because they reveal this tension between the real and the imagined self as a vital and wrenching human experience. Here are no stilted questions to testify to an inner uncertainty but the thing itself —the human emotions moving with their own logic through frustration and bewilderment to violent defiance. Here are rendered in an immediate way the two levels of reality which define in their meeting point the true Studs Lonigan, the Studs who has become enraged at the world and has created out of his rage an image of himself as the destroyer, and the Studs from whose young body the strength is ebbing. An inchoate, struggling, and doomed young man, Studs had lived always in a kind of darkness, moving aimlessly towards a destiny he could not see or command. These last compelling scenes show him sinking into a final void perhaps no more terrible than that in which he had lived all his life. The immediacy with which Studs emerges in these scenes reveals the strongest elements in Farrell's art—his penetration of the common urban mind, his ability to give literary importance to everyday people who in real life may be dull, prosaic, and of narrow vision, and his deep moral concern over the spiritual destiny of modern man that enables him to make urban manners an implicit condemnation of the destructive elements in urban life.[71]

[71] As Farrell returns to the familiar material of South Side Chicago in his latest novel, *The Face of Time* (New York, Vanguard Press, 1953), he achieves once again an intimate and sympathetic ecological study of urban childhood and of the simple working folk who are victimized by time. The story of Tom O'Flaherty's "transfiguration" by time, revealed on the one hand as age brings him illness and lingering death, and on the other as memories of his young manhood set the contrast between past and present, is a moving life-history of the Irish immigrant in America. But it is more than an individual tale, for as it is an antecedent enactment of the tragedy of Jim O'Neill (particularly as seen in *Father and Son*), it becomes a prototype of the pattern of struggle and defeat of the laboring man. The sympathy that exists between Tom O'Flaherty and his son-in-law Jim is a tacit recognition of the fate they have in common. The gradual decline of Louise O'Flaherty into the apathetic stages of consumption fortifies the theme of sickness and death as the ironic consequence of poverty and ignorance in the past. Although *The Face of Time* adds little to our essential knowledge of South Side Chicago, it creates these two new characters who are in themselves vivid and pathetic, and who become, moreover, part of Danny O'Neill's education as he witnesses the waste of young life and the suffering of age in this bewildering and destructive world of his childhood.

CHAPTER 7

RECENT TRENDS:

1943-1953

The Novel of Sentiment and the Novel of Violence

THE forty-three years between Dreiser's first novel, *Sister Carrie,* and *My Days of Anger* in Farrell's Danny O'Neill series constitute a literary period in the development of twentieth-century city fiction. In that period the modern city novel emerged and developed as a genre with characteristic themes, materials, and modes of expression, and with a clearly articulated purpose. City fiction of the last decade derives from and continues the tradition of this genre. It also marks a new stage in its development—not only because it is derivative but also because in further developing elements implicit in the form, it has given the city novel a new emphasis upon either violence or sentiment.

The essence of violence and sentiment as they function in the city novel is contained in two complementary images— that of Carrie Meeber, young, naïve, and helpless, stepping off a train into the Chicago of her dreams, and that of Danny O'Neill walking out defiantly on the Chicago of his days of anger. In her helpless capitulation to the city, Carrie is the distant prototype of the "hero" of the current novel of violence, the man overpowered and victimized by the city.

Carrie's own victimization is not a violent one, but nevertheless it is real: it is implicit in the constant evasion of her deepest desires for beauty and self-fulfillment. From Carrie, the lineage of urban victims descends not only through Dreiser's other victims (from Jennie through Clyde to Steward Barnes) but also through the confused and wounded Jimmy Herf (as well as all the futile people of *Manhattan Transfer*) to the doomed Studs Lonigan. It is with these victims of city life that the protagonist of the novel of violence of the forties and early fifties has his strongest affinitive ties.

Young Danny O'Neill, however, belongs to a different strain of fictional character. Like the urban victim, he too is helplessly subjected to a city's mortal influences; but as he learns to recognize these as part of a dead and yet virulently destructive world, he begins to free himself from them. Out of his daily experiences of South Side Chicago, Danny moves to maturity and social awareness; and the anger that grows with his awareness immunizes him against the city's further effects. This anger becomes also an aggressive force, for it commits him to the struggle for social change. The difference between Carrie, the victim, and Danny, the saved, is that she remains passive and responsive, while he becomes active and antagonistic. She is socially unconscious and therefore defenseless; his consciousness is his weapon. Her action is willless and negative: it is to submit. His is deliberate—to commit himself as artist and man to his social responsibility; and it is this commitment that leads to his final repudiation of the city.

But Danny's repudiation marks the end, rather than the beginning, of an action, just as it also marks the end of a period in the development of city fiction. His repudiation brings to an end his helpless submission to Chicago, but the new action in which his deliberate commitments should involve him remains yet unrealized. It is significant that Bernard Carr, the socially conscious writer who carries out Danny's

229

program, is a rather colorless and inept hero, and—even more important—that the militant artist as hero does not figure at all in city fiction of the last decade. In his sense of social responsibility, Danny contrasts with the heroes of current novels of violence and of sentiment, as well as with the earlier urban protagonist like Carrie. The commitment he finally makes characterizes him as a character of the thirties, with clear-cut affinities to the heroes of the proletarian novel of that decade. The city novel of the forties and early fifties has not picked up the theme of social awareness as it has the theme of urban victimization.

Yet in his achievement of maturity, Danny suggests a pattern of characterization in the novel of sentiment. The novel of sentiment, like the Danny O'Neill novels, traces against a background of urban disorder the individual's growth to certainty and self-possession. The theme of the novel of sentiment is aptly summarized in the title of Betty Smith's second novel, *Tomorrow Will Be Better.* The protagonist of the novel of sentiment, having moved through difficulties and confusions, arrives finally at an optimistic belief in his future. Significantly, however, the factor that will make for a better tomorrow is not, as it was in *My Days of Anger,* the social awareness that promises to lead to reform; it is the factor of personal adjustment involved in an individual process of growth to maturity. Growing up, in the novels of sentiment, implies hope and self-possession: one comes to feel, despite whatever experiences one has had, that he can cope with his fate, that having been lost he is now somehow miraculously found. While in Farrell's novels the daily content of experience produced the final resolution (just as Studs' experiences doomed him, Danny's motivated him to his social and aesthetic commitments), in the tomorrow-will-be-better novels, the daily experiences seem somehow discontinuous with the ultimate hopeful resolution. How, for example, can Margy

230

Shannon's experiences in *Tomorrow Will Be Better*—her childhood in Brooklyn's slums, her unsatisfactory relationship with a frustrated and dominating mother, her disillusioning marriage with a potential homosexual, and finally, the loss of her baby—be reconciled with the abrupt realization on which the book ends that "she would never be lost again"?[1] The consequences of experience seem here, as in other novels of sentiment, wonderfully avoided, while quick and unexpected reversals either in fortune or in attitude produce a happy ending. Paradoxically, the strength of these novels lies in the vivid portrayal of the destructive elements of city life; yet the tomorrow-will-be-better conclusion comes to invalidate this portrayal as the action of the city fails to have meaning in terms of the character's response. Whatever moral victory the protagonist seems to achieve in his hopeful reconciliation to life is so facile that it can hardly be considered a victory. To pass unmoved through experiences, to arrive at affirmations when one has not been deeply affected by the continual stream of daily life, is hardly an achievement of moral growth. Moreover, there is no legitimate warrant for arousing the reader's sentiments of pity, sympathy, and sometimes even horror, since the ugliness of the protagonist's environment and experience has left upon him no significant effect.

If the theme of the novel of sentiment may be summarized in the phrase "tomorrow will be better," that of the novel of violence may be summarized as "tomorrow will be worse." For the characters of the novel of violence there is no escape from the consequences of a chaotic and destructive way of life. Nick Romano, Frankie Machine and his wife Sophie, young Chico and his friend Angel, Boxie Fields—they are like Clyde Griffiths and Studs Lonigan the city's victims, doomed by everyday acts of conformity to the ways of their world. And

[1] Betty Smith, *Tomorrow Will Be Better* (New York, Harper and Brothers, 1948), 274.

their world is the city's back alley, slum, or Skid Row. Characteristically, the novel of violence explores a level of society
which had usually been dealt with in twentieth-century fiction
in a cursory manner, when it had been dealt with at all. Drei-
seir's Hurstwood had sunk to Skid Row, but Dreiser gave only
fleeting glimpses of these lower depths; and while George
Webber prowled the back alleys of Brooklyn at midnight,
Wolfe too recorded only surface horrors. The novel of violence moves into this back alley world to explore its manners,
speech, atmosphere, and tensions. The epigraph to Willard
Motley's novel *Knock on Any Door* summarizes this interest
in the city's lower depths, and it serves as a fitting epigraph
to the genre of the novel of violence: "... the city lies in splendor and squalor. There are many doors to the city. Many
things hide behind the many doors. More lives than one are
lived in the city, more deaths than one are met within the
city's gate. . . . The people come and go, the visitors. They
see the front yard. But what of the city's backyard, and the
alley? Who knows the lives and minds of the people who
live in the alley?"[2]

The unifying element in the social world of the novel of
violence is disorder. All normal social ties have been severed.
The family has fallen apart: the children are alienated from
their parents and from each other; the marriages of the young
people fail in the most sordid and dismal ways. The failure
of personal love is part of a more fundamental failure, the
failure in the basic drive to life, particularly as it is manifested in the sex impulse. In Dreiser, sex had been a positive
and forceful motive for action; in Farrell it was related to
wider needs—to Studs' adolescent need for romantic love,
Margaret O'Flaherty's need for motherhood, or Jim O'Neill's
healthy male need for woman. But in this new fiction, sexual

[2] Willard Motley, *Knock on Any Door* (New York, D. Appleton-
Century, 1947), n.p.

232

incapacity is a significant symptom of personal defeat. The life force has been drained out of the inhabitants of the city's back alley, so that they lack the desire for sexual pleasure and for propagation. They are a suicidal people, killing themselves with dissipations.

The drive towards death is revealed in their deliberate efforts to escape from reality. In their need to forget gnawing guilts and inadequacies, they seek the stupefaction of whiskey, the momentary exhilarations of brutality, or the ecstasy and violet sleep of drugs. The need to escape from consciousness is not, however, a merely personal matter. It is integrally related to the larger failure within the social environment, just as Carrie's or Clyde's desire for money and fashion is related to the basic materialism of the urban world. The novel of violence is premised upon the belief in the social causations of crime and personal disorder. The forces of the external world are as irresistible as they were in Dreiser's novels; but they have become more terrible and destructive, more of a nightmare reality. And they are so pervasive that even the avenues of temporary escape, drink and fornication, which functioned, for example, in *Manhattan Transfer,* cannot bring a deep enough forgetfulness. The need to lose one's self is always immediate and pressing—and the door to the back room of the dope peddler leads to annihilation. Thus, drug addiction is the characteristic malady in the novel of violence.

Crime, murder, and suicide are also integral to the plot. As soon as the pattern of personal dissolution has been firmly established, the basic pattern of action becomes that of the chase. For instance, in *Knock on Any Door* or in *The Man With the Golden Arm,* first the protagonist takes the irretraceable steps towards crime and self-destruction, and then the police undertake the chase that is to bring Nick to the electric chair and Frankie to suicide. The process of disintegration is recorded with the nicety of detail, the objectivity, and the accuracy that characterize Dreiser's descriptions. Above all, there is the same fidelity to the facts of real life—and the justification for these haunting and repulsive pictures of human defeat and degradation must be the realist's justification: that he is merely telling us a truth about the life of our times.

Both the novel of sentiment and the novel of violence are ecological studies of city life; that is, like Farrell's novels, they re-create the manners and tensions of a confined social world that exists as a unit within the city. They present neither the broad contrasts between rich and poor, between surface glamour and underlying destructiveness, of Dreiser's portrait novels, nor the sweeping panoramas of place and time of Dos Passos' synoptic novels. Their tendency is to limit—to select a small, distinctive area with ethnic, religious, or social unity —and to concentrate—to explore manners and typifying speech and thought patterns in greatest detail. Broad generalizations about city life may be implicit in these novels (in a novel like *Knock on Any Door* they are also made very directly), but the literary and sociological interests are primarily in the exploitation of manners, rather than in the disclosure of underlying truths.

Perhaps one reason for the popularity of the ecological form is that the characteristic theme of the portrait novel—the naïve country boy's seduction by the city—has lost the historical immediacy it had in Dreiser's time. The early century saw the mass exodus from the farm to the city, and the story of youth's failure, as well as his extraordinary success, in the glamorous urban centers had current appeal. Today, the assumption of naïvety, upon which this novel of discovery is based, cannot readily be accepted. The country boy has developed a more sophisticated and realistic attitude towards the big town. He is no longer so completely isolated from it: he knows it, if not immediately then at least vicariously, through the movies, radio, and even through the urban novel.

234

That there is, as Wolfe believed, something perennial about the theme of the country youth's quest in the city may be true. The novel *Only An Inch From Glory* by Albert Halper shows that interest in the theme is still current—and significantly, the novel follows the now conventional pattern of antagonism between the aspirant and the city. It is New York that destroys Dorothy Lynch, the small-town girl who comes to the city to seek fortune and personal freedom. Thus, her father's conclusion is the typical and conventional one: " 'My daughter,' he said, . . . 'was the victim of a big city.' "[3] But this is a single novel, and the trend has been away from the portrait study towards a form which allows for the presentation of the more modern circumstances of city life, as well as for the creation of a larger social framework.

The synoptic novel, on the other hand, which offers the novelist a structure upon which to create a broad social world, has also found few, if any, recent exponents. Outside of city fiction, Dos Passos' form for *U.S.A.* has been modified to new material to serve Norman Mailer in *The Naked and the Dead;* and outside of America, it has been adapted by Jean-Paul Sartre in his novels of postwar Paris. The synoptic form places extremely heavy demands upon the novelist—upon his knowledge of the many-faceted city, as well as upon his ability to unify and interpret a complex way of life. Dos Passos' equipment was singular: he had this extensive knowledge and the social viewpoint which organized it into a coherent whole. Yet he no longer finds tenable the Spenglerian and Marxian theses which sustained and unified his novels through *U.S.A.;* nor can the younger writers turn to these interpretations of our times for a unifying framework within which to encompass a synoptic view of the modern city in its varieties and complexities. Out of the forties has come such an isolated

[3] Albert Halper, *Only an Inch From Glory* (New York, Harper and Brothers), 272.

novel as Marcia Davenport's *East Side, West Side,* which has, as the title implies, synoptic intentions; but this is a piece of slick, commercial writing (already made into a Hollywood movie) and hardly significant to current trends.

The ecological structure has a peculiar appropriateness both to the present urban situation and to the background and talents of the recent city novelists. Neighborhoods have grown more sharply defined, so that while particular areas have been invaded by new groups and so changed, the fact of ecological grouping is firmly established. Moreover, the newer writers like Willard Motley, Nelson Algren, Hal Ellson, and Leonard Bishop are native to the city, and they knew their neighborhoods with the same intimacy and insight that went into Michael Gold's knowledge of East Side New York or Meyer Levin's or Farrell's knowledge of Chicago. Also, the form that can contain and give dramatic meaning to this kind of knowledge has reached a full development, chiefly in Farrell—and Farrell is imitable. His use of an episodic structure, of alternating point-of-view characters, and of urban speech patterns as indications of manners, his adaptation of a case history technique with its objectivity and assumption of sociological conditioning, his method of exploring urban institutions and of incorporating locale into consciousness—all these can be, and to a remarkable extent have been, taken over by later novelists. Even specific incidents have been imitated. Moreover, Farrell gives the contemporary city writer the fullest and most explicit statement of literary justification. His prefaces and critical writings are a rationale for the novel of sentiment in its exploration of the prosaically commonplace aspects of city life and for the novel of violence in its exploration of the degradation and brutalities hidden in the back alleys of the city slums.

"Tomorrow Will Be Better"

THE MOST colorful of the novels of sentiment is Betty Smith's slick best-seller *A Tree Grows in Brooklyn*. It is the story of survival in the slums; and the tree, unwatched and uncared for, growing out of cement or cellar grates, is the symbol of survival. Just as "nothing could destroy it,"[4] nothing can destroy the children of Brooklyn's slums, Francie Nolan (or Margy Shannon in *Tomorrow Will Be Better*)—not poverty and hunger, not the bleakness of Brooklyn's cold-water flats, not the disappointments of young love. Both *A Tree Grows in Brooklyn* and *Tomorrow Will Be Better* thus negate, or perhaps simply ignore, the premise traditional to slum fiction (which can be found even in such early fiction as Jacob Riis' "Skippy of Scrabble Alley" and Stephen Crane's *Maggie*)—that is, that the slum destroys its children. This is, of course, the premise in the novels of violence contemporary with Betty Smith's work, such as *Knock on Any Door* and *The Golden Spike*. In *A Tree Grows in Brooklyn,* Francie survives cold and hunger, the brutalities in her school, the attack of a sexual pervert, the immediate squalor of her home; in *Tomorrow Will Be Better,* Margy survives her mother's nagging, the insufficiencies in her marriage to a young man who cannot give normal love, and the death of her baby. Both girls face the future with the belief that "tomorrow will be better." And the materials of these novels are so arranged that the belief may be justified.

The imagination of childhood—and the ignorance of childhood—can color and heighten the facts of the outside world: they can make a shabby public library a place as awesome as a church, a pink and white peppermint as delectable as the most expensive sweet, and an afternoon on a fire escape

---

[4] Betty Smith, *A Tree Grows in Brooklyn* (New York, Harper and Brothers, 1943), 420.

237

that overlooks a dirty, noisy street as adventuresome as a romance. What is simple, sordid, or merely the necessity of poverty, can be converted by the child's imagination into a fairy tale; and the memories of childhood can thus later become sweet and romantic instead of bitter. So childhood in Williamsburg, Brooklyn, in the early 1900's, becomes in Betty Smith's novel a romance, in a way that childhood in Farrell's Chicago had never been. When Francie looks back at her past, now that she is sixteen and about to leave Brooklyn, she sees that "Brooklyn was a dream. . . . It was all dream stuff."[5] And the reason it could be a dream was not only that the realities were always colored by the imagination of childhood but also that the realities never really left any indelible mark. All that the children went through, the strain and uncertainties of their daily lives, was like a soft smoke through which they safely walked and out of which they moved towards light. Consequently, Francie grows up to be, as her mother realizes, ". . . a girl who had come face to face with some of the evil of the world and most of its hardships, and yet had remained curiously untouched."[6] She comes into young womanhood innocent, sweet, a little saddened by a brief romantic failure, but strong and hopeful. If one can remain thus "curiously untouched" by the insistent and daily pressures of poverty and struggle, then one's past can seem indeed a romance of the city slums.

Perhaps the story of childhood would not turn into this romance if it did not have its happy ending. The ending of *A Tree Grows in Brooklyn,* like that of *Tomorrow Will Be Better,* introduces a rather well-to-do *deus ex machina.* Michael McShane, who has waited years for Katie, offers her security and her daughter a chance to go to the university. Mr. Prentiss, Margy's boss, is someone Margie can only vaguely hope to marry, but with a hope that is not entirely unfounded,

[5] *Ibid.,* 407   [6] *Ibid.,* 397.

in spite of immediate obstacles. (What might have happened, one wonders, to young Studs Lonigan if some kindly magician had entered into his life at a crucial moment and offered him the warmth and guidance that his narrow, incapacitated parents could not supply?) So here the young people are saved by the almost miraculous appearance of a savior; and the past can become mellow and sweet because there is a way to escape from it. The future shines bright for the youngest children: indeed, the baby is the living symbol of the belief that tomorrow will be better. Francie's baby sister Laurie will never suffer hunger, cold, and poverty: " 'She'll never have the hard times we had . . . ,' " says Francie to her brother; and he replies, " 'No. And she'll never have the fun we had, either.' " Francie's comment, as she considers all her little sister will miss is, " 'Poor Laurie.' "[7] In *Tomorrow Will Be Better,* the baby represents Margy's belief in the future. " 'I needed it [she says] to prove something; to prove that this could be a good world.' "[8] Her baby dies, but its death marks the end of Margy's sterile marriage, and so helps to liberate her from the past and move her towards a future with new babies and Mr. Prentiss.

A Tree Grows in Brooklyn softens and sentimentalizes the life it presents; yet it is the picture of this life that gives it literary validity as well as its popular appeal. Almost no city novel of the last decade re-creates the everyday details of a pattern of life with such wealth. We know exactly what the Nolans eat, the varieties of foods they make from stale bread, and how Francie gets the bread from the factory and a free soupbone from the butcher; we know how she takes a "pick" at the corner candy store; how she has to ask to leave the room at school; how the families behave on the yearly outing given by Tammany Hall; how the children celebrate Thanksgiving

[7] *Ibid.,* 404.
[8] *Tomorrow Will Be Better,* 250.

Day with masks and how they play "potsie" on the street. These details merge into a colorful genre painting upon which the plot, with its story of final success, seems almost an imposition—for it is the picture, and not the successive chain of action, that is important. And it is the child's romanticized view of her everyday adventure, whether she is buying a Jewish pickle in the delicatessen or sitting on the fire escape, that gives the picture its charm.

Humor adds to the effect of this charm. In *Tomorrow Will Be Better,* Miss Smith has apparently attempted a more serious approach and a more realistic psychology, with the result that the novel does not have humorous characters such as those who brighten her first novel. Humor lies in the situation of Uncle Willie, who drove a horse that hated him but fell in love with his wife, and in the antics of Aunt Sissy, who is generous, scandalously promiscuous, and deeply maternal. This play upon humor makes *A Tree Grows in Brooklyn* not far removed from the comic novels of city life which recreate with warmth and affection the foibles and plights of the city's idiosyncratic folk; for example, the comic novels of Jewish life, Ethel Rosenberg's *Go Fight City Hall* and Arthur Kober's novels about Bella from the Bronx. Humor need not deny a novel a basic seriousness; in Betty Smith's work it is not the humor but the underlying sentimentality which gives the novel its quality of make-believe, despite the obvious reality of many of its details. As Francie had said, this is a dreamworld; many of its details are peculiar and sharp, as they might be in a dream, but they leave no effect. The failure to project a serious concern over this life of struggle and poverty makes these novels slick accounts of city life, rather than important commentaries. Out of the slums comes unaccountable good with an ease that suggests that the author has not evaluated with any moral concern the conditions of life which she so colorfully portrays. The emphasis is indeed upon color, local color, and not upon the price man pays for what may indeed be colorful (the word need not signify moral value) aspects of a way of life which offers as its daily experience a contest with hunger, ignorance, and ugliness.

The novels of Jewish life that have come out of the forties lack the comprehensive scope of Meyer Levin's *The Old Bunch,* but within a limited framework they present realistic situations and reach to certain basic problems of the Jewish family in America. One of the basic problems, presented with varying degrees of emphasis in such novels as *The Sidewalks Are Free, My Son, the Lawyer, Asphalt and Desire,* and *East River,* concerns the conflict between the ideals of the old world and those of a new, aggressive, and materialistic society. This conflict is presented almost conventionally in the opposition between the immigrant parents: the father, learned in Hebrew lore, intellectual, and unaggressive, represents an old way of life; the mother, frustrated at her poverty, ambitious, driving, avid for a share in the wealth of America, reflects the values of the new world.

In *The Sidewalks Are Free,* the young boy Hershy Melov is caught between the antithetical drives of his parents, and his first step towards maturity is the crystallization of his sympathies with his father. David Melov had been a Talmudic student in the old country; here in America, he earns his living as a cabinet-maker. Out of the creative element in his work he draws an inner contentment which he values far above money. But his wife wants to move to a better neighborhood, have finer clothes and better furniture, and keep up with socially higher neighbors: she has caught the American disease of the desire for things. When David receives $10,000 as insurance money from his brother's death, his wife sees the way open to the fulfillment of her desires, and she nags him into investing the money in a laundry business. This money, coming from death, takes on a symbolically ominous mean-

241

ing. It brings change and destruction, for once David has bought his laundry, he is enslaved to the machine. He loses the inner fulfillment his craft had given him, his peace of mind, his health, his leisure, his relationship to his son, and he almost loses his life. The plot of the novel, built upon the chain of events that follow the inheritance, is a simple working out of the theme that money is the root of evil. Yet for all its simplicity of theme and plot, the novel presents a complex pattern of conflicting values: the ideal of inner content against the ideal of material accumulation; the value of craftsmanship and joy in labor against the sterility of the machine; age-old wisdom, as written in the Talmud, against the cheap smartness of the modern go-getter.

The meaning of this conflict is reflected in the responses of young Hershy Melov. He sees the invidious and corrupting influence of money; and inadvertently, he becomes the instrument to free his father from its terrible hold. When he falls asleep over the controls of the laundry machine, he causes an explosion that destroys in one devastating action all that the $10,000 had bought and achieved. The explosion becomes a moment of liberation, for though the family has lost its capital resources, it has gained the opportunity to make a new life for itself, this time according to David's ideals. The novel ends with an affirmation of life, not only as David recovers from pneumonia (the result of long hours, unhealthy conditions of work, and a loss of the will to live) but also as the new baby is born, and as Hershy has the sense of his own rebirth.

The theme of conflicting values is interrelated with the theme of growing up. Hershy goes through certain experiences which have recurred so often in novels of city childhood that they may be considered literary conventions. For example, there is the gang attack upon the Jewish boy that recalls incidents of violence in *Studs Lonigan,* and the venturing into alien neighborhoods where newcomers are greeted with stones and blows. There is the typical adolescent crush on the girl with the pretty curls, the good little girl who becomes symbolic, as was Studs' Lucy, of the purity of desire as opposed to the boy's lurid curiosities over sex. There is the change of seasons, sharp and definitive in Chicago, the excitement of winter and its Christmas scenes, and the brutality of summer that makes the laundry insufferable. On the whole, however, the study of manners is neither as extensive nor as brilliant as in other novels of childhood; and there is little of the humor or charm that makes *A Tree Grows In Brooklyn* gracious reading, for all that it may be trivial. It is the serious approach to the fundamental problems of the impact of modern city life upon an old world culture that gives *The Sidewalks Are Free* its place in recent city fiction. That the solution to this problem is facile—that a conflict can be resolved by an explosion which happily wipes out the family's capital and so removes the possibilities of an alternative way of life—is symptomatic of the weakness in both the art and the sociological insight of the novel of sentiment.

My Son, the Lawyer by Henry Denker gives a genre picture of middle-class Jewish family life in New York. The family is typically drawn together by sacrifice: the father quietly working away his years for his wife and children until one day he quietly dies; the mother scrimping and scheming for her son; the son dutifully giving up his own dreams in order to fulfill the one dream of his mother—that he become a lawyer; and the sister postponing love and marriage so that she can continue to help her family with her weekly paycheck. All of these people are decent and warm-hearted, but they are living through a depression era and making an arduous adjustment to what they conceive to be the demands and standards of twentieth-century New York. Because Mrs. Brown wants her son to attain these standards—to have

243

money, prestige, and status—she works and plots to have him go through law school. She represents the type of Jewish parent to whom the way of success is inevitably the way of the professional, of the doctor, the dentist, the teacher, or the lawyer. Her triumph comes when she lies in the hospital, close to death, and proudly boasts to the nurses of her wonderful and successful son, the lawyer.

The price for this triumph is a high one. David's family, as well as his fiancée, must sacrifice to make it possible. And David himself must give up his cherished dream to become a writer in order to grind through school and nightwork to his degree. The pathos of his situation is that one wrong act, committed through love for his mother, is to cost him his hard-earned career as a lawyer. In order to pay for his mother's operation, he accepts a bribe, and although he is working for a lawyer who has made his wealth from bribery and has always escaped its consequences, he must pay the heavy price of disbarment. Circumstances seem to contrive against the good people, for David is being punished for the inveterate corruption of others. His mother dies without ever learning that the final comforts her son has been able to give her do not come as the fruit of his success but as the price of his disgrace; she feels that all her efforts and sacrifices for him have been vindicated.

That the honest people suffer is again demonstrated in the contrast between David and Herm, his high school friend who sets out to make money and succeeds—at the expense of his honesty. The novel presents two alternative paths to material success: the grueling way of the student who seeks success through a legitimate profession, and the easier and more remunerative way of the wise go-getter who works the rackets. Only at the end is a third alternative opened, the only one that can bring happiness. It is to be true to one's dream and one's desire. This is what David is finally prepared to do at the end of the novel—to follow his inner desire and to fulfill himself in his own, not in his mother's, way. The courage to do this, after the failure of the grinding efforts of the last eight years, springs from what may be a perennial hope of youth, that tomorrow will be better. The novel gives no strong warrant for this conclusion, for what lies ahead, actually, is a new, and perhaps even more difficult, struggle than the one that has ended in failure.

Frederic Morton's *Asphalt and Desire* presents a situation somewhat parallel to that in *My Son, the Lawyer*. The story starts with Iris Leavis' graduation from Hunter College, just as the other begins with David's graduation from high school. While David's process of self-discovery takes eight years, Iris' exploration of mature life is limited to only five days. These days show her venturing into the complex worlds of business and of love. Again there is a mother ambitious for her children; complaining and domineering, she is driven by a sense that her own life, limited by what her husband could give her, was wasted. Again the young protagonist has the somewhat typical adventures of her class: the wisecracking farewell at Hunter College, the interchange of nagging and affection at home, the humiliations of job-hunting, and the first encounter with love. Through her brief romantic interlude and her new understanding of her relationship to the real world (as different from the artificial little world of Hunter College), Iris achieves insight into the nature of maturity. To her adolescent mind, life had seemed an infinity of possibilities, but even a tentative exploration of the world of adults brings this "secret of maturity"—that one must have the "courage for compromise" and accept a vision of life from which "tremendousness was gone."[9] This willingness to face life on its own terms signifies a development from ado-

[9] Frederic Morton, *Asphalt and Desire* (New York, Harcourt, Brace and Company, 1952), 278.

lescence to maturity. Aside from the theme of youth's initiation, the outstanding element in *Asphalt and Desire* is style—the breathless, vivid, wisecracking and sensitive style of Iris' idiom, through which action and scene are projected.

Of more comprehensive scope than any of these three novels of Jewish life is Sholem Asch's *East River*. The scenes of New York's tenement district are once again created: the clamorous, crowded streets, the sultry flats, the cluttered local stores, the scorching fire escapes on which people seek relief from the still summer heat, the sweatshops with their imminent terror of fire. The conflicts within the neighborhood—between Jew and Gentile, between respectable and promiscuous—are also exploited. As in the other novels, the contrast between the Jewish father, learned, spiritual, and ineffectual in the new world, and the mother, practical and dominating, focalizes a contrast between two sets of values. In the sons, this contrast takes another typical form, that between the idealistic, radical labor organizer and the aggressive, rising capitalist. The development of the sons gives the underlying direction to the plot, which is involved by the ill-starred crossing of lovers, as the heroine marries the wrong brother. Nathan, forced by paralysis to become a reader and a thinker, develops in the pattern of the proletarian hero of the thirties —that is, he arrives at social awareness and commits himself to the struggle for social justice and the improvement of the condition of the worker. His brother Irving, also driven by an intimate knowledge of poverty, takes another direction: to help his parents, he tries to make money however he can, and eventually, the drive for money makes him a successful and prosperous dress-manufacturer. In the end, the two lines of progress of the brothers meet. Irving becomes a benevolent capitalist who realizes the evils of exploitation and agrees to allow his workers to unionize. Thus, the novel ends on a variation of the tomorrow-will-be-better theme as both

246

brothers arrive, after the struggles of self-discovery, at a mature reconciliation to their duties in life.

But *East River* also goes beyond the theme of youth's reconciliation to life to present a higher experience of reconciliation—that which exists when man's spirit is united with God. The novel ends with Moshe Wolf's religious ecstasy as he experiences union with the Zaddick, the Saint, and through him, with God. It is through love that this union is achieved. The novel ends on the theme of religious love and the hope it holds forth for man's eternal tomorrow. As Moshe Wolf dies, in his ecstatic vision of Heaven, his hope is fulfilled, for he is eternally united with God.

A curious ecological novel—curious because of the alien pattern of life it presents—is John Kafka's *Sicilian Street*. The novel is about life in the Piazza, a street in upper New York where the Sicilians have not only established their old way of life but have even re-created the physical features of their old Piazza in Sicily. Sileno, the puppeteer, is an important figure in maintaining the old traditions, for as his puppets re-enact the stories and myths which had passed down the generations in Sicily, they provide a cultural bond with the past. As in most city novels that deal with the immigrant and his American-born children, there is a conflict between the old and the American way of life. Sileno's daughter Piero wishes to break away from the past and to establish in the Piazza a shiny modern drugstore that will symbolize the new way of life. What can be more typically American than the gaudy splendor of chrome and marble, the ice-cream sodas, the patented medicines and scientifically prepared prescriptions? Help comes to her through an outsider as George Northill, sent by the bank to foreclose the family house, is so moved by Piero's dream that he buys the mortgage to the house in order to give her the money to open her store. But Piero encounters obstacles to her plan. There is naturally the

247

resistance of her people to something new. More serious, however, is her own strange illness: she has fallen into a trance in which she relives the part of the puppet-heroine of her father's show. Happily, all problems are finally resolved, but not before a series of melodramatic events take place: the discovery of hidden crimes and murder, the open fight between the hero and the villain, and the sensational recovery of the heroine. In the end, Sicilian Street—the street that had seen the gay carnivals, pushcarts, and street shows of old Sicily— succumbs to the forces of twentieth-century city life. The drugstore opens its doors. The children who flock in will be assimilated to the American way of life by an introduction to giant ice-cream sodas. Their parents will be weaned from their old superstitions by an introduction to antiseptically prepared medicines. Trivial and melodramatic as the novel is, it yet has interest if only because it achieves what the ecological novel can achieve: a vivid picture of everyday life in a great city's peculiar and isolated neighborhoods.

"But What of the City's Back Yard and the Alley?"

Knock on Any Door is the counterpart among the city novels of violence of the forties to Dreiser's *An American Tragedy*. Like the earlier novel, it makes a dramatic statement of the premise that individual crime is rooted in social conditions, and that individual guilt, therefore, constitutes a public accusation. Although Dreiser's novel indicts society as a whole for its economic inequality and materialism, and Motley's novel deals more specifically with poverty and the slums, both generalize the significance of their particular dramatic situation by stressing its typicality and inevitability to the times. In both novels the main action consists less of

248

what the protagonist does, as an individualized being, than of what society does to him through its combined and pervasive forces. Thus Clyde Griffiths and Nick Romano are registers of their environments; and they are doomed because they accept uncritically and unconditionally standards and goals of the world in which they live. Without premeditation—without any real awareness of what is happening to them—they both turn into destructive agents: this is the consequence of their compliance. And yet they themselves are also the pitiable victims of uncontrolled destructive forces.

Characteristically, *Knock on Any Door* is a much more violent novel than *An American Tragedy*. Motley presents the violence of the back alley and the city's lower depths. There is criminal assault, jack-rolling, and murder. There is the degradation of self-prostitution and suicide. And most condemnable, there is the brutality of organized authority, which subjects the children in reformatories and the underworld captives in prisons to sadistic beatings with hose, blackjack, and fists and to merciless grillings undertaken with a heartless scientific precision.

Yet even though the structure of *Knock on Any Door* includes a pattern of violence (in *An American Tragedy* even the murder is nonviolent), the novel is simpler than its prototype. In order to stress the sociological thesis, it has reduced character, situation, and setting to skeletal essentials. Thus, Nick is a stereotype of the juvenile driven to delinquency through bad influence. He lacks the individuality that Clyde had by virtue of his peculiar romantic and sensuous temperament, the special endowment of all Dreiser's protagonists. Nick is first a perfectly unequivocal "good boy," devout, happy with his family, school, and priest, tenderhearted and innocent—not at all like the malcontented, rather neurotic Clyde. Also, the influences that change Nick are much more specific, and hence more simplified, than those

249

that act on Clyde. First it is poverty, with its consequences of bad environment and bad companions, and then the brutality of the reformatory that turn Nick against the social order. The action of these influences is concentrated, so that Nick suffers under their impact in intense and unforgettable moments, as when his friend Tommy dies in the reformatory or when he returns to the raucous, dirty, evil slum that is his home. While the influences that act upon Clyde are cumulative, they are diffused through a life's experience, short though it was; and they have the apparent aimlessness which they have often in life. It is only when we see and appreciate their cumulative effect in *An American Tragedy* that we are horrified by the undercurrent of destructive forces in the modern urban world. Even the tone of *Knock on Any Door* has been reduced to one single expression, whereas in Dreiser's novel, there are the nuances of pity, anger, irony, despair, pathos—and horror. Nick kills out of his obsessive hatred of the law, because of what it has come to symbolize to him. Clyde's crime comes about through a series of involuted acts, and even the crime itself has its complexities, as Clyde finds himself curiously more a witness to the murder than its perpetrator. Finally, the range of Nick's reactions is limited, and it fits a strict stereotyped pattern of the sociological case history. Clyde may experience mainly the emotions of a "moral coward"—regret, fear, yearning, anxiety—but his emotional pattern is always complex because he is caught in conflict and indecision; and he never is as unequivocally good or bad as Nick. The secondary characters in *Knock on Any Door* are also reduced to a sociological stereotype: the bad companion, the pure young wife, the not-understanding father, the hard-working brother, the socially conscious writer (who comments upon the action), and the brutal policeman.

Whatever effect of richness the novel has is achieved mainly through setting. Since environment plays the role of antagonist, it is fully realized as a dramatic entity. The style, however, is as bleak as the story. Short declarative sentences carry the main burden of the narrative; and while these may be a fitting vehicle for expressing Nick's limited thought and sensibility, they tend to become monotonous. There is the recurrent imagery of a small trapped animal, which comes to symbolize the trapped child Nick, as well as all of the innocent children caught and brutalized by the slums. Nick is always to remember the wounded mouse he had once rescued from a tormenting cat, and the dead dog lying in the street: these images merge with that of himself as he is finally caught and trapped and prepared for death in a prison cell.

Structurally, the novel follows a unilateral pattern of social causation; and the theme is that of social guilt. This theme is made explicit by the defense attorney who presents the theory that the "real" Nick Romano is not guilty of murder: ". . . he is guilty of having been reared in desperate poverty in the slums of a big city. He is guilty of having had the wrong environment and the wrong companions. He is guilty of the poolrooms and the taverns whose doors were open to him from the time he was fifteen. He is guilty of learning about sex on street corners. . . . He is guilty of learning police procedure by having been picked up and beaten by the police whenever they chose. He is guilty of the foul treatment of a reform school. . . ."[10] The defense ends with the dramatic accusation against society, the murderer of the "real" Nick Romano, the saintly child at the church altar. " 'Nick Romano was murdered seven years ago! . . . Society . . . murdered!— Nick Romano! . . . We brutalized and murdered him and we made this rendezvous with him seven years ago. . . .' "[11] The opening and closing epigraphs to the novel sustain this conclusion. Motley here makes his social point explicitly: one can knock on any door in the city's back alley and find a

[10] *Knock on Any Door,* 451.   [11] *Ibid.,* 452.

Nick Romano, perverted, brutalized, made murderous by hatred and frustration.

The fullest treatment of the disorganized world of violence within the city, the Skid Row world of the socially dispossessed and the inwardly dissociated, of petty thieves, punks, winos, prostitutes, gamblers, dope-peddlers, and junkies—of the city's lost people, living in twilight fantasies of whiskey, morphine, or half-madness—is in Nelson Algren's *The Man With the Golden Arm.* This is the outstanding city novel of the last decade. It marks a creative victory over the most sordid, degraded, and violent material which the modern city has to offer to fiction. The victory is made possible by Algren's gifts as a writer: his intimate knowledge of his material; his sympathy, which throws a phosphorescent glow over the gray alleys and the gloomy shadowed rooms and decaying people of whom he writes; and his power of expression, which transforms ugly fact into evocative image and creates, as an emotionally sustaining framework, a pattern of rhythm, verbal repetition, alliteration, and tonal variations. Sometimes Algren's virtuosity with language results in overdrawn purple passages and intrusive tricky verbal manipulations; these are faults of excess, but the vitality from which this excess flows is a creative source.

Like most recent city fiction, *The Man With the Golden Arm* follows the ecological pattern. It deals with a localized area in Chicago and the way of life of the people who belong here. But what unifies this area is not a common ethnic, religious, or racial bond; it is the common background of disorder. By the disorder within their personal lives, the people of this novel establish their place within the disorganized world of Skid Row. As in *Knock on Any Door,* the society is composed of failures, mainly, the self-defeated; but what has reduced the people of Algren's novel is not simply poverty. Rather it is some inexplicable, irrational destructive force loosed in the world, which drives people on to frenzied and unrelenting acts of self-destruction. Sophie's sense of this world comes closest to an explicit description of its peculiar aura; she wonders plaintively: ". . . why did it feel as though the all-night movies had all been emptied, why did it feel they must be showing broken reels to empty rows and that the all-night bakery fires had gone out: that the loaves would grow cold and mold slowly to dust in ten thousand rusting stoves?"[12] Her conclusion, with which the reader can agree, is that " 'it's just the way things would be if that Nifty Louie [the dope-dealer] was God 'n Blind Pig [his repulsive helper] was Jesus Christ.' "[13]

Early in the novel, Algren proposes one explanation for the doom of his people. The men of Skid Row, islanded within a larger society which evaluates men according to what they own rather than what they are, are ruined by the guilt of dispossession—"the great, secret and special American guilt of owning nothing, nothing at all, in the one land where ownership and virtue are one."[14] The pervasive atmosphere of guilt is reinforced by the attitude of the obsessed Police Captain. He feels that he shares in the guilt of the dispossessed who daily troop before him to be condemned; and sometimes he feels himself the guiltiest among them. As a character strategic in reinforcing the atmosphere of guilt, his role in the novel is clear; and yet the personal meaning of his obsession with guilt is ambiguous. Is he showing understandable human strain, or is he to be equated symbolically with organized society, which, like him, condemns Skid Row (whenever it bothers to become conscious of it) while it shares the guilt for its existence? The larger social implications of the atmosphere of guilt are not clearly enough

[12] Nelson Algren, *The Man With the Golden Arm* (New York, Doubleday and Company, 1949), 122.
[13] *Ibid.*, 123. [14] *Ibid.*, 17.

defined. Indeed, after the early statement of dispossession, little more attention seems to be given it. The secret guilt of Frankie Machine, the man with the golden arm, is always hereafter associated with his part in the accident that leads to the crippling of Sophie; it is guilt for her ruined life that he feels most deeply and that he tries hardest to escape.

Yet even dispossession in a materialistic society, significant as it is, cannot fully explain this total collapse of man's inner and outer world. Somehow this collapse defies rational explanation. We can explain rationally—as Farrell, for instance, has done in his prefaces—why Studs Lonigan is doomed; or we can explain in a systematic and clear-cut manner why Nick Romano had his rendezvous with the electric chair. But we cannot aggregate sociological factors to an explanation of Skid Row. Within the limits of *The Man With the Golden Arm* the matter of *why* Skid Row exists is not completely comprehensible. The matter of *what* it is, however, is dealt with with a mastery not equaled in city fiction of the lower depths. Algren knows of what this world is comprised: dirty rooms in a tenement, each with its secret history of violence and perversion; saloons peopled with dribbling, forsaken, sullen drunks; depressive jails full of stench, walls covered with obscene legends; hopeless back rooms of the dope-peddler; cramped, hellish dance clubs filled with the modern frenzy of jazz and despair. And besides the settings, Algren knows the speech of Skid Row, racy, brutal, illiterate, vivid—and humorous: the prisoner insists he is a "case of misidentity"; Sparrow is accused of "moral warpitude"; Old Stash is forbidden to throw another "tandem."

Perhaps Algren's greatest mastery over his material lies in the way he makes his degenerate characters real and sympathetic. Even the lowliest being, the chinless, half-goofy, half-shrewd, homeless punk that is Sparrow, is a character whose humanity we recognize. For even the fall of this lowly

254

Sparrow has taken place under God's eyes; and all the people in this book, the maimed, blind, and lost, are still God's children. Some of the minor characters are grotesque and revulsive, like Blind Pig and Nifty Louie; some are humorous, like Vi and Old Stash; but all are colorful. Of the central characters, the women are perhaps most credible. Sophie, fat, sloppy, tirelessly carping, is an obsessed woman, with a crazy childlike shrewdness that is to keep her forever on guard against the ministers of the sane world who try to redeem her. Her "perverted victory"—the unbreakable hold upon Frankie which her psychopathic invalidism gives her—dooms the two of them. Molly, who tries to save Frankie, is closest to a recognizable character of the civilized world beyond Skid Row. What she wants most is a man and a baby; and the weak and guilt-ridden Frankie offers her fulfillment as a woman. Frankie Machine is perhaps the most unfathomable character. Physically, he is clearly defined; and the temptations of his addiction, as well as the sufferings that result from it, are real and understandable. But his relationship to Sophie, from its beginning, has something about it as irrational and inexplicable as the whole atmosphere. Why had he deliberately humiliated Sophie in their early relationship and so engendered the resentment which never left her? It is almost as though he had deliberately spoiled something for no reason except that the destructive instinct is in him; and later this instinct is turned against himself. Yet for all that remains unmotivated in Frankie, his disintegration is poignant and pathetic, if not tragic; for he has abilities, even if they are those valued only in Skid Row. He is the Dealer, the man with the golden arm, whose strength and virtue lie in the flick of a wrist. And when his golden arm begins to tremble, when his dealer's nerve begins to fall apart, we are watching a process of human disintegration that somehow matters.

255

Although *The Man With the Golden Arm* is the most accomplished city novel of the last decade, winner of the 1950 National Book Award, it has certain structural weaknesses that make it upon second and third reading a more tenuous and uncertain literary work than it had seemed at first. Its impact is undeniable: as one reviewer has said, "Reading it is like stepping into the arms of an octopus."[15] It is gripping and immediate. But it lacks organic structure; and for this reason it is successful as a description, not as an interpretation, of an aspect of modern city life. The parts of the novel fit together like pieces of mosaic, some of which are not properly proportioned to maintain the basic design. For example, the comic episodes with Stash and Violet and the jail scenes with Lester are too long. One guesses that Algren has put together this novel out of smaller fragments instead of creating it out of a central organic core. The section on the Captain, for example, is surely taken from his earlier sketch "The Captain Has Bad Dreams," in *The Neon Wilderness,* just as certain descriptive passages of Frankie are taken from his poem "The Man With the Golden Arm"—and one suspects that the incidents with Vi and Stash are also reshaped from early separate pieces. The unity of the novel lies in the unity of the material; it is not essentially different from that achieved in his collection of short stories and sketches, *The Neon Wilderness.* The stories belong together because they are all about the neon wilderness within Chicago; and the same may be said about the incidents and characters in *The Man With the Golden Arm:* they belong together less by virtue of structural necessity to theme, plot, and characterization than by relevance to setting. The deficiency is, then, in novelistic technique as distinct from short story technique; and its effect can be felt in a certain haziness of meaning. It is almost as though

[15] "Review of *The Man With the Golden Arm,*" San Francisco *Chronicle,* October 9, 1949, 27.

intensity of tone and atmosphere substitute for—and also obscure the absence of—sustained theme. What Algren has been able to do with his horrible and horribly fascinating material is an unquestionable achievement. He has humanized the lowest kinds of degenerates, enveloped them in pity and sympathy, and created—with more than authenticity, with imagination and poetic vision—their world, their speech, the atmosphere of guilt within which they move. But we have yet to see Algren put to use his knowledge, feeling, and creative ability to a further achievement: to the exploration of lower city life not only in order to tell us what it is but also to interpret, within a larger frame of reference, what it means.

It was fitting that one of the reviewers for Hal Ellson's recent novel *The Golden Spike* should have been Nelson Algren, for *The Golden Spike* like *The Man With the Golden Arm* presents one of the squalid isolated slum worlds within the city and the people who try to escape from it through drug-induced dreams. Here the ecological unit is the "Puerto Rican ghetto" in New York. The Puerto Ricans, newest immigrants to the slums, live through the typical experiences of the city's poor and alien minorities, the Jews, Negroes, Italians, or Polish. Their circumstances have been described in almost every city novel of immigrant life—tenement poverty and its social isolation, shame, frustration, and the need for forgetfulness and escape. In the novels of the thirties, the young people sought escape through concerted social action or through art dedicated to a social purpose; they proposed to fight the tenement world, crush it, and so not only escape from it themselves but also take with them all its underprivileged and exploited people. In *The Golden Spike,* however, escape is typically into unreality, through the deadening influence of drugs.

What keeps *The Golden Spike* from being merely a problem novel on juvenile drug addiction is that it relates the

257

need for escape to the fundamental condition of "second-class citizenry"[16] in the city. Ellson is revealing more than an isolated evil of urban life: he is projecting a particular situation against a larger view of the city and so giving it generalized significance. The people of the novel, flown into New York from their homes in Puerto Rico (presumably to supply cheap labor) become part of the city's lost people. Chico, the protagonist, thinks of himself as "arriving along with thousands of others by plane, no, by magic carpet, from that warm tropic island, escaping its poverty to find a new kind in a huge city that swallowed them as ruthlessly as it had swallowed others before."[17] Once here, the newcomers found that nothing was theirs "but dirt and poverty, dismal tenements, dark halls, broken stairs and the invisible iron bars of this newest ghetto that imprisoned them all and labeled them spiks."[18] The feeling this huge and terrifying city engenders in young Chico is not essentially different from that which Chicago had once produced in Dreiser's Carrie: fear, futility, and helplessness. To Chico, the "city loomed, impregnable and too vast, an overwhelming giant."[19] He could not fight against it: he could only try to escape from his consciousness of it.

Escape through drugs is the monotonous motif of the novel. The days pass in the pattern of addiction, of never-ending need and submission, of regret, shame, resolution, and craving need again. The pattern cannot be broken, neither by the intervention of the family, too much weakened to exercise control, nor by the individual will, also weakened with a terrible finality, nor by a removal from the conditions

[16] This is Algren's term in his review, "Spoon-fed Universe," *Saturday Review,* December 6, 1952, 35.

[17] Hal Ellson, *The Golden Spike* (New York, Ballantine Books, 1952), 24.

[18] *Ibid.,* 25.

[19] *Ibid.*

that create the need for escape. So the cycle becomes a desperate one, as the need grows stronger and more irresistible and the means to satisfy it more limited. Inevitably there is violence, assault, pursuit by police, the hell of drug-hungry sickness in the jail, and finally condemnation—an ironic justice. Nelson Algren has pointed out that "Hal Ellson cuts in pretty close to case-recording on occasion and hurries his case at its close."[20] Like an unrelieved case history, the novel has little variation in pace, tone, or action; the characterization is static, for Chico has reached a point where all he can do is conform to the addict's pattern of need and satisfaction. And as in a case history, the personal background helps to explain the present situation. For Chico there is the memory of home—of safety and belonging-ness on the island of his people. There is the memory of a father, now lost forever, of security, and of family. All of these are destroyed, and their destruction means the destruction of the young people transplanted to the filth of an isolated slum-city, alien and despised. The novel contributes to the annals of the city's lost. Chico is lost in a peculiar way and under the peculiar circumstances of his people, the latest newcomers to the city. From the first day when he found himself in a crowd of strangers searching for a familiar face he knew he was already lost; and he remained lost, "from that day on . . . searching for something which he had never found—never would find, either."[21]

Leonard Bishop's recent novel *Down All Your Streets* brings together the two parallel developments of sentiment and violence. Like the tomorrow-will-be-better novel of the forties it tells the story of a woman, Lil Lewis, who emerges from a life of poverty, shame, and violence to face a brighter future: "For her there was something ahead of today and

[20] "Spoon-fed Universe," *Saturday Review*, December 6, 1952, 35.
[21] Ellson, *The Golden Spike*, 100.

259

more in front of tomorrow."[22] Contrapuntal to her story runs that of her husband, Burt, who lives in the shadowed underworld of alleys, saloons and dope-peddlers' back rooms, the world of *Knock on Any Door* or *The Man With the Golden Arm*. His destiny, like that of the victim of the novel of violence, is to blunder from one act of self-destruction to the next and more violent one, to seek escape and forgetfulness, to writhe helplessly with the need of drugs, to know jail and its brutality, to make the too-late futile effort at self-redemption, and finally to meet the doom of madness and prison. Through the contrapuntal stories of Lil and Burt the themes of sentiment and violence are woven together—or rather, are laid out side by side—so that *Down All Your Streets* unites the two trends of city fiction of the forties and early fifties.

So much in this novel can be discussed in terms of a now established tradition that we could easily lose sight of what is individual about it. Yet we cannot ignore its striking similarities to Farrell's novels nor to the novels of sentiment and violence. While *Down All Your Streets* treats of Jewish life instead of Irish and of New York instead of Chicago, it is, like Farrell's novel, an ecological novel of manners that reveals the same intimate insider's knowledge of an everyday way of life. It is based upon the same episodic structure (although the episodes are longer) and uses alternating point-of-view characters. It too relies heavily upon dialogue, always authentic and varied, from the bitter wisecracking of young Stan to the Yiddish inflections of Lil and the cheap hard gangster talk of Burt. As in Farrell, the characters are created mainly through their speech, whether it is their outer dialogue or the interior dialogue in terms of which their thoughts and emotions are expressed and the outer scene realized. There is the same close documentation in the recording of everyday

[22] Leonard Bishop, *Down All Your Streets* (New York, Dial Press, 1952), 425.

trivial facts—the same unabashed recording of the characters' concern with physiological facts of life. Aside from specific incidents which recall those in Farrell (like the New Year's Eve Party, similar to the wild affair in *Studs Lonigan,* or the family gathering on Ella's birthday, similar to the O'Flaherty's Christmas dinner), there is an extraordinarily close resemblance to the basic family situation in the tetralogy. Like the O'Neill family, the Lewis family is broken, and the young sons must rely upon the aunt (Ella is like Margaret O'Flaherty, childless and neurotic) and upon the uncle (Alvin is like Al O'Flaherty, a pontifical bachelor). These characters are more grotesque than Farrell's, and less sympathetic, but their role and relationship are the same. An important difference is that Jim O'Neill was a decent, hard-working father, ruined by social circumstances beyond his control; and Lizz remained always slatternly and trapped in her circumstances. Burt is below decency, a convict and drug addict, a small man trying to prove how tough he is, and yet, an understandable, even at times almost a lovable, human being. Lil achieves through will and the help of her family a victory over her circumstances which lifts her above the poverty and shame of her married life. Characteristically, all of the people in Bishop's novel, unlike those in Farrell's, have the ability to laugh at themselves.

The integral element of Farrell's novels that is missing here is the deliberate social intention. Like other novels of the forties, *Down All Your Streets* incorporates the tomorrow-will-be-better motif and its assumption that the past of hardship and worry can be absolved if one makes the effort to better one's life. Lil's solution, and also that of her sons, is not identified with a social cause, as was Danny O'Neill's. There is no necessity to change a world that destroys people, because these people are not destroyed; like Francie in *A Tree Grows in Brooklyn,* they emerge "curiously untouched."

261

Lil has what seems to her sister an "oxlike courage," like that
of women of the old country which "made them immune
to hardship."[23] Perhaps one of the least satisfactory aspects
of the novel is the way Stan moves through his period of
initiation and somehow solves the inner problems that have
built up the tensions within him and kept him from freely
giving of himself even in love. Just what solves his problems
Bishop does not say; we know only that he comes back from
the CCC camp somehow stronger, mature, and resolved. In
some inexplicable way the elder brother, Lester, also arrives
at a satisfactory solution to his problems: he determines to
give up the business career foisted upon him by his aunt and
uncle and study to become a gym teacher. It is only with
Lil that we see the more laborious steps to a victory over tomorrow, as she becomes a scrub-woman, then learns how to
sew and works in a cloak factory, moves to a better neighborhood, and gradually frees herself from Burt. Her affair with
Fred, the accomplished, gentlemanly lover, is perhaps a gra-
tuitous reward, although we know that despite her degra-
dations, she has remained, like the mothers in Betty Smith's
novels, shapely and appealing. She has progressed so far in
her victory over circumstances that she can even toy with
the idea of a respectable marriage to Fred. Symbolically, her
last act represents her release from the past and victory over
tomorrow: as she puts her name in the letter box she knows
that she is free from further fear of Burt and of the violence
and degradation he had brought into her life.

Through Burt, the theme of violence is developed. The
craving need for drugs and the horrors and horrible ec-
stasies of the dream world are re-created as graphically as in
The Man With the Golden Arm. Physical violence, stemming
from a need for self-assertion, is expressed in Burt's unpro-
voked attack upon a negro, in his beating the victim of his

[23] *Ibid.*

robbery, and in his fights with his pal Mac and his children. Brutality is intrinsic to the world into which Burt must inevitably move: it pervades Riker's Island (with its junkies, fags, and sadistic guards) the dope addict's back rooms, and prison. In the hospital ward and in Riker's Island there are enacted almost unbearable nightmare scenes of a modern kind of hell; they go deeper into horror than scenes of *The Man With the Golden Arm* and are paralleled only by some of the sketches in Algren's *The Neon Wilderness*. Burt's disintegration gives the pervasive tone to the novel; it cannot be fully balanced by the victories of Lil and her children. His final submission to Mac, when he goes back on drugs and ultimately agrees to peddle marijuana to school children, marks the end of his sense of decency, which he had somehow never completely lost. And his desperate decline into madness, as he creates a private dreamworld from which he is never to escape, summarizes the theme of urban victimization which for over fifty years the city novel has developed as its most serious condemnation of twentieth-century American city life.

SUGGESTED

BACKGROUND READINGS

Works on the Sociology, History,
and Topography of the City
and Miscellaneous Works

Algren, Nelson. *Chicago: City on the Make.* New York, Doubleday and Company, 1951.

Allen, Frederick Lewis. *The Big Change.* New York, Harper and Brothers, 1952.

——. *Only Yesterday: An Informal History of the Nineteen-Twenties.* New York, Harper and Brothers, 1931.

Anderson, Nels, and Eduard Lindeman. *Urban Sociology, An Introduction to the Study of Urban Communities.* New York, A. A. Knopf, 1928.

Beard, Charles and Mary. *The Rise of American Civilization.* New York, The Macmillan Company, 1942, revised and enlarged. Vol. II.

Blumenthal, Albert. *Small-Town Stuff.* Chicago, University of Chicago Press, 1932.

Brown, Lawrence Guy. *Social Pathology: Personal and Social Disorganization.* New York, Croft Publications, 1946.

Burgess, Ernest, and Harvey Locke. *The Family: From Institution to Companionship.* New York, American Book Company, 1945.

Carpenter, Niles. *The Sociology of City Life.* New York, Longmans, Green and Company, 1931.

265

Cavan, Ruth Shonle. *Suicide*. Chicago, University of Chicago Press, 1928.

Churchill, Henry. *The City is the People*. New York, Reynal and Hitchcock, 1945.

Commager, Henry Steele. *The American Mind: An Interpretation of American Thought and Character Since the 1880's*. New Haven, Yale University Press, 1950.

Cooley, Charles Horton. *Social Process*. New York, Charles Scribner's Sons, 1918.

Dunlap, George Arthur. *The City in the American Novel, 1789–1900: A Study of American Novels Portraying Contemporary Conditions in New York, Philadelphia and Boston*. Published Ph.D. dissertation, University of Pennsylvania, 1934.

Gillin, John Lewis and John Philip. *An Introduction to Sociology*. New York, The Macmillan Company, 1942.

Gist, Noel, and L. A. Halbert. *Urban Society*. Revised ed. New York, Thomas Crowell Company, 1946.

Grey, Lennox Bouton. "Chicago and the Great American Novel." Unpublished Ph.D. dissertation, University of Chicago, 1935.

Hansen, Harry. *Midwest Portraits: A Book of Memories and Friendships*. New York, Harcourt, Brace and Company, 1923.

Horney, Karen. *The Neurotic Personality of Our Time*. New York, Norton and Company, 1937.

———. *Our Inner Conflicts*. New York, Norton and Company, 1945.

Howe, Frederick. "The City as a Socializing Agency," *American Journal of Sociology,* Vol. XVII (March, 1912), 590–601.

Hurwitz, Julius. *The City*. Cleveland, World Publishing Company, 1953.

Kazin, Alfred. *A Walker in the City*. New York, Harcourt, Brace and Company, 1951.

Lynd, Robert. *Knowledge for What?: The Place of Social Science in American Culture*. Princeton, Princeton University Press, 1946.

Maurice, Arthur Bartlett. *New York in Fiction*. New York, Dodd, Mead and Company, 1901.

———. *The New York of the Novelists.* New York, Dodd, Mead and Company, 1916.

Park, Robert. "The City: Suggestions for the Investigation of Human Behavior in the City Environment," *American Journal of Sociology,* Vol. XX (March, 1915), 577–612.

Park, Robert, Ernest Burgess and Roderick McKenzie. *The City.* Chicago, University of Chicago Press, 1925.

Parrington, Vernon. *Main Currents in American Thought.* New York, Harcourt, Brace and Company, 1927. Vol. III.

Riesman, David. *Faces in the Crowd.* New Haven, Yale University Press, 1952.

———. *The Lonely Crowd.* New Haven, Yale University Press, 1950.

Schlesinger, Arthur Meier. *The Rise of the City: 1878–1898.* New York, The Macmillan Company, 1933.

Thrasher, Frederick. *The Gang: A Study of 1313 Gangs in Chicago.* Chicago, University of Chicago Press, 1927.

Wilson, Rufus Rockwell and Otilie Erickson. *New York in Literature.* New York, Primavera Press, 1947.

Wirth, Louis. "Urbanism as a Way of Life," *American Journal of Sociology,* Vol. XLIV (July, 1938), 1–24.

Woolston, H. B. "The Urban Habit of Mind," *American Journal of Sociology,* Vol. XVII (March, 1912), 602–14.

Zorbaugh, Harvey Warren. *The Gold Coast and the Slum.* Chicago, University of Chicago Press, 1929.

A SELECTIVE LIST OF
CITY FICTION

Most of the works listed here are city novels in the sense in which the term is defined in Chapter I. Some, however, do not come strictly within that definition. They are included (as certain novels of questionable literary merit are also included) because they have significance as city fiction. They either exploit the main themes of twentieth-century urban literature or they belong structurally in one of the three categories of city fiction discussed in Chapter I, or else they use unusual or original techniques to create the urban scene, atmosphere, or way of life. All of the novels of Dreiser, Dos Passos, and Farrell are also listed here, even though, obviously, not all of them are city novels.

Algren, Nelson. *The Man with the Golden Arm*. New York, Doubleday and Company, 1950.
———. *The Neon Wilderness*. Garden City, New York, Doubleday and Company, 1947.
Anderson, Sherwood. *Dark Laughter*. New York, Boni and Liveright, 1925.
———. *Many Marriages*. New York, B. W. Huebsch, Inc., 1923.
———. *Poor White*. New York, B. W. Huebsch, Inc., 1920.
Asch, Sholem. *East River*. Trans. by A. H. Gross. New York, G. P. Putnam's Sons, 1946.

Bishop, Leonard. *Days of My Love.* New York, Dial Press, 1953.

———. *Down All Your Streets.* New York, Dial Press, 1952.

Boyd, Thomas. *In Time of Peace.* New York, Minton, Balch and Company, 1935.

Cahan, Abraham. *Yekl: A Tale of the New York Ghetto.* New York, D. Appleton and Company, 1896.

Churchill, Winston. *The Dwelling-Place of Light.* New York, The Macmillan Company, 1917.

Crane, Stephen. *Maggie, A Girl of the Streets.* New York, D. Appleton and Company, 1896.

Dahlberg, Edward. *Bottom Dogs.* New York, Simon and Schuster, 1930.

Davenport, Marcia. *East Side, West Side.* New York, Charles Scribner's Sons, 1947.

Dell, Floyd. *The Briary Bush.* New York, A. A. Knopf, 1921.

Denker, Henry. *My Son, the Lawyer.* New York, Thomas Crowell Company, 1950.

Dos Passos, John. *Adventures of a Young Man.* New York, Harcourt, Brace and Company, 1939.

———. *Chosen Country.* Boston, Houghton Mifflin Company, 1951.

———. *The Grand Design.* Boston, Houghton Mifflin Company, 1949.

———. *Manhattan Transfer.* New York and London, Harper and Brothers, 1925.

———. *Number One.* Boston, Houghton Mifflin Company, 1943.

———. *One Man's Initiation—1917.* London, George Allen and Unwin, Ltd., 1920.

    There is a reprint of this novel called *First Encounter* (New York, Philosophical Library, 1945) that contains an important introduction by Dos Passos: "A Preface Twenty-Five Years Later."

———. *Streets of Night.* New York, George H. Doran Company, 1923.

———. *Three Soldiers.* New York, George H. Doran Company, 1921.

270

The Modern Library edition, published in 1932, contains a new introduction.

——. *U.S.A.* New York, Harcourt, Brace and Company, 1938.

The 42nd Parallel. Published originally New York and London, Harper and Brothers, 1930.

1919. Published originally New York, Harcourt, Brace and Company, 1932.

The Big Money. Published originally New York, Harcourt, Brace and Company, 1936.

Dreiser, Theodore. *An American Tragedy.* New York, Boni and Liveright, 1925.

——. *The Bulwark.* Garden City, New York, Doubleday and Company, 1946.

——. *The Financier* New York, Harper and Brothers, 1912.

——. *The 'Genius.'* New York, John Lane Company, 1915.

——. *Jennie Gerhardt.* New York and London, Harper and Brothers, 1911.

——. *Sister Carrie.* New York, Doubleday, Page and Company, 1900.

——. *The Stoic.* Garden City, New York, Doubleday and Company, 1947.

——. *The Titan.* New York, John Lane Company, 1914.

Eastman, Max. *Venture.* New York, Albert and Charles Boni, 1927.

Ellson, Hal. *Duke.* New York, Charles Scribner's Sons, 1953.

——. *The Golden Spike.* New York, Ballantine Books, 1952.

Farrell, James T. *Bernard Clare.* New York, Vanguard Press, 1946.

——. *Ellen Rogers.* New York, Vanguard Press, 1941.

——. *The Face of Time.* New York, Vanguard Press, 1953.

——. *Father and Son.* New York, Vanguard Press, 1940.

——. *Gas-House McGinty.* New York, Vanguard Press, 1933.

——. *My Days of Anger.* New York, Vanguard Press, 1943.

——. *No Star Is Lost.* New York, Vanguard Press, 1938.

——. *The Road Between.* New York, Vanguard Press, 1949.

——. *Studs Lonigan.* New York, Vanguard Press, 1935. A trilogy comprising:

271

Young Lonigan, a Boyhood in the Chicago Streets.
Vanguard Press, 1932.

The Young Manhood of Studs Lonigan. Vanguard
Press, 1934.

Judgment Day. Vanguard Press, 1935.

———. *This Man and This Woman.* New York, Vanguard Press,
1951.

———. *Tommy Gallagher's Crusade.* New York, Vanguard Press,
1939. A novelette.

———. *A World I Never Made.* New York, Vanguard Press, 1936.

———. *Yet Other Waters.* New York, Vanguard Press, 1952.

Ferber, Edna. *Nobody's in Town.* Garden City, New York,
Doubleday, Doran and Company, 1939.

Ferber, Nat. *New York: A Novel.* New York, Covici-Friede, 1929.

Fitzgerald, Scott. *The Beautiful and Damned.* New York, Charles
Scribner's Sons, 1922.

———. *The Great Gatsby.* New York, Charles Scribner's Sons,
1925.

———. *This Side of Paradise.* New York, Charles Scribner's Sons,
1920.

Frank, Waldo. *City Block.* Darien, Connecticut, Waldo Frank,
1922.

———. *The Death and Birth of David Markand.* New York,
Charles Scribner's Sons, 1934.

Friedman, Isaac Kahn. *Poor People: A Novel.* New York and
Boston, Houghton Mifflin, 1900.

Fuller, Henry B. *The Cliff-Dwellers.* New York, Harper and
Brothers, 1893.

———. *Under the Skylights.* New York, D. Appleton and Company, 1901.

Gold, Michael. *Jews Without Money.* New York, Horace Liveright, 1930.

Gollomb, Joseph. *Unquiet.* New York, Dodd, Mead and Company, 1935.

Halper, Albert. *Only an Inch From Glory.* New York, Harper and
Brothers, 1943.

———. *Union Square.* New York, The Viking Press, 1933.

Harris, Frank. *The Bomb.* New York, Mitchell Kennerley, 1909.

Hecht, Ben. *Eric Dorn.* New York, G. P. Putnam's Sons, 1921.

———. *A Thousand and One Afternoons in Chicago.* New York, Covici-Friede, 1922.

Herrick, Robert. *A Life for a Life.* New York, The Macmillan Company, 1910.

———. *Memoirs of an American Citizen.* New York, The Macmillan Company, 1905.

Howells, William Dean. *A Hazard of New Fortunes.* New York, Harper and Brothers, 1889.

Hurst, Fanny. *Mannequin.* New York, A. A. Knopf, 1926.

Kafka, John. *Sicilian Street.* New York, Coward-McCann, 1949.

Kantor, MacKinlay. *Diversey.* New York, Coward-McCann, 1928.

Kober, Arthur. *Bella, Bella Kissed a Fella.* New York, Random House, 1951.

Lardner, Ring. *The Big Town.* Indianapolis, The Bobbs-Merrill Company, 1921.

Levin, Meyer. *Citizens.* New York, The Viking Press, 1940.

———. *The Old Bunch.* New York, The Viking Press, 1937.

Morris, Ira. *The Chicago Story.* New York, Doubleday and Company, 1952.

Morton, Frederic. *Asphalt and Desire.* New York, Harcourt, Brace and Company, 1952.

Motley, Willard. *Knock on Any Door.* New York, Appleton-Century Company, 1947.

———. *We Fished All Night.* New York, Appleton-Century-Crofts, 1951.

Norris, Frank. *McTeague.* New York, Doubleday and McClure Company, 1899.

———. *The Pit.* New York, Doubleday, Page and Company, 1903.

———. *Vandover and the Brute.* Garden City, New York, Doubleday, Page and Company, 1914.

O'Hara, John. *Butterfield 8.* New York, Harcourt, Brace and Company, 1935.

O. Henry. *The Four Million.* New York, Doubleday, Page and Company, 1906.

———. *The Voice of the City.* Garden City, New York, Doubleday, Page and Company, 1919.

Payne, Will. *The Story of Eva: A Novel*. Boston and New York, Houghton Mifflin Company, 1901.

Petry, Ann. *The Street*. New York, Houghton Mifflin Company, 1946.

Poole, Ernest. *The Harbor*. New York, The Macmillan Company, 1915.

———. *The Voice of the Street*. New York, A. S. Barnes and Company, 1906.

Rice, Elmer. *Imperial City*. New York, Coward-McCann, 1937.

Richardson, Dorothy. *The Long Day: The Story of a New York Working Girl As Told by Herself*. New York, The Century Company, 1905.

Riesenberg, Felix. *East Side, West Side*. New York, Harcourt, Brace and Company, 1927.

Riis, Jacob A. *Children of the Tenements*. New York, The Century Company, 1897.

Robbins, Harold. *A Stone for Danny Fisher*. New York, A. A. Knopf, 1952.

Rosenberg, Ethel. *Go Fight City Hall*. New York, Simon and Schuster, 1946.

Ross, Sam. *The Sidewalks Are Free*. New York, Farrar, Strauss, 1950.

Salinger, Jerome. *The Catcher in the Rye*. New York, Little, Brown and Company, 1951.

Saxton, Alexander. *The Great Midland*. New York, Appleton-Century-Crofts, 1948.

Schneider, Isidor. *From the Kingdom of Necessity*. New York, G. P. Putnam's Sons, 1935.

Shulman, Irving. *The Amboy Dukes*. New York, Doubleday and Company, 1947.

Sinclair, Upton. *The Jungle*. New York, Doubleday, Page and Company, 1906.

———. *The Metropolis*. New York, Moffat, Yard and Company, 1908.

Slesinger, Tess. *The Unpossessed*. New York, Simon and Schuster, 1934.

Smith, Betty. *Tomorrow Will Be Better*. New York, Harper and Brothers, 1948.

———. *A Tree Grows in Brooklyn*. New York, Harper and Brothers, 1943.

Van Vechten, Carl. *Nigger Heaven*. New York, A. A. Knopf, 1926.

———. *Parties: Scenes from Contemporary New York Life*. New York, A. A. Knopf, 1930.

Wharton, Edith. *The Age of Innocence*. New York, D. Appleton and Company, 1920.

———. *The Custom of the Country*. New York, Charles Scribner's Sons, 1913.

———. *The House of Mirth*. New York, Charles Scribner's Sons, 1905.

———. *Hudson River Bracketed*. New York, D. Appleton and Company, 1929.

Wolfe, Thomas. *Of Time and the River*. New York, Charles Scribner's Sons, 1935.

———. *The Web and the Rock*. New York, Harper and Brothers, 1939.

———. *You Can't Go Home Again*. New York, Harper and Brothers, 1940.

Wouk, Herman. *The City Boy*. New York, Doubleday and Company, 1952.

Wright, Richard. *Native Son*. New York, Harper and Brothers, 1940.

Yaffe, James. *The Good-For-Nothing*. Boston, Atlantic-Little, Brown and Company, 1953.

Yezierska, Anzia. *Salome of the Tenements*. New York, Boni and Liveright, 1923.

Zugsmith, Leane. *A Time to Remember*. New York, Random House, 1936.

INDEX

287

Ward, Mrs. Humphry, referred to by Dreiser: 61
Warner, Charles Dudley, referred to by Dreiser: 61
Web and the Rock, The: 99, 121, 122, 129
Wharton, Edith: ecological form of, 13, 107; relevance to city fiction, 95, 97; as novelist of fashionable New York, 107–19; her statement of intention, 107; role of money in, 109, 112–13; theme of social void in, 111–12, 113–15; role of inheritance in, 113; theme of renunciation in, 113, 119; significance of taste in, 116–17
Whitman, Walt: 71
Wilson, Edmund: 139, 161
Winesburg, Ohio: 96
Wirth, Louis: 29, 30, 31, 35; *see also* Urbanism
Wolfe, Thomas: 11, 20, 232, 235; relevance to city fiction, 95, 97–98; his symbolic use of the city discussed, 119–32; impact of the depression upon, 126–27; evaluation of as city novelist, 131–32

You Can't Go Home Again: 99, 127, 128

Znaniecki, Florian: 29
Zorbaugh, Harvey: 29, 32